EVERYDAY *flexitarian*

CALGARY PUBLIC LIBRARY

APR   2011

EVERYDAY *flexitarian*

recipes for vegetarians & meat lovers alike

NETTIE CRONISH & PAT CROCKER

whitecap

Copyright © 2011 by Nettie Cronish and Pat Crocker
Photos copyright © 2011 by Pat Crocker
Whitecap Books

All rights reserved. No part of this publication may be reproduced, stored in a retrieval system, or transmitted in any form or by any means, electronic, mechanical, photocopying, recording, or otherwise, without the prior written permission of the publisher. For more information contact Whitecap Books, at 351 Lynn Avenue, North Vancouver, BC, Canada V7J 2C4.

The information in this book is true and complete to the best of the authors' knowledge. All recommendations are made without guarantee on the part of the authors or Whitecap Books Ltd. The authors and publisher disclaim any liability in connection with the use of this information. Opinions expressed in this book do not necessarily represent the views and opinions of Whitecap Books. Whitecap Books does not review or endorse the contents of the websites listed in this book. Whitecap Books assumes no liability for any content or opinion expressed on these websites, nor does it warrant that the contents and links are error or virus free.

Whitecap Books is known for its expertise in the cookbook market, and has produced some of the most innovative and familiar titles found in kitchens across North America. Visit our website at www.whitecap.ca.

EDITED BY Holland Gidney
COPY EDITED BY Grace Yaginuma
BOOK DESIGN BY Mauve Pagé
FOOD PHOTOGRAPHY AND STYLING BY Pat Crocker

The Canadian Organic Food Standards on pages 264–65 are reprinted by permission from the Canada Organic Trade Association (www.ota .com/otacanada.html).

Printed in Canada at Friesens

LIBRARY AND ARCHIVES CANADA CATALOGUING IN PUBLICATION

Cronish, Nettie, 1954–
    Everyday flexitarian : recipes for vegetarians & meat lovers alike / Nettie Cronish and Pat Crocker.

Includes index.
ISBN 978-1-77050-021-1

    1. Vegetarian cooking. 2. Cooking (Meat). 3. Cookbooks.
I. Crocker, Pat II. Title.

TX837.C757 2011   641.5'636   C2011-900234-5

The publisher acknowledges the financial support of the Government of Canada through the Canada Book Fund (CBF) and the Province of British Columbia through the Book Publishing Tax Credit.

11 12 13 14 15   5 4 3 2 1

ENVIRONMENTAL BENEFITS STATEMENT

Whitecap Books Ltd saved the following resources by printing the pages of this book on chlorine free paper made with 10% post-consumer waste.

TREES	WATER	SOLID WASTE	GREENHOUSE GASES
19 FULLY GROWN	8,815 GALLONS	535 POUNDS	1,830 POUNDS

Calculations based on research by Environmental Defense and the Paper Task Force. Manufactured at Friesens Corporation

*Cooking great meals is not difficult. It just takes
thought and care and respect. This book
is dedicated to those people who think and care
and hold a deep respect for food, for they are the
ones most likely to create a tolerant kitchen.*

INTRODUCTION

The ancients did it, Einstein recommended it, and David Suzuki supports it. The trend of eating less meat is centuries old, but for many North Americans it is a new way of life. Every year more and more people move toward a healthier, plant-based diet. There is no doubt that the earth and its inhabitants fare better when meat is not a priority at dinner (or at lunch or breakfast, for that matter). We aren't saying you must eliminate meat completely—in fact, for some body types, responsible consumption of small amounts of organic beef, lamb, chicken, and fish may be beneficial. What we see evolving is a flexible way of thinking about food, cooking it, and serving it to family and friends.

Everyday Flexitarian allows you to adjust your personal meal plan so most of the time it consists of vegetables and grains, beans, soy, and/or pasta. We encourage you to eat smaller portions of animal-based proteins and larger portions of vegetables, raw and cooked.

WHAT IS A FLEXITARIAN?

The truth is, a lot of people eat meat and would have a hard time removing it from their diets completely. Awareness is growing, however, and many meat eaters are mindful of where and how their meat is raised. In addition, there is a growing number of people who are eating more vegetarian meals because they recognize the health and environmental benefits.

We can put these people under the category *flexitarian*—that is, those who have moved closer to being vegetarian but who sometimes consume meat, poultry, or fish. And it's also people who identify themselves as meat eaters but replace meat with meat alternatives for at least some meals. This can mean two to four (or more!) meatless meals per week. It is estimated that 30 to 40 percent of the population of the United States and Canada are flexitarian, and the numbers keep growing.

In this book, we carefully consider how we use meat in recipes and in our diet. Our take on cooking puts the focus on humane stewardship of animals and land, on *quality* meat, and on smaller amounts of meat. We reappraise the amount of animal protein that should be served with a meal, positioning meat as just one of the ingredients rather than as the central one.

Meat is better savoured. We both agree that one eats and drinks not just for sustenance. We have written a book for people who cook with passion, not for technicians of the table. In our cooking classes, seminars, and workshops, we meet a lot of flexitarians. And they're always looking for recipes that combine time-saving strategies, affordable ingredients, and great taste. We wanted to write a cookbook with recipes that could serve both the vegetarian and the meat eater.

WHY SHOULD I REDUCE OR ELIMINATE MEAT IN MY DIET?

The market for meatless meals is growing by 40 percent annually, largely due to mounting scientific evidence that higher fat and meat-based diets are factors in heart attacks and strokes. It has been scientifically proven that eating more fruits and vegetables and consuming less fat and more fibre may lead to a decreased incidence of Type 2 diabetes, cancer, and obesity. More recently, environmental issues such as factory farming, and moral concerns over animal cruelty, are having an impact on eating habits.

CAN VEGETARIAN AND MEAT RECIPES CO-EXIST IN THE SAME KITCHEN?

In a word: *yes.*

The food we eat is a result of many choices we make and have made. Over the years, we have been introduced to many food reform movements: Slow Food, vegan, organic, local, Whole Beast, seasonal, raw, Terroir, vegetarian, and 100 Mile, most of them highly politicized. But there are many reasons other than politics that help us choose the food we eat, including nutritional, spiritual, social, and ecological reasons. Often people feel anxious about their food choices; they may also feel guilty or feel judged. Such feelings are not exactly life-enhancing.

Food is so essential to daily life that how we think about it and engage with it has a huge effect on our mental and physical health. It's time to push away pressures of guilt and anxiety and embrace open and relaxed discussion and debate about food and food choices. This book is an invitation to create a healthy and relaxed dialogue about food and the food choices that are open to us all.

Nettie has been teaching vegetarian cooking classes for 25 years and she is often the only vegetarian in the class. Some of the recipes and ideas in this book evolved because people attending her classes told her that they were sometimes cooking three different meals for their loved ones. Wouldn't it be great if they had a cookbook that offered them choices and allowed them to prepare one recipe two ways?

THE FLEXITARIAN WAY: IT'S ALL ABOUT CHOICE

The flexitarian meal idea evolved over time, not only in my classes, but also in my own home. I have three children, and each of them was vegetarian until the age of six. Once they started going to school, birthday parties, and other kids' homes, they were introduced to many kinds of foods not eaten in our home. My breast-fed, raised-on-organic children were soon sampling candies, sugar-sweetened cereals, deep-fried foods, and, to my dismay, meat.

At mealtimes we spoke a lot about choice. I explained my reasons for being a vegetarian, and they dutifully listened, but whether it was peer pressure or simple curiosity, they crossed the line and began eating meat socially. At the time, I was very angry. My husband pointed out that I needed to "pick my battles." Indeed, battling with my children on the issue of eating meat would make life for our family much more difficult. Was I to tell every playdate and caregiver that my kid was not allowed to eat meat? Or drink milk? Or eat sugar-sweetened cookies?

As the kids got older they told me they felt that restrictions on meat eating had been forced on them without their say. I began to suspect this was less about eating meat and more about my kids wanting to make their own decisions. They were maturing as teenagers.

Initially I would not allow meat in our house, but as the kids approached their teenage years and began cooking for themselves, I realized I needed to become more tolerant. I have my children to thank for this book, for it is rooted in an attitude of flexibility surrounding food choices, an attitude I had to develop out of respect for them. Once I learned to respect their approach to food, I had to figure out ways the family kitchen could function for all of us.

Would I have liked a totally vegetarian family? Of course. I am a member of several vegetarian societies and organizations. Information, books, and videos all geared for kids were at my disposal. As I explained my ethical and philosophical reasons for being a vegetarian, my children asked questions. We talked about feedlots crammed with cows destined for their plates; I compared meat to cigarettes, cocaine, and white sugar. Alas, life does not always work out the way you want it to. Should I have clubbed them over

(continued)

(continued from previous page)

the head with pictures of cruelty to animals or taken them to a slaughterhouse? Some of you may say yes, but instead I chose to open the lines of communication, talking to them about why I am a vegetarian and listening to their ideas. This dialogue is ongoing.

My family will eat any vegetarian meal I prepare. They do not eat a lot of meat overall, but meat *is* part of our household meal plan, and the discussion never ends. We talk about a lot of food issues. We consider the origins of seed stock and the agricultural methods used to grow food. Can organic certification be standardized? What are humane standards for raising animals? How animals are raised, how they died, and how meat tastes are centrepiece conversations around our dinner table.

Flexitarian cooking is about choice, tolerance, and good health. My kids—two of them now in university—are conscious about all things that cross their forks. But they're not afraid of food. Quite the opposite. They enjoy it and understand it and appreciate it, and not just the taste of food or food as physical nourishment, but also its larger meaning. Food can reflect how we relate to one another and to the world around us.

That's what this book is all about: taking pleasure in our food while being flexible and tolerant and informed about the food choices we have. I hope it inspires dialogue around your dinner table, mindful eating, and delicious flexitarian meals. —NETTIE

HOW DO THE RECIPES WORK?

Pat Crocker and I worked as a team to create a repertoire of flexitarian recipes. Drawing on my years as a natural foods and vegetarian chef, I developed delicious and nutritionally balanced vegetarian meals; Pat added meat portions. The "right" amount is a healthy portion that will not overwhelm your plate (or your waistline). Straightforward cooking instructions let you prepare the recipe to suit the needs of both vegetarians and meat eaters. —NETTIE

The vegetarian recipes are the foundation of this book, and I expect that more often than not they will be prepared without adding the meat, whether or not the people gathered around the table are all vegetarians.

I envisioned the meat sometimes acting as a condiment or a "flavour spike" that adds to the core vegetarian recipe; other times as a "protein finish," in the same way that a fine wine completes the total meal experience. I think of my meat suggestions as a pairing of fine flavours to fit in with the star vegetarian dish. In other words, in this book, the meat is not the main attraction but simply a minor ingredient in a world of delicious plant-based choices. —PAT

HOW MUCH PROTEIN IS ENOUGH?

The word *protein* comes from the Greek *proteios*, meaning "of first importance." Proteins are the basic structure of all cells and are necessary for healthy growth, cell repair, reproduction, and protection against disease. The building blocks of protein are amino acids.

Your body can manufacture most of the amino acids it needs. However, there are nine essential amino acids that your body cannot manufacture, and these must come from the food you eat.

Protein in foods of animal origin, such as meat, dairy products, eggs, and fish, provides all nine essential amino acids in the proportions that build and repair tissue. Plants also contain all the essential amino acids but not always in the proportions the body requires.

In 1971, Frances Moore Lappé's book *Diet for a Small Planet* raised awareness of complimentary protein: since plant proteins are limited in one or more of the essential amino acids, a food limited in one amino acid should be combined with another that is abundant in that amino acid. For example, grains are high in methionine but low in lysine, but legumes are low in methionine and high in lysine, so a dish of rice and beans provides complete protein.

As long as you eat a variety of vegetables, grains, beans, peas, nuts, and seeds in quantities sufficient to meet your energy (calorie) needs, it is unlikely you will be deficient in protein. Some vegetarians also include dairy products and eggs in their diet. Compared to those who eat meat, vegetarians get smaller amounts of protein from a wide variety of sources.

So how much essential amino acid protein do we need to eat to be healthy? Health Canada's Nutrition Recommendations tell us that a safe goal for adults is 0.3 oz (0.86 g) of protein per day for every 2.2 lb (1 kg) of body weight. For most people, that translates to a range of 1½ to 2¼ oz (45 to 70 g) per day, depending on your age, gender, and the amount of exercise you do.

Canada's Food Guide recommends two to three servings of meat or a meat alternative daily, where a serving is equal to 2½ oz or ½ cup (75 g or 125 mL) of cooked fish, shellfish, poultry, or lean meat; ¾ cup (185 mL) of cooked beans; 2 eggs; or 2 Tbsp (30 mL) of peanut butter. It is estimated that North Americans eat about 50 percent more than the recommended daily amount of protein.

The amount of animal protein I recommend for the non-vegetarian portions in this book may look small to some people, and they are small in comparison to most other recipes, because I have attempted to keep them within the nutrition guidelines. Also, almost all of our main-course vegetarian dishes deliver complete protein by combining two complimentary plant proteins, which makes the meat superfluous.

HOW IMPORTANT IS IT TO EAT ORGANIC?

From the Organic Consumers Association (www.organicconsumers.org):

- Organic foods contain higher levels of beta carotene, vitamins C, D, and E, and essential minerals.
- Organic foods are free of food additives (such as colour dyes), flavour enhancers (like MSG), artificial sweeteners (like aspartame and high-fructose corn syrup), contaminants (like mercury), and preservatives (like sodium nitrate).
- Organic animals are drug free: they are not given antibiotics, growth hormones, arsenic, or genetically modified vaccines; they are not fed slaughterhouse waste, blood, or even manure (chicken manure is reportedly used sometimes as a supplement to a cow's diet), thus eliminating the risk of Creutzfeldt-Jakob Disease, aka mad cow disease.
- More than 400 chemical pesticides are used in conventional farming, and residues remain on or within the cell walls of produce even after washing. Children are especially vulnerable to pesticide exposure.
- Organic food is not genetically modified.

We have a lot more to say about organic food, but the Canada Organic Trade Association says it best. See their comments in the appendix on page 264.

Anaheim   NuMex Big Jim   Cayenne   Cherry Bomb   Chile Andy

Goliath Griller   Holy Molé   Hungarian Wax   Jalapeño   Kung Pao

Lemon Drop   Paper Lantern   Poblano   Serrano   Thai Hot

THE ENLIGHTENED PANTRY

BROTHS, BOUILLON CUBES, AND POWDER

If you do not have the time to prepare stock from scratch (page 40 to 48), you can easily find good-quality vegetable stock, powder, and cubes at supermarkets and whole food stores. Read the labels of these products very carefully. Always check the amount of salt on the label—"no salt added" is the best option. Remember, you can always add a small amount of salt during cooking.

These products sometimes have questionable additives that are not natural and may include MSG (monosodium glutamate). The worst culprit is hydrolyzed vegetable protein, which is made from vegetables past their prime. Their nutrients are extracted through a process called hydrolysis, which requires the manufacturer to boil the vegetables in acid. The acid is then neutralized by a caustic soda. The resulting brown sludge is dried into a brown powder. We don't like the process and would not recommend buying any products that list this ingredient on the label.

CANNED FOODS

Many cans have a toxic coating on the inside containing something called bisphenol A (BPA). Only buy canned foods that are labelled "BPA-free" or do not have this coating.

CHILE PEPPERS

Chiles are available in several forms, whether fresh, dried, ground, or canned. Jalapeño, serrano, chipotle, ancho, and poblano chiles are the varieties used

Chiles for sale in late September at the annual Hudson Valley Garlic Festival, Saugerties, New York

most often as they are relatively easy to find, but there are many other chile peppers. Look for them in specialty food stores and farmers' markets.

Anaheim • These long and tapered chiles are pungent and mildly hot.

NuMex Big Jim • This mildly hot chile, a relative of the Anaheim, is good for roasting or for salsa. Some pods grow to 2 to 3 feet (60–90 cm) long.

Cayenne • These are small, thin, bright red when mature, and often curled and twisted. They are hot peppers that are used fresh and dried (whole or ground).

Cherry Bomb • The thick flesh, red colour (green when unripe), and small size of these very hot peppers make them good for using whole in recipes.

Chile Andy (aka Chile Andy F1) • A long and tapered bright-red pepper that grows to 8 inches (20 cm) long. (The one pictured is maturing to red.) Great for preserving and drying.

Goliath Griller • As the name suggests, these chile peppers are great for grilling.

Holy Molé • These are hot with a crisp texture, and are good for chile sauce and chilli dishes containing beans.

Hungarian Wax • These start as a canary yellow and turn bright red when ripe. These great-looking, mildly hot chiles are a versatile ingredient for vegetarian recipes.

Jalapeño/Chipotle • Along with poblano, jalapeños are one of the most popular of the chiles. Green and red jalapeños are versatile and enliven many dishes including salsa, black bean soups, and burritos. These bullet-shaped chiles have a medium-to-hot heat level (red ones pack more heat than green ones) and a bell pepper–like flavour.

Very good stuffed and baked, and often pickled.

Chipotles are large, cherry-red jalapeño peppers that have been dried and smoked. The distinctively smoky flavour partially obscures their heat. The chiles are available dried and canned; canned chiles are usually in a tomato-based adobo sauce. (Leftover sauce can be transferred to a covered glass jar and kept in the refrigerator for up to three months.)

Kung Pao • A very hot chile that is often used fresh in Szechuan dishes. This chile has thin walls and dries very easily. But it's best used fresh (for salsa, for example).

Lemon Drop • Does not have a distinct lemon flavour but does have a unique taste. A hot pepper that is good raw in salsa.

Paper Lantern • An elongated habañero type, these are very hot—mouth-blistering, in fact. Due to their heat rating, be very careful when handling and using them.

Poblano/Ancho • These dark-forest-green pods have an anvil shape with broad shoulders,

HOW TO ROAST BELL PEPPERS AND CHILE PEPPERS

Roasting peppers not only provides an easy method of peeling them but also intensifies their nutty flavours, caramelizes their sugars, and makes them soft and tender. Choose thick-walled fresh peppers for roasting. Roasted peppers may be canned or frozen to preserve them for future use.

1. Preheat the oven by setting it to Broil (500°F/260°C). Wash and dry peppers. If roasting bell peppers, cut in half lengthwise and remove stem, membrane, and seeds. If using chile peppers, leave whole with stem intact. Arrange cut side down on a lightly oiled

rimmed baking sheet. Brush lightly or drizzle with olive oil.

2. Roast on top rack in an oven for 10 to 12 minutes, or until skins blacken and blister. (You will need to turn whole chile peppers once or twice during roasting.)

3. Cover with a clean kitchen towel, or place in a paper bag, and let cool. If you are planning to freeze roasted peppers, cool and seal in a freezer bag without removing the skins, which will slip off easily upon thawing. Skins should rub away or pull off easily.

4. Cut off stem ends of chile peppers,

and remove seeds if desired, but leave chile peppers whole. Slice bell peppers, quarter them, or leave as halves.

HARISSA

MAKES: ½ cup (125 mL)

Popular in Morocco, Tunisia, and Algeria, harissa is a fiery sauce used in almost the same way that North Americans use ketchup. It is used as a dip for grilled vegetables, put into couscous, stirred into soups and stews, or used as an ingredient for dips and sauces.

12 dried red chile peppers

¾ cup (185 mL) boiling water

1 Tbsp (15 mL) whole coriander seeds

2 tsp (10 mL) whole cumin seeds

1 tsp (5 mL) whole fennel seeds

½ tsp (2 mL) whole fenugreek
seeds (optional)

2 cloves garlic

½ tsp (2 mL) salt

½ cup (125 mL) olive oil

TRIM STEMS OFF chiles and discard along with some of the seeds. Using kitchen scissors, cut chiles into small pieces. Place in a small bowl and pour boiling water overtop. Soak until soft, about 30 minutes. Drain.

Meanwhile toast coriander, cumin, fennel, and fenugreek (if using) seeds, in a small dry heavy skillet over medium heat for about 3 minutes, or until fragrant and light brown. Remove from heat and let cool.

Using a mortar and pestle or a small food processor, pound or process garlic with salt. Add toasted spices and drained chiles and pound or process until smooth. Add olive oil slowly and grind or process until sauce is well mixed. Harissa should have the consistency of mayonnaise. Store harissa in a small jar with a lid in the refrigerator for up to 3 weeks.

and are also called "Super Chile" when fresh and "ancho" when dried. They mature from green to red. Poblano peppers have a raisin-like flavour and range in heat from mild to hot; their delicate flavour makes them useful in preserve recipes, but they are often roasted. Most poblano hybrids will be mild but if crossed with serrano, will be hot.

The name *ancho* means "wide" or "broad," which describes the shoulders of the pepper. Ancho peppers are burnt-red and have wrinkled skin. They have a mild heat, and are toasted in a dry skillet and rehydrated before using.

Serrano • These small, narrow green (or red) chiles have a sharp, prickly heat, which quickly fades. Because they are small and finger-shaped, they're great for pickle recipes and when you want even crosswise slices. The pods have a dense core of seeds that should be removed before using it in a dish. Also available dried.

Thai Hot • Pungent and five times hotter than jalapeños. Be sure their heat level is what you want before adding them to salsa and chilli dishes.

COCONUT MILK

When fresh coconut pulp or meat is ground with hot water and then squeezed completely dry, the resulting liquid is referred to as coconut milk. If left to stand, it separates into a layer of fatty "cream" and a layer of thinner "milk." With canned coconut milk, always check the expiration date and shake the can well before using.

CONDIMENTS

Hoisin Sauce • Dark brown with a reddish tint, hoisin is a soybean-paste sauce that contains garlic, vinegar, and chile peppers—it's sweet, salty, and spicy. Always check the best-before date and refrigerate once opened.

Mirin • A sweet rice wine used in Japanese cooking. It is used to balance the saltiness of other seasonings like miso and soy sauce. We use it in vinaigrettes, sauces, and glazes. Although naturally brewed mirin is made from water, sweet brown rice, and rice culture (*koji*), much of the mirin sold in Asian supermarkets is sweetened with sugar or corn syrup. Another reminder to read labels carefully.

Nutritional Yeast • Nutritional yeast comes in flakes or a powder that is pale golden with a distinct but pleasant aroma. Not to be confused with baking yeast, nutritional yeast is a condiment, not a leavening agent, added to sauces, casseroles, and salads for its nutritional value and cheese-like flavour. Available in stores under the brand name Vegetarian Support Formula (T-6635+) Primary Grown Nutritional Yeast, made by Red Star Yeast and Products.

See also **tahini** on page 6.

FATS

Olive Oil • As early as 6000 BC, ancient peoples spread the olive tree along the shores of the Mediterranean. Due to their deep roots, trees can withstand extreme temperatures, frost, and drought. They are well known for their longevity. The olive tree is an evergreen; its leaves are a light silvery green. The fruit has a fleshy pulp and the colour ranges from black to mustard yellow and green.

Olive oil is pressed from olives, which are, botanically speaking, a fruit. Over the centuries the fruit has been picked and processed in the same way to make olive oil, and these methods are still in use today. Historians over the ages have sung the praises of olive oil. Consider its many uses: as a fuel, for skincare and medicine, and as a condiment. According to the International Olive Oil Council, olive oil has potential in the prevention and control

of diabetes and in warding off the effects of aging (*Olive Oil, Quality of Life*, 2000). The health benefits of olive oil are backed by scientific research.

When tomatoes are paired with olive oil, the health-inducing lycopene in the tomatoes is more readily absorbed. (Lycopene is a powerful antioxidant linked to the prevention of prostate, cervical, and digestive-system cancers.) Garlic, long revered as another potent antioxidant and mainstay of alternative medicine, is the perfect complement to both olive oil and tomatoes. Here is a win-win situation. Not only does olive oil taste terrific, it brings out the best in other ingredients, too.

Non-Hydrogenated Shortening • Earth Balance shortening (containing no trans fats) is made from non-GMO palm fruit, soybean, canola, and olive oils. Keep it refrigerated and always check the expiration date before purchasing. There are four ½-cup (125 mL) sticks in a package.

Sesame Oil • An aromatic oil expressed from sesame seeds. Light sesame oil has a golden colour and a mild, nutty taste and is best for sautéing and for dressings. Dark sesame oil, pressed from roasted seeds and sometimes  called "toasted sesame oil," is deep brown, has a strong, smoky flavour, and is used for cooking and seasoning.

GREENS

Cruciferous Vegetables • The word *cruciferous* is derived from the Latin name for "cross" (*crux*), which the four petals of flowers form. Also referred to as "crucifer plants," members of the *Cruciferae* family of vegetables include arugula, bok choy, broccoli, Brussels sprouts, cabbage, cauliflower, collard greens, horseradish, kohlrabi, mustard (both the seeds and the greens are used), radishes, rutabaga, turnip, and watercress.

Kale • Dark, ruffled Lacinato kale is sold under a number of different names—Black, Tuscan, and Dinosaur—and shares the nutritional make-up of cruciferous vegetables. Kale grows well in produce-starved winter months, which is great because it is free of fat and cholesterol, rich in fibre, low in fat, and high in vitamin A. Its rich, full-flavoured contribution to minestrone, risotto, calzones, and lasagna reflects its versatility and adaptability. (See the sidebar on page 153 for more information on greens.)

LEGUMES (BEANS)

Legumes or beans (sometimes called "pulses") are plants that have pods that split open when ripe to reveal a row of edible seeds.

Beans are high in protein, fibre, and starch and low in fat, and an excellent source of iron, B vitamins, potassium, riboflavin, niacin, and folic acid. When sprouted they have the added bonus of vitamin C. They have long been an alternative to costly animal protein, and have deep roots in the cuisines of Asia, Central and South America, and the Mediterranean.

Beans also contain oil. Legumes that produce oil crops, such as peanuts and soybeans, are the most economically viable, and are used industrially and as livestock feed.

Choose dried beans that are bright in colour and uniform in size and shape. And why do we need to soak dried beans? To shorten the cooking time, to enable some beans to hold their shape, and to remove the complex sugars (*raffinose*) that pass undigested into our lower intestines and encounter bacteria there that cause them to ferment and release gas. Dried beans may be stored for a year in airtight containers in a cool, dark place. Cooked beans may be frozen in sealed packaging for up to six months.

Adzuki Beans • Small, deep-maroon, and peppercorn-sized beans of Japanese origin. They are used in candied desserts and as a base for hot drinks. Easy to prepare and a staple in macrobiotic cuisine. Often sprouted.

Black Beans • Small, plump, kidney-shaped beans with a shiny black-blue coat and an earthy flavour.

Chickpeas (Garbanzo Beans) • Round, medium-sized, tan-coloured beans with a firm shape and nutty flavour. Garbanzos have been grown for 9,000 years. The botanical name *Cicer arietinu* comes from the bean's Latin name, *cicer*, which means "ram-like" and refers to the bean's resemblance to a ram's head, with curling horns. *Garbanzo* is the Spanish name for chickpeas.

Kidney and Pinto Beans • Grouped together because they can be used interchangeably in many recipes. Kidney beans, named for their shape, are medium-sized beans with a soft texture and come in four different colours: red, pink, brown, and white. White beans are called cannellini. They retain their shape well in long-simmering dishes.

Pinto beans (see page 143) are half the length of kidney beans and oval-shaped. They can have pinkish tan, speckled coats, or be all brown or all cranberry-coloured. *Pinto* means painted in Spanish. They have been grown for 10,000 years.

Lentils • A type of legume that is small and disc-shaped with a firm texture. Whole lentils are made up of two lens-shaped sides. Lentils are also sold without the husk, making them smaller and finer-textured. India consumes half the world's lentil crop.

There are many kinds and colours of lentil: brown, black, red, and green. Nettie's favourite is a small brown French lentil called Lentille du Puy. Pat's favourite is called Beluga (or Black Beluga), which glisten when cooked, making them resemble beluga caviar.

Unlike other legumes, lentils do not need to be presoaked and they cook faster than dried peas and beans. Because lentils are flat, with thin seed coats, they can be easily penetrated by cooking water. Simmer lentils gently in roughly three times as much water. Season with salt or other ingredients only *after* cooking because salt, and other acidic ingredients, halts the cooking and turns legumes tough.

NUT (AND SEED) BUTTERS

Pastes made from finely ground nuts or seeds are called "butters." Peanut butter is the best-known example. Commercial food companies have made a fortune adding sugar and refined oils. Who knew that ground nuts could achieve junk-food status?

Almond (smooth and crunchy), cashew, macadamia, hazelnut, sunflower, sesame, pumpkin, and sunflower are but a few examples of nut and seed butters available for cooking and eating. Most nuts average about 60 percent fat (by weight) while seeds are lower (50 percent). The fat of nuts and seeds is mono- and polyunsaturated and contains no cholesterol; compare this to other protein foods such as meat and cheese, which contain saturated fats. That said, nut and seed butters are best used in small portions.

Tahini • A thick, smooth paste made of hulled and ground sesame seeds. A Middle Eastern staple, tahini is used as a spread and as an ingredient in dressings, sauces, and dips.

CASHEW CREAM

MAKES: 1⅓ cups (330 mL)

Use as a cream substitute in soup and sauce recipes. Toast the cashews first for a deeper, richer flavour.

⸻

¾ cup (185 mL) cashews
1 cup (250 mL) rice milk or plain soymilk

⸻

COMBINE NUTS AND milk in a blender. Blend on high until nuts are completely puréed and cream is smooth.

Store cream tightly covered in the refrigerator for up to 1 week.

CASHEW CREAM TOPPING

MAKES: 1⅓ cups (330 mL)

Flavourful and rich, this sweet topping may be used as a whipped cream substitute for sweet dishes.

⸻

⅓ cup (80 mL) brown rice syrup
¼ cup (60 mL) rice milk or plain soymilk
1 cup (250 mL) cashews
1 tsp (5 mL) pure vanilla extract
Pinch of salt

⸻

COMBINE RICE SYRUP and milk in a saucepan and heat over medium-high heat, stirring constantly, for about 2 minutes or until the syrup is dissolved.

Grind nuts in a food processor until very fine. With the motor running, add milk mixture through the opening in the lid. Blend on high until nuts are completely puréed and cream is smooth. Stir in vanilla and salt.

Store cream tightly covered in the refrigerator for up to 1 week.

SAUCES, PASTES, SEASONINGS, GLAZES, AND MARINADES

As the author of both a vegetarian and a vegan cookbook, I have found that paying attention to seasonings, herbs, sauces, glazes, and marinades is critical for those making the transition from a meat-based to a plant-based diet. For this reason, we have included these basic recipes that really pack a punch and that you'll definitely want to have on hand. —PAT

BARBECUE SAUCE

MAKES: 2 cups (500 mL)

With no preservatives or additives, this zippy sauce lends a complex and slightly sweet taste to foods. Regular Worcestershire sauce contains anchovies, so use soy sauce if you want to make this 100 percent vegetarian.

  1 Tbsp (15 mL) olive oil
  1 cup (250 mL) finely chopped onion
  2 cups (500 mL) vegetable stock
    (see page 40 for homemade)
    or chicken stock (page 45)
  ¾ cup (185 mL) ketchup
  ¼ cup (60 mL) lightly packed brown sugar
  2 Tbsp (30 mL) Worcestershire-style sauce
  2 tsp (10 mL) Dijon mustard
  ½ tsp (2 mL) salt
  ¼ tsp (1 mL) freshly ground pepper

HEAT OIL IN a heavy saucepan over medium heat. Add onion and cook, stirring frequently, for 10 minutes or until softened. Whisk in stock, ketchup, brown sugar, Worcestershire sauce, mustard, salt, and pepper. Bring to a boil, reduce heat, and simmer, stirring occasionally, for 25 minutes or until thickened and reduced to about 2 cups (500 mL).

SWEET AND SOUR SAUCE

MAKES: 2 cups (500 mL)

To give dishes a spike of Asian flavour, this easy-to-make sauce is essential.

  1 tsp (5 mL) peanut oil or olive oil
  1 clove garlic, minced
  1 tsp (5 mL) minced fresh ginger
  1½ cups (375 mL) apple juice
  2 Tbsp (30 mL) maple syrup
  2 Tbsp (30 mL) apple cider vinegar
  2 Tbsp (30 mL) tomato paste
  2 Tbsp (30 mL) tamari or soy sauce
  1 Tbsp (15 mL) Dijon mustard
  1 tsp (5 mL) toasted sesame oil
  2 Tbsp (30 mL) arrowroot flour (or cornstarch)
  2 Tbsp (30 mL) water

HEAT OIL IN a saucepan over medium-high heat. Add garlic and ginger and sauté for 1 minute. Add apple juice, maple syrup, vinegar, tomato paste, tamari, mustard, and sesame oil. Bring to a boil, reduce heat, and simmer, stirring frequently, for 5 minutes.

Combine arrowroot flour and water in a bowl. Whisk to dissolve arrowroot. Whisk into simmering sauce and cook, stirring constantly, for 3 to 5 minutes or until sauce thickens.

PEANUT LIME SAUCE

MAKES: 1¼ cups (310 mL)

You can tailor the taste of this piquant sauce by using milder-tasting almond or cashew butter instead of peanut butter. Increase or decrease the heat by adjusting the amount of chile flakes.

  ½ cup (125 mL) smooth peanut butter
  ½ cup (125 mL) coconut milk
  ¼ cup (60 mL) tamari or soy sauce

3 Tbsp (45 mL) brown sugar

2 Tbsp (30 mL) fresh lime juice

2 Tbsp (30 mL) rice vinegar

1 Tbsp (15 mL) toasted sesame oil

1 tsp (5 mL) minced fresh ginger

⅛ tsp (0.5 mL) dried red chile flakes

ADD ALL INGREDIENTS to a blender or food processor. Process for about 1 minute or until blended and smooth.

Store in an airtight container in the refrigerator for up to 2 weeks. Bring to room temperature and mix well before using.

POMEGRANATE GLAZE

MAKES: 2 cups (500 mL)

A glaze is thicker than a sauce, and something you can spread or "glaze" over ingredients. This sauce is sold commercially as pomegranate molasses.

4 cups (1 L) pomegranate juice

½ cup (125 mL) granulated sugar

¼ cup (60 mL) fresh lemon juice

COMBINE ALL INGREDIENTS in a heavy-bottomed saucepan. Bring to a gentle boil over medium-high heat, stirring until sugar is dissolved. Reduce heat and keep simmering gently for about 1 hour, or until thick and syrupy. Liquid should be reduced by at least one-half.

Pour the hot liquid into a canning jar before cooling. Cap, label, and let cool.

Use immediately, or store in the refrigerator for up to 2 weeks.

SWEET THAI CHILE SAUCE

MAKES: 2 cups (500 mL)

You will often find this spelled "chilli sauce" on labels of the store-bought version of this sauce. If you wish, use Thai basil or flat-leaf parsley in place of the cilantro.

⅔ cup (160 mL) granulated sugar

4 tsp (20 mL) cornstarch

1 tsp (5 mL) salt

⅔ cup (160 mL) water

½ cup (125 mL) rice vinegar

3 Tbsp (45 mL) red or green curry paste (page 9 for homemade)

2 cloves garlic, minced

¼ cup (60 mL) chopped fresh cilantro

COMBINE SUGAR, CORNSTARCH, and salt in a bowl. Set aside.

Combine water, vinegar, curry paste, and garlic in a saucepan. Bring to a boil over medium-high heat, stirring often. Stir in sugar mixture. Reduce heat and simmer, stirring constantly for 5 minutes or until thickened. Cool and stir in cilantro.

Store in an airtight container in the refrigerator for up to 2 weeks. Bring to room temperature and mix well before using.

TERIYAKI SAUCE

MAKES: 1½ cups (375 mL)

Double or triple this recipe for marinating tofu, tempeh, chicken, or fish.

1 cup (250 mL) tamari or soy sauce

⅓ cup (80 mL) liquid honey

3 cloves garlic, minced

2 Tbsp (30 mL) rice vinegar

2 tsp (10 mL) toasted sesame oil

COMBINE ALL INGREDIENTS in a bowl and mix well.

Use immediately, or cover and store in the refrigerator for up to 2 weeks.

GREEN CURRY PASTE

MAKES: 1 cup (250 mL)

This is modelled on the classic green curry paste but uses North American ingredients. The Asian ingredients are given in parentheses should you wish to use them. Using hot green chiles gives this sauce its colour and a good deal more heat than the red curry paste that follows.

3 cloves garlic

1 slice candied ginger (1 Tbsp/15 mL grated fresh ginger)

½ onion

2 anchovies (1 tsp/5 mL shrimp paste) (optional)

15 green chile peppers

12 fresh or dried lemon verbena leaves (4 stalks lemongrass, minced)

6 sprigs fresh cilantro or flat-leaf parsley

3 sprigs fresh rosemary (1 Tbsp/15 mL minced kaffir lime leaves)

1 tsp (5 mL) Brazilian green peppercorns, cracked

1 tsp (5 mL) ground coriander

1 tsp (5 mL) ground cumin

½ tsp (2 mL) salt

1 tsp (5 mL) toasted sesame oil

IN A FOOD processor, combine garlic and ginger. Process until finely chopped. Add onion and anchovies (if using). Process until finely chopped.

Add chile peppers and process until finely chopped. Add lemon verbena, cilantro, rosemary, peppercorns, coriander, cumin, and salt. Process. With the motor still running, add the sesame oil through the opening in the lid. Continue processing until a smooth paste is achieved.

Spoon into serving dish, cover, and refrigerate until serving, or spoon into a sterilized jar and cap with the lid. Store in the refrigerator for 3 to 4 weeks.

RED CURRY PASTE

MAKES: 1 cup (250 mL)

This is a hot but not blistering sauce. As with the green curry paste, the Asian ingredients are given in parentheses. If you can only get dried cayenne peppers, slit them in half and soak them in warm water for 20 minutes. Drain and use as directed. And if you cannot find lemon verbena leaves or even lemongrass, use a tablespoon (15 mL) of lemon or lime zest.

3 cloves garlic

1 slice candied ginger (1 Tbsp/15 mL grated fresh ginger)

½ red onion

2 anchovies (1 tsp/5 mL shrimp paste) (optional)

15 fresh red cayenne peppers

12 fresh or dried lemon verbena leaves (4 stalks lemongrass, minced)

6 sprigs fresh cilantro or flat-leaf parsley

3 sprigs fresh rosemary (1 Tbsp/15 mL minced kaffir lime leaves)

1 tsp (5 mL) Malabar black peppercorns, cracked

1 tsp (5 mL) ground coriander

1 tsp (5 mL) ground cumin

½ tsp (2 mL) salt

1 tsp (5 mL) toasted sesame oil

IN A FOOD processor, combine garlic and ginger. Process until finely chopped. Add onion and anchovies (if using). Process until finely chopped. Add cayenne peppers and process until finely chopped. Add lemon verbena, cilantro or parsley, rosemary, peppercorns, coriander, cumin, and salt. Process. With the motor still running, add the sesame oil through the opening in the lid. Continue processing until a smooth paste is achieved.

Spoon into serving dish, cover, and refrigerate until serving, or spoon into a sterilized jar and cap with the lid. Store in the refrigerator for 3 to 4 weeks.

TOASTED CUMIN DRY RUB

MAKES: about ¾ cup (185 mL)

Toasting the seeds brings out their nutty flavour.

⅓ cup (80 mL) whole cumin seeds

3 Tbsp (45 mL) whole coriander seeds

2 Tbsp (30 mL) green or black peppercorns

1 Tbsp (15 mL) granulated sugar

2 tsp (10 mL) salt

COMBINE THE CUMIN, coriander, and peppercorns in a spice wok or small heavy-bottomed skillet. Dry-roast, stirring constantly over medium-high heat for 3 to 6 minutes, or until fragrant and the seeds begin to pop. Remove from heat before spices begin to smoke.

Cool and then grind using a mortar and pestle, blender, or spice grinder. Transfer to a small bowl and stir in the sugar and salt.

Store in a glass jar in a cool dark place for up to 6 months.

KAFFIR LIME

This citrus fruit is similar to the common lime but it has a very knobby and fragrant skin and virtually no juice. The skin or rind is often grated and added to food, and the fragrant leaves are used in soups and curries, or finely shredded and added to salads. Substitute dried leaves for fresh ones.

LEMONGRASS

Lemongrass is a tropical plant that matures into a woody but fragrant, lemon-scented herb, resembling a miniature leek. Lemongrass gives a citrus aroma and flavour to the dishes of Southeast Asia. Remove the dry, fibrous outer layers and top of the herb and use only the lower 6 inches (15 cm) of the interior of the stalks. Slice paper-thin or pound into a paste and add to rice, soup, casseroles, and other Asian dishes. Whole stalks will keep in the fridge for two weeks if wrapped well.

SEA VEGETABLES

Long before the development of agriculture, coastal peoples harvested a variety of nutritious vegetables from the sea. Sea vegetables are rich in essential minerals, vitamins, and proteins and important trace elements, which land vegetables are lacking in because of soil demineralization. Sea vegetables are important in a non-dairy, grain-based vegetarian diet because they provide calcium, iron, and iodine. They also have an abundance of vitamins, including niacin, vitamin C, and folic acid.

Arame • A dark-brown sea grass that is sold shredded, resembling black angel-hair pasta. It has a mild aroma and taste. Arame needs to be soaked in cold water for five minutes and drained before being used in recipes. Its sweet taste is due to the presence of mannitol, a non-caloric sugar, which is present in many brown sea grasses.

Kombu • An essential ingredient in the preparation of *dashi* (Japanese stock). Do not soak, wash, or rinse kombu before using it, as some of the components that account for the flavour are water-soluble and could be washed away. Main courses with kombu will require lengthy sautéing or boiling in a more highly seasoned liquid.

Nori • A sea vegetable that has been dried and pressed into sheets. It is most commonly used to wrap rice or as the exterior of sushi rolls. Nori has many health benefits, with a wide range of nutrients including calcium, iron, and vitamins A, B, and C.

Nori sheets should be greenish-black. It should be lightly toasted prior to use, or buy it already toasted. To toast nori, pass an unfolded sheet briefly over a gas flame or electric burner until the colour changes to a brilliant green and the nori becomes crispy and fragrant. Nori may be used in lots of ways. It can be crumbled or cut into strips and used to garnish soups and noodles. It is also sold as flakes.

SOY

Soy foods contain many healthy ingredients, including high-quality protein, fibre, lecithin, vitamin B12, vitamin E, calcium, zinc, and iron. The protein in soybeans has all of the essential amino acids necessary for nutritional health. Soybeans also contain omega-3 fatty acids, and around 50 percent of the fat in soybean oil is linoleic acid, which is an essential nutrient that the body cannot create.

We recommend only organic soybeans and soy products because most of the soybeans grown today are genetically modified and are produced using high amounts of pesticides. Also avoid textured vegetable protein (TVP) made from soybeans because it is produced using chemicals and harmful techniques and is not considered a whole food. Do not consume excessive amounts of soy during pregnancy, and completely avoid soy-based baby formulas.

Overreliance on soy foods may cause nutritional deficiencies, and, in fact, these foods can interfere with the normal functioning of the thyroid gland. In this book, we use small amounts of soy intelligently and provide balanced protein recipes.

Edamame • Edamame is the name for the smooth green soybeans in the soybean pod. They are available fresh or frozen. Caution: Fresh soybeans contain enzyme inhibitors that block protein digestion and may cause serious gastric distress and organ damage.

Miso • Miso is to vegetarian cooking what beef bouillon or gravy is to a meat-centred diet. This salty, fermented paste is made from cooked, aged soybeans and grains. Miso is thick and spreadable and used for flavouring a wide variety of dishes (replacing salt in many recipes) and for making soup stocks. It must never be boiled. It is available in several varieties: barley, rice, and chickpea miso are dark and salty with a strong flavour because they are aged for several years; white miso has a mild, less-salty taste because it is only aged for three months. Buy unpasteurized, refrigerated miso. Store in the fridge for up to six months.

Soymilk • As the name suggests, soymilk is a non-dairy beverage made from cooked, strained soybeans and water. The name *soymilk* might imply that it tastes beany, although the taste varies depending on the oil and sweetener content, and the new varieties are very pleasant. It can be used in similar ways to dairy milk but has no cholesterol or lactose. Plain or "original" flavour works best in most savoury recipes; vanilla and other flavours may work in dessert recipes. Drink chilled. Available fortified with calcium and B vitamins. Soymilk is sold fresh, or in aseptic packages that usually last about a year (check the expiration date). Once opened, it keeps for one week if refrigerated. For baking recipes you can interchange soymilk with other non-dairy beverages such as almond, rice, hemp, and coconut milk.

Soy Sauce (Tamari) • Made from soybeans, wheat, and salt. The traditional brewing process begins with toasting the cracked wheat and steaming the soybeans. These are then mixed together and inoculated with spores of an *Aspergillus* mould. A three-day incubation period is needed for the *koji* (mould) to grow. Once the *koji* has formed, the mixture is added to a brine to make a liquid mash, which is fermented in large tanks for one to two years. Next, it is placed in  cotton sacks and pressed to extract a dark liquid, a combination of soy oil and soy sauce. The oil rises to the surface and is removed. The sauce is ready for pasteurization and bottling.

Soy sauce is high in glutamic acid (a natural form of monosodium glutamate), which is used as a flavour enhancer, often used for marinating, pickling, and sautéing. Purchase organic soy sauce made from whole soybeans; it's worth it.

Tamari is a Japanese word that best describes a dark, rich soy sauce. Read labels carefully: good-quality tamari contains no preservatives, food colouring, or sugar.

Tempeh • A cultured food invented in Indonesia made from soybeans and grains. Tempeh is traditionally made by culturing cooked, cracked soybeans with the mould *Rhizopus oligosporus*. It becomes a dense, protein-rich square of fermented soybeans. Tempeh has a firm, chewy texture. It is commonly used to replace ground beef, chicken, or fish in recipes. Sold fresh or frozen. Do not eat uncooked tempeh.

Tofu • Tofu, often called bean curd, is a beige, neutral-tasting soy food that is easily digestible, is high in protein, and contains no cholesterol. To make tofu, soybeans are soaked, drained, and then ground. The ground beans are placed in water, strained, and pressed to produce soymilk. A coagulant is then added to the soymilk to cause curds to form—the amount of coagulant and water used determines the texture of the tofu.

Tofu is available in several varieties, including soft, firm, and extra firm. Soft and silken types are best in sauces, smoothies, and desserts. Firmer types are best for stir-fries and marinades. Only buy tofu made from organic soybeans.

Once opened, tofu will last one week in your refrigerator. To store unused tofu, put it in a covered container and cover it with cold water.

Refrigerate tofu this way for up to seven days, changing the water daily. We often use leftover tofu to make smoothies. If you have not used up all the tofu by Day 7, it may be frozen.

Freezing tofu changes its texture (renders it chewy) and colour (from white to amber). Frozen tofu resembles ground beef in recipes. Defrosting frozen tofu is easy. Remove any wrapping and place in a deep bowl. Cover with boiling water and let stand for 10 minutes. Drain. Rinse with cool water and divide tofu into small pieces, squeezing out excess water into a bowl and crumbling remaining tofu. Use frozen tofu in pasta sauce, chilli, or bean and rice dishes.

SWEETENERS

Agave Syrup • Made from the sap of a plant that has been used medicinally in Mexico for decades. Agave plants must be seven to ten years old before they are ready for harvesting. Plants are 5 to 8 feet (1.5 to 2.4 m) tall and have a diameter of 7 to 12 feet (2.1 to 3.6 m). This natural sweetener is used as a vegan alternative to honey. It does not crystallize nor solidify when cold, is sweeter than sugar, and has a three-year shelf life. It is sold in light, amber, dark, and raw varieties. A general substitution is to use one-third less agave than you would white sugar and one-fourth less than other liquid sweeteners. Also, baked goods made with agave brown more quickly, so reduce oven temperatures by 25°F (14°C).

Apple Syrup • Apples, sugar, and water are heated and strained to produce a sweet, apple-tasting syrup.

Barley Malt Syrup • A natural sweetener, similar to molasses in colour, made from sprouted dried barley. It is the predecessor of modern corn syrups. Malt syrup is used in malted milk, malt balls, and for making homemade beer, but can act as a replacement for other sweeteners in cooking and baking.

Brown Rice Syrup • A thick syrup made from cracked brown rice and barley. It has a mildly sweet taste and is used in desserts and sauces. A good substitute for honey (one to one ratio). Stored in a cool, dark place, it has a long shelf life.

Brown Sugar • Most brown sugar is refined white sugar with molasses added. Available in light and dark varieties. The darker the colour, the more intense the flavour.

Confectioners' Sugar • Confectioners' sugar (usually called icing sugar in Canada) is sugar that has been ground into a fine powder, with corn-starch added to prevent crystallization. It is used mostly in icings because it dissolves very easily; it can also be sifted over desserts.

Demerara Sugar • Amber brown, coarse, and dry. It retains 15 percent of the natural molasses it contains. Deep toffee flavour. Large crystals make it suitable for decoration and toppings, and it dissolves easily into batter.

Honey • The product of bees, honey is a natural sweetener. Nettie's local health food store, the Big Carrot, has a terrific relationship with a bee farmer who practises humane bee husbandry. The source of the nectar determines the flavour of the honey. Nettie's favourite is clover honey.

Maple Syrup • A sweet syrup made from boiling the spring sap tapped from sugar maple trees (Acer). Maple syrup is graded according to colour, flavour, and sugar content. Grade A is the lighter, more delicately flavoured designation. Grades B and C are stronger in flavour, and are more often used for cooking and baking. Today, many producers use energy-efficient, reverse-osmosis kits to remove the sap water, and then boil the sap to develop its flavour.

Molasses • Molasses is a by-product of the

sugar-refining industry. It is the syrup left over in cane-sugar processing once the sucrose has been removed from the boiled juice. Used as a background flavour in many foods—such as gingerbread, baked beans, barbecue sauces, and licorice—it also helps to retain moisture in food. It can be stored in a cool, dark cupboard for up to six months.

Muscovado Sugar • Known as Barbados sugar, this sugar is moist, fine grained, and dark in appearance. Best used in spice cakes, fruit fillings, and baked goods that can absorb its distinct molasses flavour.

Stevia • Stevia, sold as a liquid and as a powder, is a natural sweetener derived from a sweet herb, whose dried leaves are 10 times sweeter than sugar. Only use small amounts or your recipe will be overwhelmed by the sweet flavour. Stevia has a distinct flavour that not everyone enjoys. On the plus side, it contains few calories and is often used by diabetics.

Sucanat • Sucanat is the brand name for organically grown sugar-cane juice that has been dried and thus contains all of its natural ingredients. Often substituted for refined white sugar (one to one ratio).

VINEGARS

The word *vinegar* comes from the French *vin aigre* meaning "sour wine." The process of producing vinegar involves fermentation to cause the grape or grain sugars to break down into ethyl alcohol and carbon dioxide gas. During a second fermentation, bacteria assist the alcohol to react with oxygen in the air to form acetic acid.

Commercial vinegars range from 4 to 9 percent acetic acid. This level of acidity makes vinegar useful in preserving food, as bacteria cannot grow in such strong acid. The acidity also enhances the flavour of food, so use it often. Always keep vinegar in

---

BASIC BALSAMIC VINAIGRETTE

MAKES: ½ cup (125 mL)

⅓ cup (80 mL) balsamic vinegar
3 Tbsp (45 mL) fresh lime juice
1 Tbsp (15 mL) tamari or soy sauce
1 tsp (5 mL) mirin
1 tsp (5 mL) rice vinegar
¼ tsp (1 mL) freshly ground pepper

IN A SMALL bowl, whisk together all the ingredients.

Store covered in the refrigerator for up to 3 days.

---

non-reactive glass containers, with corks or lined metal lids. Store in a cool, dark place.

Balsamic Vinegar • (level of acidity: 6 percent) Made from extremely sweet Trebbiano grapes (skins and juice) that are crushed and fermented in wooden casks in the Italian region of Emilia-Romagna, near the town of Modena, Italy.

Cider Vinegar • (level of acidity: 5 percent) Very fruity vinegar made from a base of yeast and fermented apple juice. It is often cloudy.

Malt Vinegar • (level of acidity: 4 to 8 percent) Made from sprouted barley, cereal grains, and un-hopped beer. Soft acidity, and balances the heaviness of deep-fried foods.

Rice Vinegar • (level of acidity: mild, usually around 4 percent) Made from fermented rice. The starches of rice grains are reduced to sugar using a mould culture. Do not buy "seasoned" rice vinegar—the seasoning interferes with the naturally light, sweet flavour.

Sherry Vinegar • (level of acidity: mild, usually around 4 percent) Nettie's absolute favourite. Expensive and delicious, sherry vinegar is blended with older batches and can mature for years in wooden barrels. Extended contact with microbes and wood leave the vinegar with high levels of amino acids. Your best bet is *vinaigre de Jerez*, which is produced in Spain.

Wine Vinegar • (level of acidity: 6 to 7 percent) Made from red or white wines. The taste ranges from mild to strong depending on the type of grape used and the length of fermentation. The deeper the colour, the stronger the flavour.

HOW DO THE SERVINGS WORK?

The majority of the recipes in this book are designed to serve six people. For the recipes that can serve both the vegetarian and the meat eater (featuring a mix of regular and blue text, the latter signifying the meat portion of the recipe), here are some guidelines:

- If you want to make these dishes completely vegetarian, simply follow the recipe, *but ignore all of the blue text* (which denotes the extra ingredients and prompts needed to make the meat version of the dish). You will usually end up with six servings.

- If you are serving a few meat eaters, follow the recipe, *but pay attention to the additional ingredients and prompts in blue text.* You will end up with two meat servings and four vegetarian servings—six servings in total.

- Simply double the ingredients listed in blue if you wish to prepare four meat servings instead of two. You DO NOT need to double any of the other ingredients, but you will be doubling whatever is "set aside" for the meat servings. You will end up with four meat servings and two vegetarian servings—six servings in total.

Ignore the blue text if making the vegetarian version of the dish.

APPETIZERS

RICE PAPER ROLLS WITH SWEET RED CHILE SAUCE

When you see how easy they are to prepare, you and your kids will often have fun making these simple yet sophisticated lunch or snack rolls. Use your imagination and fill them with raw or cooked vegetables in any combination. I prefer to chop the lettuce and use 2 Tbsp (30 mL) per roll, while Pat prefers to use the whole leaf. Serve with Sweet Thai Chile Sauce or Peanut Lime Sauce. —NETTIE

SHRIMP RICE PAPER ROLLS WITH SWEET RED CHILE SAUCE

You can use any cooked fish or seafood, such as crab, snapper, and mussels. I really do love how the colour and shape of whole shrimp show through the rice paper. —PAT

RICE PAPER WRAPPERS

Rice paper wrappers are made from a mixture of rice flour, water, and salt, which is rolled out by a machine to paper thinness and then dried on bamboo mats in the sun. They are only available dried, and come in packages of 50 to 100. Store in a cool, dark place.

Wrappers must be softened before use. Carefully immerse one or two sheets in warm water. Soak them until they are soft, about 10 to 30 seconds, just until softened. Drain them on a towel before rolling.

1 lb (500 g) rice vermicelli

2 Tbsp (30 mL) rice vinegar

1 Tbsp (15 mL) toasted sesame oil

12 rice paper wrappers

36 fresh basil leaves (more for
garnishing, optional)

12 small lettuce leaves,
chopped or left whole

¾ cup (185 mL) fermented black
bean sauce (optional)

¾ cup (185 mL) chopped peanuts

Twenty-four ½-inch (1 cm) zucchini
or carrot sticks

Twelve ½-inch (1 cm)
red bell pepper sticks

6 snow peas, halved lengthwise

4 Tbsp (60 mL) chopped
fresh cilantro (optional)

12 cooked whole shrimp or ⅓ cup
(80 mL) chopped cooked shrimp

1 cup (250 mL) Sweet Thai Chile
Sauce (page 8) or Peanut Lime
Sauce (page 7)

(continued)

(continued from previous page)

PLACE RICE VERMICELLI in a bowl and cover with very hot water. Soak for 15 minutes. Drain well, return to bowl, and toss with rice vinegar and oil.

Fill a shallow pan or bowl with very warm water. Work with one rice paper wrapper at a time. Soak wrapper in warm water for 10 seconds or until softened. Place on a damp towel.

Place 3 basil leaves in a line down the centre of the wrapper. Place a lettuce leaf, cup side up, overtop of the basil. Top with a tablespoon (15 mL) each of black bean sauce (if using) and peanuts, and then add a small pile (about ¼ cup/60 mL) of softened vermicelli noodles, 2 zucchini sticks, 1 pepper stick, half a pea pod, and 1 tsp (5 mL) cilantro (if using), creating a compact pile in the middle of the leaf. Fold in the sides and one end, and then roll up to make a compact roll.

Repeat this process for the remaining veggie rice paper wrappers, reserving 4 wrappers for the shrimp rolls.

For the shrimp rolls, place 3 whole shrimp or 4 tsp (20 mL) chopped shrimp in a line down the centre of the wrapper. Place a lettuce leaf, cup side up, overtop of the shrimp. Add a tablespoon (15 mL) of black bean sauce (if using) to the centre of the leaf.

Add a tablespoon (15 mL) of peanuts, a small pile (about ¼ cup/60 mL) of vermicelli noodles, 2 zucchini sticks, 1 pepper stick, half a pea pod, and 1 tsp (5 mL) cilantro (if using), creating a compact pile in the middle of the leaf. Fold in the sides and one end. Roll up to make a compact sausage.

Repeat this process for the remaining 3 rice paper wrappers.

Serve with Sweet Thai Chile Sauce (page 8) or Peanut Lime Sauce (page 7). Garnish with extra basil or cilantro if desired.

Veggie Rolls

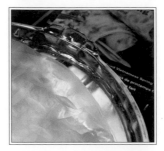

Shrimp Rolls

RICE VERMICELLI

Delicate strands of rice noodles vary in length and width. The noodles are softened in very hot water first. Dried noodles are sometimes deep-fried in hot oil and used as nests for stir-fried foods.

One 14 oz (398 mL) can black beans,
drained and rinsed

3 Tbsp (45 mL) olive oil, divided

1 clove garlic, minced

1 Tbsp (15 mL) chopped fresh basil

1 Tbsp (15 mL) + 2 tsp (10 mL)
fresh lemon juice, divided

¼ tsp (1 mL) salt

⅛ tsp (0.5 mL)
freshly ground pepper

1½ Tbsp (22 mL) water

4 cups (1 L) stemmed arugula leaves

Eight 1-inch (2.5 cm) slices whole
wheat bread or bread of your choice

2 tomatoes, thinly sliced

¼ cup (60 mL) toasted pumpkin
seeds (sidebar, page 26)

BRUSCHETTA WITH BLACK BEAN PURÉE, TOMATOES, AND ARUGULA

I have found a silicone basting brush to be the best tool to use when grilling. Its impermeable bristles won't shed and are easy to clean. Leave the real bristles with the boars.

Grilled bread makes a satisfying meal any time of day. To serve at dinner, use a loaf that is 8 inches (20 cm) long and 3 inches (8 cm) wide, slice into 1-inch (2.5 cm) slices, and serve open-faced as instructed below. You can also form these into sandwiches. —NETTIE

PREHEAT THE GRILL to medium.

Purée beans, 1 Tbsp (15 mL) of the oil, garlic, basil, 1 Tbsp (15 mL) of the lemon juice, salt, pepper, and water in a food processor. Transfer to a bowl and set aside.

In a bowl, toss arugula with 1 Tbsp (15 mL) olive oil and remaining 2 tsp (10 mL) lemon juice.

Grill bread over preheated grill for 2 minutes each side, turning once. Lightly brush grilled bread with remaining 1 Tbsp (15 mL) oil. Spread an equal amount of purée on each slice of grilled bread and top with one-eighth of the arugula, tomato slices, and pumpkin seeds.

VEGETABLE FONDUE

Switzerland is the home of fondue. Cheese, chocolate, or broth in the pot, and veggies, seafood, or meat for dipping—the choices are truly flexible. If you don't have a fondue pot, use an enamel or an ovenproof ceramic-lined pot that you can place over a tea light.

You can use pieces of potato (regular or sweet), cauliflower, mushrooms, or broccoli in addition to or in place of the vegetables listed opposite. —NETTIE

MEAT FONDUE

I love the versatility and fun aspect of this recipe and that it can cater to everyone's tastes. If your family loves seafood, use chunks of lobster, crab, shrimp, scallops, and other fresh seafood. If they prefer pork or beef or chicken or fish, those can be cooked in the broth. I have listed the amount of each variety of meat you will need to make two meat skewers. —PAT

FONDUE POT

1 Tbsp (15 mL) olive oil

½ onion, chopped

2 cloves garlic, chopped

½ cup (125 mL) sliced mushrooms

3½ cups (875 mL) vegetable stock
(page 40 for homemade)

½ cup (125 mL) Burgundy wine

Fondue pot

VEGGIE FONDUE FORKS

Eight 1-inch (2.5 cm)
chunks zucchini

4 green or wax beans, trimmed

Eight 1-inch (2.5 cm)
chunks eggplant

1 onion, quartered

4 cherry tomatoes

MEAT FONDUE FORKS
Options
(Each option makes 2 forks)

1 lb (500 g) lobster, crab, jumbo
shrimp, and/or scallops

7 oz (200 g) firm fish fillets
(cod, halibut, perch)

8 oz (250 g) boneless chicken breast,
cut into strips

8 oz (250 g) beef sirloin,
cut into strips

6 oz (175 g) boneless pork chop(s),
cut into ½-inch (1 cm) strips

(continued)

(continued from previous page)

HEAT OIL IN a skillet over medium-high heat. Add onion and cook, stirring frequently for 4 minutes. Add garlic and mushrooms and cook, stirring constantly, for 5 minutes or until vegetables are soft. Add stock and wine and bring to a boil. Transfer to the fondue pot and light the heat source to keep the stock at a brisk simmer.

Thread vegetables onto the fondue forks in the following order: zucchini, bean, eggplant, onion, eggplant, tomato, zucchini. Prepare meat fondue forks by dividing meat into 2 equal portions and threading it onto 2 fondue forks.

Cook veggie fondue forks in the simmering hot stock for about 5 minutes, or until tender-crisp. Cook meat fondue forks in the simmering hot stock, following these cooking times:

- SEAFOOD: Cook for 3 to 5 minutes, or until seafood changes colour and is firm but not rubbery.
- FISH: Cook for 3 to 5 minutes, or until fish becomes opaque and flakes easily.
- CHICKEN: Cook for 5 to 8 minutes, or until chicken turns opaque and inside is no longer pink and juices run clear.
- BEEF: Cook for 6 to 10 minutes, or until rare (120°F/46°C), medium-rare (125°F/50°C), or medium (130°F/54°C).
- PORK: Cook for 6 to 10 minutes, or until internal colour changes to white with traces of pink in the centre (160°F/71°C).

FRIED SWEET POTATO AND BEET CROQUETTES WITH GUERNSEY GIRL CHEESE

1 Tbsp (15 mL) + ¼ cup (60 mL) olive oil, divided

1 clove garlic, minced

1 cup (250 mL) thinly sliced leeks, white and pale green parts only

1½ cups (375 mL) shredded Guernsey Girl or haloumi cheese

½ cup (125 mL) all-purpose flour

3 large eggs, lightly beaten

2 Tbsp (30 mL) chopped fresh basil, plus sprigs for garnishing

¼ tsp (1 mL) salt

1 cup (250 mL) shredded sweet potato

1 cup (250 mL) shredded beets

3 cups (750 mL) torn romaine lettuce

2 limes, cut into wedges

1 cup (250 mL) plain yogurt

Guernsey Girl is the new addition to the Upper Canada Cheese company's family of artisanal cheeses. Modelled on a Cypriot-style cheese, it has a salty flavour and holds its shape when grilled or fried. The surface caramelizes evenly and the interior becomes wonderfully supple. Made with pure rich milk from a single herd of Guernsey cows, this cheese expresses the unique terroir found at the heart of the Niagara Escarpment—a "World Biosphere Reserve" as designated by UNESCO.

Serve in a pita, with pasta, or as an appetizer. These croquettes have great texture and flavour, and the shredded cheese combines well with the other ingredients. Serve with plain yogurt, salsa, or plum sauce. Move over, falafel.
—NETTIE

HEAT 1 TBSP (15 ML) of the oil in a skillet over medium heat. Add garlic and leeks and cook, stirring frequently, for 5 minutes or until soft. Cool slightly and transfer to a bowl. Add cheese, flour, eggs, basil, and salt. Mix well. Divide the mixture between 2 bowls, about 1 cup (250 mL) per bowl.

Mix shredded sweet potato into one bowl and shredded beets into the other bowl. Stir well. To form the balls, measure 2 Tbsp (30 mL) of the mixture and shape using your hands.

Heat ¼ cup (60 mL) oil in a large, heavy skillet. Fry balls in one layer, in batches, for 3 minutes each side or until browned on all sides. Lift out of oil using tongs or a slotted spoon and drain on a linen towel or on paper towels. Continue frying balls in hot oil until they all are cooked. Serve over romaine with lime wedges, yogurt, and a small sprig of basil.

EGGPLANT MANICOTTI

The very best trio of ingredients: eggplant, ricotta, and tomato sauce. Colourful and delicious, and can be served hot or cold. —NETTIE

EGGPLANT AND LAMB MANICOTTI

Any ground meat will work with this cheesy-garlicky filling, but in my view lamb (which I use here) and beef go best. —PAT

FILLING

2 cloves garlic

2 cups (500 mL) ricotta cheese

1 cup (250 mL)
lightly packed spinach

1 cup (250 mL) lightly
packed fresh basil

½ cup (125 mL) lightly
packed fresh parsley

½ cup (125 mL) shredded
Swiss cheese

¼ cup (60 mL) toasted sunflower
seeds (see sidebar)

3 Tbsp (45 mL) finely grated
Parmesan cheese

LAMB MIXTURE

1 Tbsp (15 mL) olive oil

½ cup (125 mL) chopped onion

1 clove garlic, chopped

6 oz (175 g) ground lamb
(or beef or turkey)

TOASTING NUTS AND SEEDS

Toasting nuts is a technique that intensifies their flavour and deepens their colour. Toasting may be done in the oven or on the stovetop. Usually no oil or butter is used in the toasting process, although some recipes do call for some fat. Pecans, pine nuts, walnuts, almonds, Brazil nuts, sesame seeds, sunflower seeds, and peanuts are some of the many nuts and seeds that may be toasted for extra flavour.

TO TOAST NUTS ON THE STOVE: Heat nuts in a large heavy-bottomed skillet over medium-high heat. Stir and toss the nuts for 3 to 4 minutes, or until lightly browned. (If using this method for smaller nuts and seeds, reduce the cooking time to 2 to 3 minutes.)

TO TOAST NUTS IN THE OVEN: Toast nuts in a baking pan or on a rimmed baking sheet. Place in a 350°F (180°C) oven for 4 to 6 minutes or until lightly coloured but not browned. Remove and cool.

TIP

Only purchase smooth, shiny eggplants that are firm to the touch. When you press an eggplant with your fingers, it should feel firm; the flesh should dent but bounce back. Check the fuzzy green caps and stems: they must be intact and mould-free.

MANICOTTI

2 eggplants, cut lengthwise
into ¼-inch-thick (6 mm) slices
(12 slices total)

3 cups (750 mL) tomato sauce
(page 159 for homemade), divided

¾ cup (185 mL) shredded
mozzarella cheese, divided

2 rimmed baking sheets,
lightly oiled

9- × 13-inch (23 × 33 cm)
baking dish

7-inch-square (18 cm) baking dish

PREHEAT THE OVEN to Broil (500°F/260°C) and move oven rack to top position.

MAKE FILLING: Chop garlic in a food processor. Add ricotta, spinach, basil, parsley, Swiss cheese, sunflower seeds, and Parmesan. Purée ingredients and transfer to a bowl. Cover and refrigerate until ready to use. Filling may be made up to 2 days in advance.

MAKE LAMB MIXTURE: Heat oil in a skillet over medium-high heat. Add onion and garlic and cook, stirring frequently, for 5 minutes. Add ground lamb and reduce heat to medium. Cook, stirring constantly and breaking up the clumps, for 5 to 8 minutes or until meat is browned with no pink on the inside. Using a slotted spoon to allow the meat to drain, lift the meat into a bowl. Let cool.

MAKE MANICOTTI: Arrange eggplant slices in one layer on prepared baking sheets. Broil eggplant on top rack for 3 to 5 minutes, one sheet at a time. Eggplant should be softened but not crisp. Repeat with second baking sheet. Reduce heat to 375°F (190°C) and move oven racks to centre of the oven.

Spread ½ cup (125 mL) tomato sauce on the bottom of the larger baking dish and about ¼ cup (60 mL) on the bottom of the smaller baking dish. Fill eggplant manicotti by placing 2 Tbsp (30 mL) ricotta-spinach filling at the lower end of an eggplant slice and then rolling it up around the filling. Repeat with remaining slices, reserving 4 slices for the lamb manicotti.

Add lamb mixture to remaining ricotta-spinach filling and mix well. Fill 4 eggplant slices with meat-ricotta filling and roll the eggplant slices up around the filling.

Divide rolls between baking dishes, placing meat rolls in the smaller dish. Pour 1½ cups (375 mL) tomato sauce over larger dish and remainder over smaller dish. Sprinkle ½ cup (125 mL) mozzarella cheese overtop larger dish and remainder overtop smaller dish. Bake in preheated oven for 45 minutes, or until eggplant is tender and tomato sauce is thick and bubbly. Test lamb manicotti for doneness after 35 minutes.

KALE AND FARRO RISOTTO

Farro is the Italian name for spelt. Farro and spelt are not always the same, although they are similar in appearance. Grown in Lebanon and transplanted to France, farro was very popular until the Romans introduced bread wheats. Farro has a chewy, dense texture, and is typically pearled. As a result, little of the bran layer remains and the grain cooks in less than 30 minutes. —NETTIE

1.5 lb (750 g) kale leaves, ribs and stems removed

8 oz (250 g) farro (about 1 cup/250 mL)

2 Tbsp (30 mL) olive oil

¼ cup (60 mL) chopped green onions, white part only

4 cups (1 L) vegetable stock (see page 40 for homemade) or chicken stock (page 45)

2 Tbsp (30 mL) finely grated Parmesan cheese

1 Tbsp (15 mL) butter

BRING A LARGE saucepan of salted water to a boil over high heat. Add kale and cook, stirring once, for 1 minute. Lift out using tongs (you'll be using the pot of water again) and plunge into a sink or bowl of ice-cold water. Drain and pat dry. Squeeze out excess water and chop coarsely.

Meanwhile, bring water in the pot back to a boil. Add farro and cook, stirring once, for 13 minutes or until tender. Drain and cool.

Heat oil in a skillet over medium heat. Add green onions and cook, stirring constantly, for 2 minutes.

Add chopped kale and cook, stirring constantly, for 2 minutes or until onions are soft. Add stock and bring to a boil. Reduce heat and simmer, stirring often, for about 25 minutes or until kale is tender and almost all of the stock has been absorbed.

Using a slotted spoon, transfer the kale mixture to a food processor and purée. (This step may be omitted for a chunkier result). Return purée to the same saucepan and add the cooked farro, Parmesan cheese, and butter. Stir until evenly heated through.

2 cloves garlic, chopped

4 Tbsp (60 mL) olive oil, divided

1 tsp (5 mL) coarse sea salt

2 cups (500 mL) each of the
following, cut into 2- × ½-inch
(5 × 1 cm) sticks: carrots,
parsnips, rutabagas, red beets,
golden beets, Yukon Gold potatoes
(12 cups/3 L total)

1 head roasted garlic
(sidebar, page 97)

One 14 oz (398 mL) can cannellini
beans, drained and rinsed,
liquid reserved

2 Tbsp (30 mL) fresh lemon juice

2 rimmed baking sheets,
lightly oiled

ROASTED VEGETABLE STICKS
WITH ROASTED GARLIC DIP

This recipe is such an easy way to introduce root vegetables to those who may think they don't like them. Combining Yukon Gold potato sticks with a range of veggies will encourage everyone to try it, even if it's ketchup free! The different-coloured beets add an extra dimension. — NETTIE

PREHEAT THE OVEN to 450°F (230°C).

Whisk garlic, 2 Tbsp (30 mL) of the olive oil, and salt together in a bowl. Arrange carrot, parsnip, rutabaga, red and golden beets, and potato sticks on the prepared baking sheets in one layer. Drizzle garlic-oil mixture overtop. Roast in preheated oven for 25 minutes, or until vegetables are tender but not soft.

Meanwhile squeeze the roasted garlic cloves from their skins into the bowl of a food processor fitted with a metal blade. Add 2 Tbsp (30 mL) of the olive oil, beans, and lemon juice and pulse mixture until creamy and smooth, adding a small amount of the reserved bean liquid if necessary to achieve the desired consistency. Serve as a dip with roasted vegetable sticks.

SPICY STIR-FRIED GREENS WITH PEANUTS

This recipe gives you an opportunity to use a new frozen leafy green product called Cookin' Greens. A big time saver, these greens are already thinly sliced, and so easy to use and delicious. Stir-fried greens can be added to anything. They are low in calories, fat free, high in fibre, and packed with nutrients.
—NETTIE

SPICY STIR-FRY WITH GREENS, CHICKEN, AND PEANUTS

If you have time, marinate the chicken strips in the stir-fry sauce up to two days in advance to infuse the flavour into the meat. —PAT

STIR-FRY SAUCE

3 Tbsp (45 mL) tamari or soy sauce

2 Tbsp (30 mL) rice vinegar

1 Tbsp (15 mL) fresh lemon juice

1 Tbsp (15 mL) toasted sesame oil

1 Tbsp (15 mL) brown rice syrup or honey

STIR-FRIED GREENS

2 Tbsp (30 mL) peanut oil

4 green onions, chopped

2 cloves garlic, minced

1 Tbsp (15 mL) chopped seeded serrano chiles

6 cups (1.5 L) lightly packed greens (spinach, kale, Swiss chard, broccoli rabe, or cabbage) cut into 1-inch (2.5 cm) strips

STIR-FRIED CHICKEN

6 to 8 oz (175 to 250 g) boneless, skinless chicken breast cut into 1-inch (2.5 cm) strips

2 Tbsp (30 mL) peanut oil

2 tsp (10 mL) cornstarch

6 Tbsp (90 mL) coarsely chopped roasted peanuts, for garnishing

2 Tbsp (30 mL) sesame seeds, for garnishing

WHISK TOGETHER TAMARI, rice vinegar, lemon juice, sesame oil, and rice syrup in a bowl. Set aside. If using chicken, remove about half of the sauce to a separate bowl and marinate the chicken strips, covered in the refrigerator, for 30 minutes or up to 2 days. Return to room temperature before cooking.

Heat peanut oil in a large wok over medium-high heat. Add the green onions, garlic, and chiles and cook, stirring constantly, for 1 minute. Add about 2 cups (500 mL) greens and cook, stirring and tossing, for 1 minute or until just wilted. Keep adding greens 2 cups (500 mL) at a time, stirring and tossing until all of the greens are wilted. Stir the reserved sauce into the greens and cook over high heat, stirring constantly, for about 5 minutes or until greens are tender and sauce is slightly reduced.

Heat peanut oil in a skillet over medium-high heat. Lift the chicken out of the marinade using tongs or a slotted spoon and set the bowl aside. Stir-fry the chicken in the skillet for 3 to 5 minutes, or until chicken has turned white and its juices run clear. Meanwhile whisk the cornstarch into the remaining stir-fry sauce in the bowl. Add stir-fry sauce to the chicken in the skillet and cook, stirring constantly, for 1 minute or until sauce thickens.

Divide greens between 6 bowls using a slotted spoon. Divide cooked chicken mixture in half and spoon over greens in 2 bowls. Garnish each bowl with 1 Tbsp (15 mL) chopped peanuts and 1 tsp (5 mL) sesame seeds.

WASABI AND SESAME COATED ASPARAGUS WITH SUSHI DIPPING SAUCE

You can use a variety of vegetables for this recipe. — NETTIE

PREHEAT THE OVEN to 450°F (230°C).

For the Sushi Dipping Sauce, combine all the ingredients in a bowl. Whisk until blended. Set aside.

Trim bottom end from each asparagus spear. Soak spears in cool water for a few minutes and swish under cool running water to remove all grit from tops. Drain, pat dry, and set aside.

Combine tahini, mayonnaise, wasabi, vinegar, tamari, and ginger in a shallow pie plate. Mix panko and sesame seeds in a separate shallow pie plate. Toss asparagus in tahini mixture to coat, then roll in panko mixture. Arrange on prepared baking sheet as each spear is coated in both mixtures. Drizzle with sesame oil.

Roast in preheated oven, turning once, for 15 or 16 minutes or until tender-crisp and lightly browned. Transfer to a heated platter and sprinkle salt overtop. Serve with Sushi Dipping Sauce.

SUSHI DIPPING SAUCE

½ cup (125 mL) tamari
or soy sauce

¼ cup (60 mL) toasted sesame oil

2 Tbsp (30 mL) mirin

1 Tbsp (15 mL) fresh lemon juice

1 tsp (5 mL) minced fresh ginger

1 tsp (5 mL) prepared mustard

1 tsp (5 mL) prepared wasabi

1 clove garlic, minced

1¼ lb (625 g) fresh asparagus

2 Tbsp (30 mL) tahini

2 Tbsp (30 mL) mayonnaise

1 to 2 tsp (5 to 10 mL) prepared
wasabi (to your preference;
sidebar, page 253)

1 tsp (5 mL) rice vinegar

1 tsp (5 mL) tamari or soy sauce

1 tsp (5 mL) grated fresh ginger

1 cup (250 mL) panko or homemade
breadcrumbs (sidebar, page 178)

¼ cup (60 mL) sesame seeds

2 tsp (10 mL) toasted sesame oil

Sea salt, for garnishing

¼ cup (60 mL) Sushi Dipping Sauce
(above)

Rimmed baking sheet, lightly oiled

BEAN CAKES WITH SWEET POTATO TOPPING

You can buy good-quality refried beans in a can. Read the label carefully, especially if you want to avoid lard. They are an excellent staple to have in the pantry and can transform any dull omelette or an empty pita into a delicious meal.
—NETTIE

BEAN CAKES WITH GROUND TURKEY AND SWEET POTATO TOPPING

These delicious cakes may be served as an appetizer or as a light meal. I've suggested the addition of cooked ground turkey or chicken to the list of garnishes. (See pages 138 and 139 for suggested amounts and cooking method for ground turkey.) —PAT

TOPPING

2 Tbsp (30 mL) olive oil

1 onion, chopped

3 cloves garlic, chopped

2 sweet potatoes, diced

1 to 2 jalapeño peppers, seeded and finely chopped

1 tsp (5 mL) Toasted Cumin Dry Rub (page 10) or ground cumin

½ tsp (2 mL) salt

BEAN CAKES

2 lb (1 kg) fresh masa or masa harina (see sidebar)

2 cups (500 mL) refried black beans

2 tsp (10 mL) baking powder

½ tsp (2 mL) salt

Peanut oil, for frying

Shredded lettuce

Sour cream

Tomato salsa (store-bought
or Salsa Cruda, page 220)

Pesto

Guacamole

Ground turkey, cooked
(pages 138 and 139)

FOR THE TOPPING, heat oil in a skillet over medium heat. Add onion and cook, stirring frequently, for 4 minutes. Add garlic, sweet potatoes, jalapeño peppers, cumin rub, and salt. Cook, stirring frequently, for 8 to 12 minutes or until sweet potatoes are tender. Use a potato masher to mash in the skillet until smooth.

For the bean cakes, preheat the oven to 300°F (150°C). Combine the masa, refried beans, baking powder, and salt in a bowl. Heat ½ cup (125 mL) oil in a large skillet over medium heat. Make a golf ball–sized ball of dough and pat it between your hands to make a pancake about ½ inch (1 cm) thick. Fry for about 3 to 4 minutes or until crisp and brown on one side. Flip and fry on the other side until crisp and brown on the outside but soft on the inside. Lift out to baking sheet. Cover with foil and keep cooked cakes warm in a preheated oven. Repeat until all of the dough has been shaped and fried.

Serve hot with sweet potato topping and garnishes.

MASA

Tortillas, tamales, and corn chips are made from corn grains. The corn is cooked in a solution of calcium hydroxide, aka lime (not the citrus lime). It is then left to steep and cool. After steeping, the softened hulls are washed away and the kernels (including the germ) are stone-ground to produce a dough called masa. It contains starch, protein, and oils, and calcium from the lime. Masa harina flour is a masa dried into a convenient mix for making dough. Latin American specialty stores and some whole food stores usually carry both ingredients.

SPICED BAKED SHRIMP

If you serve these shrimp with hot pita wedges, they make a pretty substantial hors d'oeuvre or starter course. You need some kind of bread to soak up the spicy juices or you could serve it over rice for a light lunch dish. — PAT

3 Tbsp (45 mL) olive oil

1 onion, chopped

½ red bell pepper, diced

2 cloves garlic, chopped

1 dried cayenne pepper, crushed (or ½ to 1 tsp/2 to 5 mL dried red chile flakes)

2 tsp (10 mL) garam masala (see sidebar)

One 28 oz (796 mL) can whole tomatoes and juice

1½ lb (750 g) large shrimp, peeled and deveined

¾ cup (185 mL) crumbled feta cheese

2-quart (2 L) shallow baking dish

PREHEAT THE OVEN to 375°F (190°C).

Heat oil in a large saucepan over medium heat. Add onion and red pep-per and cook, stirring frequently, for 4 minutes. Add garlic and cayenne pepper and cook, stirring constantly, for 2 minutes, or until onion and peppers are tender. Stir in garam masala and cook, stirring constantly, for 30 seconds.

Add tomatoes and juice and bring to a boil over high heat. Reduce heat and simmer, stirring occasionally, for about 20 minutes or until sauce is slightly thickened. Remove from heat and stir in shrimp. Transfer to baking dish and top with cheese. Bake for 12 to 16 minutes, or until shrimp has turned bright pink and flesh is opaque.

GARAM MASALA

The blend of ground spices known as garam masala, common in Indian and other South Asian cuisines, is usually a combination of cinnamon, dried red chile peppers, ground ginger, sesame, mustard seeds, turmeric, coriander, fennel seeds, and star anise. You can toast and grind whole spices using a mortar and pestle, or purchase a commercial powdered mixture.

SOUPS

VEGETABLE STOCK

Vegetable stocks are not just for vegetarians. Whether making a spicy Asian curry, a broth-y Mediterranean soup, or a hearty vegetable stew, vegetable stock makes a delicious base by adding flavour from the very beginning. Stock keeps for five days in the refrigerator. I freeze this stock in an ice cube tray. Each cube yields 2 Tbsp (30 mL) of stock, a flavourful addition to stir-fries. —NETTIE

VEGETABLE STOCK—THE ULTIMATE FLAVOUR ENHANCER

A good soup stock can enliven the flavour of more than just soup. It adds richness to sauces, stews, grain and bean entrees, salad dressings, braised tofu and tempeh, and stir-fries. Stocks add pizzazz to almost anything you cook. You can even try vegetable stock as a drink on its own.

A basic vegetable stock usually consists of allium vegetables (onions, leeks, shallots, garlic) and other vegetables (celery, carrots, mushrooms, tomatoes) at a ratio of two to one, with the addition of herbs, spices, pulses, and water. Vegetables that have a strong, dominating flavour, such as cabbage, broccoli, cauliflower, and peppers, should be avoided; they can add a bitterness to stock and overwhelm the taste of other ingredients.

Don't use them raw! However, roasting them before adding them to the stock will remove any harshness or bitterness.

The best way to make stock is to place the vegetables in a large pot, add four times the amount of water, and bring to a boil. Simmer uncovered for 30 minutes to 2 hours. (Vegetables will become bitter if simmered longer.) Strain the stock and discard the vegetables, as they will not be palatable after the lengthy cooking time. To add body, I recommend adding a small amount of miso paste or nutritional yeast after straining the vegetables from the broth.

If you are preparing soup for vegetarians, vegetable stock is what you must use. But you can use it in any rec-

ipe that calls for stock, even if you're not cooking for vegetarians.

Stock must be stored in the fridge and will keep for five days, or in the freezer for up to three months. To make frozen stock easy to use in small amounts, freeze stock in an ice cube tray. Once frozen, place the stock cubes in a reusable container and use as needed.

Nowadays, many people prepare their stocks from the ingredients they can find locally or whatever is in season. However, we are very fortunate to live in 2011. If you do not have the time to prepare stock from scratch, you can buy good-quality vegetable stock, powder, and cubes at supermarkets and whole food stores.

2 Tbsp (30 mL) olive oil

2 onions, thinly sliced

2 leeks, white and pale green
parts only, thinly sliced

2 cloves garlic, crushed

4 carrots, cut into
1-inch (2.5 cm) rounds

1 large potato, cut into
1-inch (2.5 cm) rounds

4 stalks celery, cut into
1-inch (2.5 cm) pieces

6 tomatoes, quartered,
or one 14 oz (398 mL) can diced
tomatoes and juice

8 oz (250 g) button mushrooms,
thinly sliced

⅔ cup (160 mL) green lentils, rinsed

6 sprigs fresh parsley

4 sprigs fresh basil

4 bay leaves

½ tsp (2 mL) black peppercorns

10 cups (2.5 L) water

2 tsp (10 mL) salt

HEAT OIL IN a large 3- or 4-quart (3 or 4 L) stockpot or saucepan over medium heat. Add onions, leeks, and garlic. Cook, stirring frequently, for 5 minutes or until softened. Stir in carrots, potato, and celery, and cook, stirring frequently, for 8 minutes.

Add tomatoes and their juice, mushrooms, lentils, parsley, basil, bay leaves, and peppercorns. Cover with water and add salt. Bring to a boil over high heat. Cover, reduce heat to low, and simmer, skimming often, for 30 minutes.

Strain through a large sieve placed over a large bowl, pressing against vegetable mixture with the back of a wooden spoon to extract all liquid. Discard solids and use vegetable stock immediately, or let cool, cover, and refrigerate for up to 5 days. Vegetable stock may also be frozen in individual 2- or 4-cup (500 mL or 1 L) containers (or ice cube trays) for up to 3 months.

MUSHROOM BROTH

The dried mushrooms lend a smoky and deeply earthy flavour to this rich, dark brown broth. It's a natural for using in mushroom soup or as a base for miso soup or other clear broth soups, and to add flavour to other vegetable soups or soups with red meat. —NETTIE

COMBINING FRESH AND DRIED MUSHROOMS FOR COMPLEX FLAVOUR

We can thank the Sun King (French king Louis XIV) for the now-ubiquitous button mushroom (*Agaricus bisporus*, above) being widely available all year round. We sometimes forget that mushrooms are a wild fungus that is seasonal. Because King Louis XIV loved the white button mushroom so much, he ordered his chief agronomist to find a way to grow it all year long for his table. The obliging Olivier de Serres learned how to transplant the wild white button mushroom, making it easier to harvest, and thus reinforcing the love the French people have for the fungus. Later on, toward the end of the 18th century, it was discovered that these mushrooms do not require light to grow, a significant finding that led to their being cultivated indoors.

Cremini mushrooms are a brown-coloured strain of the common domesticated *Agaricus* mushroom described above. (Both button and cremini mushrooms are the cultivated cousins of the wild Field Mushroom.) When cremini mushrooms are allowed to mature into an open-capped adult form, they are called "portobello" mushrooms. Cremini mushrooms lend a richer colour and flavour to soup stock than white button mushrooms.

The *Boletus edulis* variety of mushroom (also known as cèpe, cep, porcini, and king bolete) is considered to be one of the best in the world. Of all the mushroom varieties, *B. edulis* lends itself best to being dried or frozen. The dried form has a deeper, more concentrated musky flavour than the fresh form, making it perfect for Mushroom Broth (see above).

3 oz (90 g) dried porcini or other
dried mushrooms

3 cups (750 mL) boiling water

1 lb (500 g) cremini mushrooms

4 cloves garlic

1 onion, quartered

1 carrot, coarsely chopped

2 Tbsp (30 mL) olive oil

4 cups (1 L) vegetable stock (page 40
for homemade) or water

1 tsp (5 mL) salt

4 sprigs fresh thyme

1 sprig fresh rosemary

Roasting pan

PREHEAT THE OVEN to 350°F (180°C).

Place dried mushrooms in a bowl and pour boiling water overtop. Set aside and let soak for at least 20 minutes, or as long as a few hours.

Meanwhile, combine cremini mushrooms, garlic, onion, and carrot in a roasting pan and drizzle with oil, tossing to coat the vegetables. Roast in preheated oven, stirring once or twice, for 30 to 45 minutes or until vegetables are soft. Mushrooms should be withered and slightly charred and onions may be somewhat burnt around the edges.

Strain reconstituted dried mushrooms over a bowl, pressing out all the soaking liquid. Reserve soaking liquid and mushrooms in separate bowls.

Combine roasted vegetables, scraping up any bits from the pan, and reconstituted mushrooms in a stockpot or large saucepan. Strain mushroom-soaking liquid through a layer of cheesecloth into the stockpot. Add vegetable stock, salt, thyme, and rosemary and bring to a boil over high heat. Reduce heat and simmer, stirring once or twice, for 40 minutes.

Line a large strainer or colander with 2 layers of cheesecloth and place over a large pot. Strain the broth, pressing on the solids with the back of a spoon to release all the liquid. Discard solids and use mushroom broth immediately, or let cool, cover, and refrigerate for up to 3 days. Mushroom broth may also be frozen in individual 2- or 4-cup (500 mL or 1 L) containers (or ice cube trays) for up to 3 months.

ROASTED VEGETABLE STOCK

Why roast vegetables? To intensify the flavour! Roasting the vegetables before simmering them in water and wine results in a rich and deeply flavoured stock. This stock recipe makes a great base in ordinary recipes. — NETTIE

PREHEAT THE OVEN to 450°F (230°C) and place a rack in the middle position.

Toss mushrooms, shallots, carrots, red and green peppers, garlic, parsley, and thyme with oil in a large roasting pan. Roast in preheated oven for 40 minutes, stirring often. Some vegetables may char.

Transfer roasted vegetables and liquids to a soup pot, scraping up brown bits from the roasting pan into the pot. Stir in tomato paste and cook over medium-high heat, stirring for 1 minute. Add wine and bring to a boil over high heat, stirring constantly.

Add water and salt. Cover, reduce heat, and simmer, stirring frequently for 40 minutes.

Strain through a large sieve placed over a large bowl, pressing against vegetable mixture with the back of a wooden spoon to extract all liquid. Discard solids and use vegetable stock immediately, or let cool, cover, and refrigerate for up to 3 days. Roasted vegetable stock may be frozen in individual 2- or 4-cup (500 mL or 1 L) containers (or ice cube trays) for up to 3 months.

2 cups (500 mL) mixed portobello and cremini mushrooms, thickly sliced

4 shallots, unpeeled and quartered

4 carrots, cut into 1-inch (2.5 cm) pieces

1 red bell pepper, cut into 1-inch (2.5 cm) pieces

1 green bell pepper, cut into 1-inch (2.5 cm) pieces

4 cloves garlic, coarsely chopped

6 sprigs fresh flat-leaf parsley (including stems)

4 sprigs fresh thyme

¼ cup (60 mL) olive oil

¼ cup (60 mL) tomato paste

1 cup (250 mL) dry red wine

6 cups (1.5 L) water

1 tsp (5 mL) salt

Roasting pan

CHICKEN STOCK

4 lb (1.8 kg) leftover chicken carcasses

4 cups (1 L) coarsely chopped vegetables or vegetable trimmings (see recipe introduction)

2 Tbsp (30 mL) olive oil

10 cups (2.5 L) cold water

15 sprigs fresh parsley

4 sprigs fresh thyme

8 black peppercorns

4 whole allspice berries

2 bay leaves

2 whole cloves

1 tsp (5 mL) salt

Roasting pan, lightly oiled

Roasting the bones is a ritual of homemade soup stock that I rarely skip because it gives a richer, deeper colour and flavour to this versatile soup stock. However, if time is short, you can skip the roasting step and still make a very good stock. When you cook a whole chicken or turkey, save the carcass, neck, and giblets for this soup stock. You can also use chicken bones that are left over if you debone meat yourself. I always buy chicken breasts and thighs on the bone, even if a recipe calls for boneless breasts or thighs. Not only do I save money, I have bones to use to make stock. I discard the skin and freeze the bones (and any meat attached to them) in a Ziploc bag until I'm ready to make stock.

Because I use only organic vegetables, I feel okay about using vegetable peelings and the woody stems of broccoli and cauliflower (which I freeze) for this stock. If you do not have any frozen vegetable pieces, use a combination of the following: onions, garlic, carrots, celery, bell peppers, leeks, the outer leaves and core of cabbage, and the stalks of broccoli and cauliflower. Never omit the onions, garlic, carrot, and celery, but the other vegetables are optional. —PAT

PREHEAT THE OVEN to 350°F (180°C).

Place carcasses in prepared roasting pan and bake in preheated oven for 45 minutes, stirring once or twice. Add vegetables and drizzle with oil, tossing to coat the vegetables. Bake, stirring once, for 45 minutes or until vegetables are browned. (Bones may be charred.)

Combine baked bones and vegetables in a stockpot, scraping up any bits and liquid from the roasting pan. Add water, parsley, thyme, peppercorns, allspice, bay leaves, cloves, and salt. Bring to a boil over high heat. Reduce heat and simmer, skimming off the scum from the stock once or twice an hour for 3 hours.

Line a large strainer or colander with 2 layers of cheesecloth and place over a large pot. Strain the stock, pressing on the solids with the back of a spoon to release all the liquid. Discard solids and let stock cool. Cover and refrigerate for up to 3 days. Before using or freezing, skim and discard any fat that has risen to the surface of the stock. Chicken stock may be frozen in individual 2- or 4-cup (500 mL or 1 L) containers (or ice cube trays) for up to 3 months.

HEARTY BEEF STOCK

You don't have to use the red wine, but it does give a very professional finish to this stock; I use a hearty Bordeaux or merlot. You can include a ham or lamb bone from a roast along with the beef bones. Look for beef bones with the frozen meats or ask your meat manager for them if they are not in the fresh meat section. — PAT

PREHEAT THE OVEN to 350°F (180°C).

Place bones in prepared roasting pan and bake in preheated oven for 45 minutes, turning once or twice. Add chopped vegetables, onions, garlic, celery and carrot, and drizzle with oil, tossing to coat vegetables. Bake, stirring once, for 45 minutes or until vegetables are browned. (Bones may be charred.)

Using tongs or a slotted spoon, transfer bones and vegetables to a stockpot, discarding any grease that may have accumulated in the pan. Add water, wine, tomato paste, parsley, thyme, peppercorns, allspice, bay leaves, cloves, and salt. Bring to

a boil over high heat. Reduce heat and simmer for 4 hours, skimming the scum from the stock once or twice every hour.

Line a large strainer or colander with 2 layers of cheesecloth and place over a large pot. Strain the stock, pressing on the solids with the back of a spoon to release all the liquid. Discard solids and let stock cool. Cover and refrigerate for up to 3 days. Before using or freezing, skim and discard any fat that has risen to the surface of the stock. Beef stock may be frozen in individual 2- or 4-cup (500 mL or 1 L) containers (or ice cube trays) for up to 3 months.

4 lb (1.8 kg) beef soup bones (or a combination of beef, ham, and lamb bones)

2 cups (500 mL) coarsely chopped vegetables or vegetable trimmings (see introduction, page 45)

2 onions, quartered

6 cloves garlic, crushed

3 stalks celery, coarsely chopped

1 carrot, cubed

2 Tbsp (30 mL) olive oil

10 cups (2.5 L) cold water

1 cup (250 mL) red wine

¼ cup (60 mL) tomato paste

15 sprigs fresh parsley

4 sprigs fresh thyme

8 black peppercorns

4 whole allspice berries

2 bay leaves

2 whole cloves

1 tsp (5 mL) salt

Roasting pan, lightly oiled

2 lb (1 kg) chicken, beef, ham, or lamb bones

2 cups (500 mL) coarsely chopped vegetables or vegetable trimmings (see recipe introduction, as well as introduction on page 45)

1 onion, quartered

3 cloves garlic, crushed

2 stalks celery, coarsely chopped

1 carrot, cubed

6 cups (1.5 L) water

¼ cup (60 mL) tomato paste or 2 quartered tomatoes (optional)

4 sprigs fresh parsley

2 sprigs fresh thyme

6 black peppercorns

3 whole allspice berries

2 bay leaves

1 whole clove

1 tsp (5 mL) salt

Slow cooker

SLOW COOKER MEAT STOCK

For working cooks, this stock is a delicious alternative to a stovetop-simmered soup stock. You can combine the ingredients in the morning or evening and use the stock by the time you return home from work or get up in the morning. If you have been freezing broccoli stalks and vegetable trimmings, this method requires very little preparation. — PAT

COMBINE BONES, CHOPPED vegetables, onion, garlic, celery, carrot, water, tomato paste (if using), parsley, thyme, peppercorns, allspice, bay leaves, clove, and salt in a slow cooker. Cover and cook on the low setting for 6 to 10 hours.

Line a large strainer or colander with 2 layers of cheesecloth and place over a large pot. Strain the stock, pressing on the solids with the back of a spoon to release all the liquid. Discard solids and let stock cool. Cover and refrigerate for up to 3 days. Before using or freezing, skim and discard any fat that has risen to the surface of the stock. Meat stock may be frozen in individual 2- or 4-cup (500 mL or 1 L) containers (or ice cube trays) for up to 3 months.

ALLSPICE

Pimenta dioica (shown at left, middle top, between the mustard seeds on the left and the coriander seeds on the right) is the name of the tropical, aromatic tree that produces berries with a warm and spicy essence. When dried, the berries are larger than peppercorns and have a pleasantly peppery flavour of cloves, cinnamon, and nutmeg.

FISH STOCK

Essential to fish stew, chowder, and bouillabaisse, fish stock differs from meat stock in that the bones are not baked and the ingredients are gently simmered, never boiled. The whole process is fast and easy. Just as I freeze chicken carcasses and vegetable trimmings, I also freeze fish heads (gills removed), tails, and bones, as well as shrimp and lobster shells, until I have enough to make fish stock. You can also use pieces of fresh lean fish (such as whitefish, perch, or cod) for this stock. — PAT

3 lb (1.5 kg) fish parts

6 cups (1.5 L) cold water

1 onion, quartered

1 leek, white and pale green parts only, coarsely chopped

1 carrot, coarsely chopped

2 stalks celery, coarsely chopped

2 whole allspice berries

1 bay leaf

COMBINE FISH PARTS, water, onion, leek, carrot, celery, allspice, and bay leaf in a stockpot. Bring to a simmer over medium-high heat. Reduce heat and gently simmer for 1 hour, skimming the scum from the stock once or twice.

Line a large strainer or colander with 2 layers of cheesecloth and place over a large pot. Strain the stock, pressing on the solids with the back of a spoon to release all the liquid. Discard solids and let stock cool. Cover and refrigerate for up to 3 days. Fish stock should gel when chilled. Fish stock may be frozen in individual 2- or 4-cup (500 mL or 1 L) containers (or ice cube trays) for up to 3 months.

TORTILLA STRIPS

Thin strips cut from corn or flour tortillas are fried until lightly browned and crisp. Use them to add texture to soups and salads or chilli dishes.

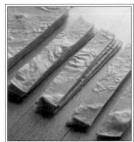

1. Fold two 6-inch (15 cm) tortillas in half. Cut each one along the fold line.

2. Stack tortilla halves and cut strips ¼ to ½ inch (6 mm to 1 cm) wide.

3. Pour vegetable oil, or peanut oil, into a heavy-bottomed skillet to a depth of about ½ inch (1 cm). Heat oil over high heat until very hot. Use one of the smallest pieces to test the heat of the oil: if the piece bubbles upon hitting the oil and browns in less than 30 seconds, oil is hot. Adjust heat to keep oil hot but not smoking.

4. Remove test piece and discard. Drop 3 or 4 pieces into the hot oil and watch carefully. Remove with tongs before strips brown.

5. As strips are being removed from oil, squeeze them in the centre using tongs to give them an interesting twist. Drain on paper towel–lined plate and sprinkle sea salt overtop while hot.

GAZPACHO

Gazpacho is a chilled tomato soup, a classic Spanish contribution to the dinner table. You will need a 12-cup (3 L) food processor, but if you have a smaller capacity food processor or a blender, divide the ingredients in half or in thirds and process them in batches. I use freshly ground breadcrumbs for this recipe, and they are simple to make—see page 178. —NETTIE

COMBINE TOMATOES AND tomato juices, olive oil, sesame oil, garlic, red pepper, cucumber, breadcrumbs, salt, and pepper in a food processor or blender and process for 5 minutes, or until smooth and well combined. Transfer to a bowl, cover, and refrigerate for at least 3 hours, or overnight.

Stir and spoon chilled gazpacho into bowls. Garnish with chives.

One 28 oz (796 mL) can diced
tomatoes and juice

One 8 oz (250 mL) can tomato juice

¼ cup (60 mL) olive oil

1 Tbsp (15 mL) toasted sesame oil

3 cloves garlic

1 red bell pepper, thinly sliced

1 cucumber or zucchini,
coarsely chopped

1 cup (250 mL) breadcrumbs (dry or
fresh; see page 178 for homemade)

1 tsp (5 mL) salt

½ tsp (2 mL) freshly ground pepper

¼ cup (60 mL) chopped chives
or green onions, for garnishing

APPLE, CARROT, AND PARSNIP SOUP

Look for firm medium-sized parsnips with smooth surfaces. Avoid the large parsnips if you can because they are often split and taste bitter, and their inner cores have a woody texture. Parsnips remind me of cream-coloured carrots you sometimes find at farmers' markets, but sweeter and more buttery. Carrots and apples round out their flavour, and add a fresh taste to this soup.

I love Belsoy soy cooking cream; because it is so concentrated I find I need to use only ½ cup (125 mL) for this recipe. You can also use any plain non-dairy milk in place of the soymilk. —NETTIE

APPLE, CARROT, AND PARSNIP SOUP WITH SMOKED CHICKEN

The smoked chicken lends a "smoked chowder" note to the sweetness of the apple and root vegetables. You don't need much to spike the soup, so if you buy more than you need, dice it all, measure it into two- or four-serving amounts, and freeze the extra. If you can't find smoked chicken or turkey, use a poached chicken breast instead (see page 183). —PAT

2 Tbsp (30 mL) olive oil

2 cups (500 mL) sliced leeks, white and pale green parts only

3 cloves garlic, minced

2 cups (500 mL) sliced parsnips (¼-inch/6 mm rounds)

1 cup (250 mL) sliced carrots (¼-inch/6 mm rounds)

1 Granny Smith apple, cut into ½-inch (1 cm) pieces

6 cups (1.5 L) vegetable stock (page 40 for homemade)

¼ tsp (1 mL) salt

⅛ tsp (0.5 mL) freshly ground pepper

⅛ tsp (0.5 mL) ground nutmeg

1 cup (250 mL) 10% cream (half and half) or plain soymilk, or ½ cup (125 mL) Belsoy soy cooking cream

⅓ cup (80 mL) diced smoked chicken (about 1½ oz/45 g)

HEAT OIL IN a large pot or Dutch oven over medium heat. Sauté leeks and garlic for 3 to 5 minutes, or until softened. Add parsnips, carrots, and apple and cook, stirring constantly, for 1 minute.

Add stock and bring to a boil over high heat, stirring constantly. Cover, reduce heat, and simmer, stirring often, for 30 minutes.

Purée in batches in a food processor, transferring purée to a bowl until all vegetables from the cooking pot have been processed. Return puréed soup to pot and heat over medium heat. Stir in salt, pepper, and nutmeg. Whisk in cream and heat through. Portion out vegetarian servings. Add the smoked chicken to the remaining soup and heat through over medium heat. Divide soup between remaining bowls. Serve immediately.

20 fresh tomatillos
(approx 2 lb/1 kg) or one 28 oz
(796 mL) can, drained

8 cups (2 L) peeled and cubed
butternut squash

1 Tbsp (15 mL) + 3 Tbsp (45 mL)
olive oil, divided

5 cups (1.25 L) diced Vidalia onions

8 cloves garlic

8 cups (2 L) vegetable stock
(page 40 for homemade)

One 28 oz (796 mL) can diced
tomatoes and juice

1 Tbsp (15 mL) chipotles
in adobo sauce, diced

**GARNISHES AND
ACCOMPANIMENTS**

½ cup (125 mL) chopped
fresh cilantro

½ cup (125 mL) corn kernels

1 avocado, cut into
½-inch (1 cm) slices

2 cups (500 mL) sour cream

2 rimmed baking sheets,
parchment-lined

TOMATILLO SOUP WITH SQUASH AND CILANTRO

Fresh tomatillos are enclosed in papery husks; you must remove the husks and rinse the peeled fruit under warm water before using. Tomatillos are available canned as well.

Squash is classified as summer squash or winter squash. My favourite varieties are the winter types: acorn, butternut, and Hubbard. They are allowed to mature before picking, resulting in thicker shells and larger seeds. Store winter squash in a dark, cool, ventilated room for up to one month. Combining sweet squash with tangy tomatillos is a delicious taste adventure. —NETTIE

PREHEAT THE OVEN to 450°F (230°C).

If using fresh tomatillos, remove and discard husks. Rinse under warm water, drain, and pat dry. Cut tomatillos in half and place cut side up in a single layer on one prepared baking sheet.

Place squash on remaining baking sheet and toss with 1 Tbsp (15 mL) of the oil. Spread squash in a single layer. Roast squash on lower rack of preheated oven and tomatillos on upper rack for 30 minutes. Remove tomatillos and check that squash is soft. If not, roast until soft.

Heat remaining 3 Tbsp (45 mL) oil in a medium-sized pot over medium heat. Add onions and cook, stirring frequently, for 5 minutes. Add garlic and cook, stirring for 1 minute, or until fragrant and onions are soft. Stir in stock and tomatoes and bring to a boil over high heat.

Cover, reduce heat, and simmer for 15 minutes. Add chipotle peppers and adobo sauce, and the roasted (or canned) tomatillos and squash. Simmer for 10 minutes.

Purée soup in a 12-cup (3 L) capacity food processor (or in batches in a smaller food processor). Return purée to pot and heat over low heat. Ladle into soup bowls and garnish with cilantro. Pass the corn, avocado, and sour cream separately as accompaniments to the soup.

WILD AND BROWN RICE SOUP WITH THREE KINDS OF MUSHROOM

How many types of rice do you have in your cupboard? You may not know it, but there's a rice revolution going on in your supermarket and whole foods store. With over 8,000 edible varieties in the world, there is a lot to choose from. We combine wild and brown rice in this soup, but you can easily combine two or more of any kind, or even just stick to one. Cremini, button, and shiitake mushrooms are a delicious combination in this soup. —NETTIE

RICE AND MUSHROOM SOUP WITH BRAISED COD

The cod is full-bodied and stands up to the earthiness of the mushrooms and the nuttiness of the rice, but if you want a subtler flavour that complements but doesn't bully the vegetables, substitute halibut. Both fish are firm-textured so they can be simmered in the soup for reheating, if necessary. — PAT

GREMOLATA

Not usually made with anchovies, gremolata is a traditional garnish for the dish known as osso buco. I have added anchovies for their saltiness, rich flavour, and paste-like texture, but for vegetarian dishes, omit them. I add a very small amount of oil to just moisten the mixture. This is not a sauce, so if you want to keep the gremolata chunky and grainy, add the oil by the teaspoon (5 mL) and stop processing before the mixture becomes smooth. You may even find that the oil in the anchovies is sufficient and that you don't need any extra oil. This mixture may be frozen and added to soups, stews, casseroles, and even to garnish pizza. —PAT

GREMOLATA

3 cups (750 mL) lightly packed
flat-leaf parsley leaves

3 anchovies, drained
and cut into pieces

2 cloves garlic, coarsely chopped
Zest of 1 lemon

Olive oil (see sidebar)

TO MAKE GREMOLATA, combine parsley,
anchovies, garlic, and lemon zest in a blender and
process for 30 seconds, or until combined. Add
oil through the opening in the lid, 1 tsp (5 mL)
at a time, and process for a few seconds or until
mixture is combined but still coarse. Store in a
covered container for up to 1 week in the refrigerator. This recipe makes about ¾ cup (185 mL).

(continued)

(continued from previous page)

RINSE WILD RICE and brown rice in a colander under cool water; drain.

Bring stock to a boil in a large pot over high heat. Stir in rinsed wild and brown rice, and 2 tsp (10 mL) oregano. Cover, reduce heat, and simmer for 45 minutes or until rice is tender. Be sure water is simmering but do not lift the lid to check on rice.

Meanwhile, heat 2 Tbsp (30 mL) oil in a heavy-bottomed skillet over medium heat. Add onion and cook, stirring frequently, for 5 minutes or until soft. Add mushrooms and remaining oregano and cook, stirring constantly for 3 minutes or until onions and mushrooms are soft. Remove half the onion-mushroom mixture and set aside.

Add remaining 3 Tbsp (45 mL) oil to the skillet and heat over medium heat. Add carrots and celery to onion-mushroom mixture remaining in the skillet. Cook, stirring constantly, for 10 to 12 minutes or until carrots are soft.

When rice is cooked, scoop out about half using a wire mesh strainer. Add scooped rice to the carrot mixture in the skillet.

Using a liquid measuring cup, transfer about a cup (250 mL) of stock from the pot into a 12-cup (3 L) food processor. Scrape vegetable-rice mixture from the skillet into the food processor and purée. Return purée to the soup pot containing remaining stock and rice. Add reserved mushroom-rice mixture, cream, parsley, wine (if using), salt, and pepper. Mix well. Keep simmering, stirring occasionally for 10 minutes or until heated through. Ladle into bowls, reserving 2½ cups (625 mL) for 2 cod servings.

Season cod with salt and pepper and place in the skillet (used to cook the vegetables). Transfer reserved soup to the skillet. Cover and simmer gently for 7 to 10 minutes, or until fish turns opaque and flakes easily with a fork. Ladle into 2 bowls. Garnish cod soup with 1 Tbsp (15 mL) gremolata, if using.

½ cup (125 mL) wild rice

½ cup (125 mL) brown rice

8 cups (2 L) vegetable stock
(page 40 for homemade)

3 tsp (15 mL) chopped fresh
oregano or marjoram, divided

2 Tbsp (30 mL) + 3 Tbsp (45 mL)
olive oil, divided

1 onion, thinly sliced

2 cups (500 mL) thinly sliced
assorted mushrooms (see sidebar)

1½ cups (375 mL) sliced carrots
(¼-inch/6 mm rounds)

1½ cups (375 mL) chopped celery

2 cups (500 mL) 10% cream
(half and half) or plain soymilk

¼ cup (60 mL) chopped
fresh parsley

½ cup (125 mL) dry white
wine (optional)

½ tsp (2 mL) salt

⅛ tsp (0.5 mL)
freshly ground pepper

Two 3 oz (90 g) fillets
of cod or halibut

Salt and pepper, for seasoning fish

Gremolata (page 55) (optional)

SOME "MEATY" MUSHROOM VARIETIES

Mushrooms are a vegetarian cook's favourite ingredient because of their chewy texture, an ingredient that can substitute for meat in so many recipes. Each variety has its own subtle flavour characteristics, but all lend a rich and earthy flavour to vegetable dishes. The following varieties are some of the fleshier types of mushrooms now available fresh from commercial growers.

CHANTERELLES *(Cantharellus cibarius)*. This is the most delicate in texture of all the mushrooms in this list. They are often used in rice and pasta dishes with eggs and cream sauces to bring out their nutty flavour. Add at the end of the cooking time to avoid having them soften and break apart.

CREMINI *(Agaricus bisporus)*, also known as Italian Brown. Similar in shape and size to the common white "button" mushroom. Cremini mushrooms have a light to dark brown cap and a rich, intensely earthy flavour. (See page 42.)

KING TRUMPET *(Pleurotus eryngii)*. The largest of the oyster mushroom species. The king trumpet has a long shelf life and is firm-textured, chewy, and tasty, which makes it a good variety for commercial sale.

LION'S MANE *(Hericium erinaceus)*. Part of a group of mushrooms known as "toothed." They have a pleasing texture that is firm and succulent (similar to tender veal), but they have very little flavour on their own. These mushrooms are best if used in combination with other flavourful mushrooms or added to highly spiced or flavourful dishes.

PORCINI *(Boletus edulis)*, also known as ceps (or cèpes) and King Bolete (U.S.). Can weigh up to 1 lb (500 g). These pungent-tasting, fat-stemmed, and meaty-textured mushrooms are used fresh or dried in soup, pasta, and rice dishes (risotto), but their expense often prevents their widespread use.

PORTOBELLO *(Agaricus bisporus)*. If the cremini mushroom is allowed to grow, it matures into a larger version with a slightly flattened cap and woody stem. The cap is light to dark brown and as it matures, the taste deepens to a musty and intense earthiness, and the texture becomes firm and meaty. Portobello caps are grilled or baked and used in place of meat in burgers and sandwiches.

SHIITAKE *(Lentinula edodes)*. These mushroom spores grow from rotting oak trees in the wild and from oak sawdust blocks in commercial operations. They range in colour from tan to dark brown. The variety shown below, light brown with white spots, is called "Snow on the Mountain." The texture is firm and meaty and their flavour is full-bodied, almost steak-like. Their woody stems are removed and used to flavour vegetable stock and broth. When the caps flatten and seem greasy, the mushrooms are past their prime. (See page 61.)

SPLIT PEA SOUP WITH SHIITAKE MUSHROOMS

This is a very easy soup to prepare. Green, red, and yellow varieties of split peas are easy to find—mix and match! After fresh peas are dried, their indigestible skins are removed and the peas are split in half. Soaked peas cook in less than 45 minutes. I soak my split peas in a pot, covered by 2 inches (5 cm) cold water, at room temperature for six hours. Can't wait six hours? Cover with boiling water and let stand for 30 minutes. —NETTIE

SPLIT PEA AND MUSHROOM SOUP WITH CRISPY PANCETTA

Traditionally, ham bones and ham hocks are simmered in recipes for baked beans and split pea soup; the combination is legendary. If you have cooked ham in the freezer, a cup (250 mL) of diced meat can be added to the soup after the vegetarian portions have been removed. Pancetta is a cured Italian bacon often used as a flavouring in pasta, vegetable, and egg dishes. —PAT

COMBINE SPLIT PEAS, barley, water, and bay leaves in a large soup pot. Bring to a boil over high heat, stirring occasionally. Partially cover, reduce heat, and simmer, stirring often, for 45 minutes.

Meanwhile, heat oil in a skillet over medium-high heat. Add onions and cook, stirring frequently, for 5 minutes or until softened. Add garlic and stir frequently, for 2 minutes. Add soy sauce, mushrooms, carrot, and dill. Cook, stirring constantly, for 5 minutes. Add vegetables in skillet and salt to split-pea mixture. Simmer, stirring often, for 20 minutes or until peas are tender but not mushy. Add pepper in the last 5 minutes of cooking.

Sauté pancetta in the skillet (used for the vegetables) over medium-high heat for 4 to 7 minutes or until crisp and most of the fat is melted. Drain on paper towels. Ladle soup into 6 bowls. Garnish 2 meat servings with crispy pancetta.

1¼ cups (310 mL) uncooked
green, red, or yellow split peas,
rinsed and soaked
(see recipe introduction)

½ cup (125 mL) pearl barley, rinsed

10 cups (2.5 L) water or vegetable
stock (page 40 for homemade)

2 bay leaves

2 Tbsp (30 mL) olive oil

1½ cups (375 mL) chopped onions

2 cloves garlic, minced

2 Tbsp (30 mL) soy sauce or tamari

1½ cups (375 mL) diced
fresh shiitake mushrooms

1 cup (250 mL) diced carrot
(¼-inch/6 mm dice)

¼ cup (60 mL) chopped fresh dill

1 tsp (5 mL) salt

⅛ tsp (0.5 mL) freshly
ground pepper

1 to 2 oz (30 to 60 g) thickly sliced
pancetta, cut into short, wide strips

BUDDHA DRAGON BOWL WITH LEMONGRASS AND RICE NOODLES

The thick, salty paste made by cooking and fermenting soybeans and grains is called miso. Like fine wines, each miso has its own distinct flavour, colour, and aroma. Miso can be used with nut butters, tapenade, and even pesto. My favourite brand is Amano, which is handcrafted and barrel-aged and keeps in the fridge for up to six months.

Similar in shape to a green onion but longer, lemongrass imparts a rich, ethereal lemon flavour not mimicked by lemon zest. Trim to the lower third of the stalk, strip away the tough outer leaves, and then chop the softer inner core.

Thin, dried rice noodles are very easy to use. They readily take on the taste of the foods with which they are cooked. Stored in a dry, cool place, they will last indefinitely. —NETTIE

BUDDHA DRAGON NOODLE BOWL WITH BACON-BROILED SCALLOPS

Use sea scallops (as opposed to bay scallops) because they are larger and more suited to the oven method and the bacon used in this recipe. If only the smaller bay scallops are available, cook the bacon in a skillet until crispy and drain on a paper towel. Sauté the bay scallops in the hot bacon fat over medium heat, turning once, for two to four minutes or until cooked through. Be careful not to overcook scallops because they will turn rubbery. —PAT

8 oz (250 g) sea scallops

1 or 2 slices side bacon

2 Tbsp (30 mL) toasted sesame oil

1 cup (250 mL) thinly sliced red onion

½ cup (125 mL) thinly sliced fresh shiitake mushrooms

1 cup (250 mL) thinly sliced red bell pepper

1 carrot, shredded

2 stalks celery, thinly sliced

⅓ cup (80 mL) finely chopped lemongrass, white parts only (about 3 stalks)

2 cloves garlic, chopped

2 Tbsp (30 mL) finely chopped fresh ginger

One 14 oz (398 mL) can coconut milk

½ cup (125 mL) unpasteurized barley miso

6 cups (1.5 L) cold water

12 oz (375 g) dried thin rice noodles

1 cup (250 mL) salted roasted peanuts, for garnishing

4 green onions, thinly sliced, for garnishing

6 Tbsp (90 mL) chopped fresh cilantro, for garnishing

¼ cup (60 mL) Sweet Thai Chile Sauce (page 8) or store-bought (optional)

Rimmed baking sheet, lightly oiled

SHIITAKE MUSHROOMS

Shiitakes are aromatic, chewy mushrooms with a brown cap that are used in traditional Japanese cuisine. They are grown commercially on hardwood logs (the variety pictured above is called "Snow on the Mountain"). These mushrooms are recognized as a symbol of longevity in Asia due to their immunity-boosting, anti-tumour, anti-cancer, antiviral, cholesterol-lowering, and liver-protective properties. Whether fresh or dried, shiitakes add a rich flavour to soups, stews, sauces, rice dishes, and noodle dishes.

Dried mushrooms must be soaked in hot water to soften before use, and very tough stems should be removed. When stored in an airtight container in a cool, dark, dry place, dried shiitakes keep for a long time. Fresh shiitakes need to be refrigerated and will keep for a week.

PREHEAT THE OVEN to Broil (500°F/260°C).

Arrange scallops in one layer on prepared baking sheet. Cut the bacon strips into 1-inch (2.5 cm) pieces and attach to the bottom or tops of each scallop, securing with a toothpick.

Broil on the top rack of the oven, turning once, for 2 minutes each side or until scallops turn opaque and are firm but not hard or rubbery. Remove and let drain on a paper towel–lined plate. Remove toothpicks and divide scallops and bacon pieces into 2 equal portions.

Heat oil in a wok or large skillet over medium heat. Add onion and cook, stirring occasionally, for 5 minutes or until softened. Add mushrooms and red pepper and cook, stirring frequently, for 2 minutes. Add carrot and celery and cook, stirring constantly, for 4 minutes or until softened.

Add lemongrass, garlic, and ginger, and stir to combine. Cook, stirring frequently, for 2 minutes. Add coconut milk, miso, and water. Lower heat and simmer, stirring occasionally, for 20 minutes.

Meanwhile, prepare rice noodles. Pour boiling water over noodles in a bowl until totally covered. Let stand for 10 minutes to rehydrate. Drain in a colander.

Divide noodles, heaping them in the centre of 6 soup bowls. Ladle soup over noodles. Garnish 2 soup bowls with scallops and bacon pieces. Garnish to taste with peanuts, green onions, cilantro, and chile sauce.

RED CABBAGE SOUP WITH CURRANTS

Cabbage comes in many shapes, sizes, and colours. Red cabbage is best cooked in broth with red wine and with sweet and sour accents as provided by spices, lemon juice, apples, and onions. This soup is aromatic and filling, and has a spicy depth to its flavour. Use sweet, firm apples such as Honeycrisp, Granny Smith, or Fuji for the best results. —NETTIE

RED CABBAGE SOUP WITH CURRANTS AND CHORIZO

The spicy chorizo sausage is a perfect match for the hearty cabbage in this soup. Cook and drain it well, but save some of the chorizo oil from the pan and lightly drizzle a teaspoon (5 mL) overtop of the soup for added richness, if desired. —PAT

2 Tbsp (30 mL) + 1 Tbsp (15 mL) olive oil

1 cup (250 mL) chopped onion

1 tsp (5 mL) ground cinnamon

½ tsp (2 mL) ground cloves

½ tsp (2 mL) ground allspice

5 cups (1.25 L) shredded red cabbage

6 cups (1.5 L) vegetable stock (page 40 for homemade) or water

1 cup (250 mL) dry red wine (optional)

¼ cup (60 mL) fresh or dried currants

2 tsp (10 mL) salt

2 cups (500 mL) apple slices, ½ inch (1 cm) thick

1 tsp (5 mL) freshly ground pepper

4 oz (125 g) chorizo, chopped into ½-inch (1 cm) pieces

2 cups (500 mL) plain yogurt, divided

2 Tbsp (30 mL) fresh lemon juice

2 Tbsp (30 mL) chopped fresh chives, for garnishing

HEAT 2 TBSP (30 ML) olive oil in a large pot or Dutch oven over medium heat. Add onion and cook, stirring frequently, for 5 minutes or until softened. Stir in cinnamon, cloves, and allspice and cook, stirring constantly, for 1 minute. Add cabbage and cook, stirring constantly, for 5 minutes.

Add the stock, wine (if using), currants, and salt. Bring to a boil over high heat. Cover, reduce heat, and simmer, stirring once or twice, for 20 minutes. Add apples and pepper and simmer uncovered, stirring occasionally, for 15 minutes.

Heat 1 Tbsp (15 mL) olive oil in a skillet over medium-high heat. Add chorizo and cook, stirring constantly, for 8 minutes or until browned and crisp. Keep heat high enough to brown the meat but reduce heat if chorizo begins to burn. Transfer to a paper towel–lined plate and let drain, reserving 2 tsp (10 mL) oil in the pan for garnishing the soup, if desired.

Remove soup from heat and stir in 1½ cups (375 mL) of the yogurt and all of the lemon juice. Ladle soup into 6 bowls. Add cooked chorizo, chives, and reserved oil (if using) to 2 bowls. Divide remaining yogurt into 6 equal amounts to garnish each soup bowl.

2 Tbsp (30 mL) olive oil

1 red onion, chopped

1 large leek, white and pale green parts only, chopped

1 clove garlic, minced

6 cups (1.5 L) vegetable stock (page 40 for homemade) or water

3 potatoes (any kind), cubed

4 cups (1 L) broccoli florets

½ tsp (2 mL) salt

1 Tbsp (15 mL) chopped fresh oregano or marjoram

1 Tbsp (15 mL) chopped fresh basil

Pinch of dried red chile flakes

2 slices side bacon or pancetta, cut into 1-inch (2.5 cm) pieces

¼ cup (60 mL) finely grated Parmesan cheese

2 cups (500 mL) milk

¼ tsp (1 mL) freshly ground pepper

½ cup (125 mL) chopped fresh parsley, for garnishing

BROCCOLI PARMESAN SOUP

Broccoli is a member of the cruciferous vegetable family, which includes cabbage, cauliflower, kale, and bok choy. The word *cruciferous* comes from the Latin word for cross, which the four flower petals form. These vegetables are free of fat and cholesterol, rich in fibre, and extraordinarily nutritious. This is an easy soup to prepare if you use a blender or food processor to purée it.
—NETTIE

BROCCOLI PARMESAN SOUP WITH BACON

Bacon or pancetta is the perfect accompaniment to broccoli and cheese soup—you will only need two slices, one per person. Diced cooked ham may be used in place of the bacon. —PAT

HEAT OIL IN a large pot or Dutch oven over medium-high heat. Add onion and leek and cook, stirring frequently, for 5 minutes or until onions are soft. Add garlic and cook, stirring constantly, for 1 minute.

Add stock and bring to a boil. Add potatoes, broccoli, and salt. Reduce heat and simmer for 15 minutes, stirring once or twice, until potatoes are soft. Add oregano, basil, and red chile flakes and cook, stirring constantly, for 1 minute.

Arrange bacon pieces in a single layer on a grill or skillet, making sure pieces don't touch. Cook, tossing and turning using tongs or a slotted spoon, over medium-high heat for 3 to 5 minutes or until bacon is browned and crisp. Lift out using a slotted spoon and drain on paper towel–lined plate.

Purée soup in batches in a food processor or blender. Return to the pot and keep hot over medium heat until all soup has been puréed. Stir in cheese, milk, and pepper. Bring to just under a boil, stirring constantly. Ladle soup into 6 bowls and garnish each one with parsley. Divide bacon into 2 equal portions and use it to garnish 2 of the bowls.

DRIED SHIITAKE MUSHROOM, ADZUKI BEAN, AND CARROT SOUP

Dried mushrooms add a deep, concentrated flavour to soups and noodle dishes. With dried mushrooms, look for thick, lightly spotted caps with cracks. The cracks indicate a late fall harvest, when less moisture in the air results in more cracks on the surface of the dried caps. Adzuki beans are small, oval, burgundy-coloured beans that are easy to digest. —NETTIE

SHIITAKE, ADZUKI BEAN, AND CARROT SOUP WITH SAUTÉED SHRIMP

Storing shrimp (cooked or raw) in the freezer makes a lot of sense for a flexi-tarian cook. As a protein, shrimp is an excellent alternative to beef and pork; shrimp is low in calories and saturated fats yet satisfying and tasty—and being firm and boneless, easy to prepare. —PAT

1 oz (30 g) dried shiitake (sidebar, page 61) or porcini mushrooms

2 cups (500 mL) boiling water, for mushrooms

2 Tbsp (30 mL) + 2 Tbsp (30 mL) olive oil

1 cup (250 mL) chopped onion

1 cup (250 mL) diced zucchini (¼-inch/6 mm dice)

1 cup (250 mL) shredded carrot

1 cup (250 mL) diced red bell pepper (¼-inch/6 mm dice)

2 + 2 cloves garlic, minced

½ cup (125 mL) corn kernels (fresh, frozen, or canned)

1 Tbsp (15 mL) finely chopped fresh ginger

One 14 oz (398 mL) can adzuki beans, with liquid

8 cups (2 L) vegetable stock (page 40 for homemade)

¼ cup (60 mL) tamari or soy sauce

¼ tsp (1 mL) cayenne pepper

8 oz (250 g) dried thin rice noodles

6 oz (175 g) shrimp,
peeled and deveined

1 tsp (5 mL) chopped fresh
rosemary

2 Tbsp (30 mL) fresh lemon juice

6 sprigs fresh cilantro, for garnishing

4 green onions, thinly sliced,
for garnishing

COVER MUSHROOMS IN a bowl with boiling water, and soak for about 20 minutes or until completely softened. Set a cheesecloth-lined sieve over a separate bowl and strain mushrooms, reserving the soaking water. Remove and discard stems from mushrooms. Thinly slice mushroom caps and set aside.

Heat 2 Tbsp (30 mL) olive oil in a large skillet over medium heat. Add onions and cook, stirring frequently, for 5 minutes or until soft. Add zucchini, carrot, red pepper, and 2 cloves minced garlic and cook, stirring constantly, for 5 minutes.

Transfer vegetable mixture to a soup pot. Add corn, ginger, beans and liquid, stock, softened mushrooms, reserved mushroom-soaking liquid, tamari, and cayenne. Bring to a boil over high heat, reduce heat, and simmer for 15 minutes.

Meanwhile, bring a kettle of water to the boil. Pour over noodles in a bowl until totally covered. Let stand for 10 minutes to rehydrate and then drain.

Heat 2 Tbsp (30 mL) olive oil in a heavy-bottomed skillet over medium-high heat. Add shrimp, lower heat to medium-low, and cook, turning once for 2 minutes on each side. Add 2 cloves minced garlic, rosemary, and lemon juice and cook, tossing and stirring for 1 or 2 minutes or until shrimp is firm, opaque, and bright pink.

Divide noodles among 6 soup bowls. Divide shrimp evenly and spoon into 2 bowls. Ladle soup into bowls and garnish with cilantro and green onions.

MUSHROOM PROVENÇAL STEW

Mix your mushrooms—button, shiitake, portobello, cremini, and oyster—in this flavourful stew. They have a rich "meaty" texture that establishes their savoury, intense flavour. Prepare vegetable stock from scratch (page 40) or use vegetable broth powder, bouillon cubes, or Tetra Pak stock. Cut the vegetables the same size, about ½-inch (1 cm) dice, for even cooking. Vegetables, except for potatoes, can be prepared up to two days ahead if you cover and refrigerate them. —NETTIE

MUSHROOM PROVENÇAL STEW WITH LAMB SHANKS

I suggest that you marinate the lamb shanks overnight in the removable crock of a slow cooker (see page 68). Turn the slow cooker on in the morning (medium heat) and by the late afternoon, the lamb will be fork-tender and ready to serve with the mushroom stew. —PAT

½ cup (120 mL) olive oil, divided

1½ cups (375 mL) finely chopped Vidalia onion

2 cloves garlic, chopped

3 cups (750 mL) mushrooms (about 1½ lb/750 g), thinly sliced

1 cup (250 mL) chopped carrot

1 cup (250 mL) chopped celery

1 cup (250 mL) chopped red bell pepper

10 cups (2.5 L) vegetable stock (page 40 for homemade), divided

1 bottle (750 mL) dry red wine, divided

1 tsp (5 mL) tamari or soy sauce

1½ lb (750 g) Yukon Gold potatoes, diced

1 Tbsp (15 mL) fresh thyme leaves

1 Tbsp (15 mL) fresh chopped oregano or marjoram

Pinch of cayenne pepper

1 tsp (5 mL) salt

½ tsp (2 mL) freshly ground pepper

¼ cup (60 mL) all-purpose flour

½ cup (125 mL) tomato paste

2 Lamb Shanks (next page), warm

HEAT ¼ CUP (60 ML) of the oil in a large skillet over medium heat. Add onion and cook, stirring frequently, for 5 minutes or until tender. Stir in garlic and add mushrooms in 2 or 3 batches, starting with about 1 cup (250 mL). Cook, stirring constantly, for 3 to 5 minutes or until softened. Add remaining mushrooms and cook, stirring constantly, for 3 to 5 minutes or until softened.

Stir in carrot, celery, red pepper, and 1 cup (250 mL) of stock. Simmer for 15 minutes or until vegetables are softened.

Combine 7 cups (1.75 L) of stock, 1 cup (250 mL) wine, tamari, skillet vegetables (including liquids), potatoes, thyme, oregano, cayenne, salt, and pepper in a large pot. Bring to a boil over high heat. Cover, reduce heat, and simmer, stirring once or twice, for 10 minutes or until potatoes are tender.

Meanwhile, heat remaining ¼ cup (60 mL) oil in a saucepan over medium-low heat. Whisk in flour and cook, whisking constantly for 1 minute. Add tomato paste and whisk for 1 minute. Add 1 cup (250 mL) stock and cook, whisking constantly, for 1 minute. Add remaining stock and cook, whisking constantly, for 2 minutes or until thickened. Stir into vegetable stew. Cover, reduce heat, and simmer, stirring once or twice, for 15 minutes.

Ladle stew into 6 bowls. Add lamb to 2 bowls.

(continued)

(continued from previous page)

LAMB SHANKS

MAKES: 2 (or 6) servings

When I cook lamb shanks, I always cook six shanks at a time and freeze the extra portions in two-serving containers. To cook six shanks, you only have to increase the water in this recipe (to cover the meat), not the other ingredients. If time is tight, you don't have to marinate the meat overnight, but marinating does help to tenderize the meat and cuts down on the actual cooking time. Long, slow simmering is the best way to cook this cut of lamb. The bonus is that you will also have a delicious and richly flavoured lamb stock to use in future meat recipes. — PAT

2 (or 6) lamb shanks, about 8 oz (250 g) each (see Tip)

1 carrot, coarsely chopped

1 onion, quartered

3 cloves garlic, crushed

3 whole allspice berries

2 whole cloves

2 cups (500 mL) dry red wine

Beef stock (page 46 or 47 for homemade) or water, to cover

Slow cooker with detachable crock (or roasting pan for oven cooking)

COMBINE LAMB, CARROT, onion, garlic, allspice, cloves, and wine in the detachable crock of a slow cooker (or roasting pan). Pour enough beef stock overtop so meat is covered. Cover and refrigerate for at least 6 hours, or overnight.

Return crock to slow cooker and cook on "medium" setting for 4 to 6 hours, or until meat is fork-tender. Lift meat out of pan liquids and slice off the bone. (If cooking in the oven, preheat the oven to 350°F (180°C) and cook, stirring once or twice, for 2 to 3 hours or until meat is fork-tender.) Add to 2 bowls of the vegetable stew in the last step of the Mushroom Provençal Stew recipe.

Line a large strainer or colander with 2 layers of cheesecloth and place over a large bowl. Strain the cooking liquids, pressing on the solids with the back of a spoon to release all of the liquid. Discard solids and let liquids cool. Cover and refrigerate for up to 3 days. Skim and discard any fat that has risen to the surface of the liquids before using or freezing. Lamb cooking liquids may be used to make gravy or as a meat stock. Freeze in individual 2- or 4-cup (500 mL or 1 L) containers (or ice cube trays) for up to 3 months.

TIP

The size of lamb shanks varies, but generally speaking, if you are health-conscious, the meat from one large shank could serve two people. If you are planning to use one shank per person, look for small shanks that weigh no more than ½ to ¾ lb (250 to 375 g) each with the bone in.

CHICKEN NOODLE SOUP

3 oz (90 g) dried egg noodles

2 Tbsp (30 mL) olive oil

1 onion, chopped

2 cloves garlic, chopped

2 stalks celery, diced

1 carrot, diced

2 Tbsp (30 mL) chopped
fresh parsley

1 Tbsp (15 mL) fresh thyme leaves

½ cup (125 mL) dry white wine

7 cups (1.75 L) chicken stock
(page 45 for homemade)

2 boneless, skinless chicken breasts,
cut into ½-inch (1 cm) dice

1½ cups (375 mL) frozen peas

Salt and pepper, to taste

As in any soup, the key to a really good chicken soup is the stock. If you can start with homemade chicken stock the taste will be enhanced. This is a brothy soup (as opposed to a creamy soup), and the one ingredient that sets it apart from most other chicken-soup recipes is the dry white wine. — PAT

BRING A POT of salted water to a boil and cook egg noodles for 3 to 6 minutes, or until al dente. Drain and set aside.

Meanwhile heat oil in a large heavy saucepan over medium heat. Add onion, garlic, celery, and carrot. Cook, stirring frequently, for 6 minutes or until vegetables are softened but not browned. Add parsley, thyme, and wine. Cook, stirring constantly, for 1 minute or until wine has bubbled for 30 seconds.

Add chicken stock and bring to a boil over high heat. Stir in chicken and peas. Reduce heat and simmer, stirring occasionally, for 5 minutes or until chicken is firm and showing no pink. Stir in cooked noodles and heat through. Season to taste with salt and pepper.

BEEF AND BARLEY SOUP

Barley thickens and adds body to soups and stews. I prefer to use
Scotch barley if I can get it because it is less refined. I love the
sweetness of the butternut squash and parsnips, but you could
substitute carrots and turnip instead. For a richer, earthier base,
you can use mushroom broth (page 42) in place of the beef stock,
or use half beef stock, half mushroom broth. — PAT

HEAT OIL IN a soup pot over medium-high heat. Add beef
and cook, turning every few minutes, for 5 minutes or until
well browned on all sides. Transfer to a plate using tongs or a
slotted spoon. (Alternatively, grill the beef on a hot grill pan
until there are grill marks on all sides.)

Reduce heat to medium-low and add onion. Cook, stirring
and scraping up the browned bits, for 5 minutes or until softened. Add garlic and mushrooms and cook, stirring frequently,
for 3 to 4 minutes or until mushrooms are soft.

Add beef stock and bring to a boil over high heat. Add
browned meat, squash, parsnips, barley, bay leaf, and cinnamon
(if using). Cover, reduce heat, and simmer for 40 to 50 minutes
or until vegetables are tender and barley is swollen and soft.
Discard bay leaf, season to taste with salt and pepper, and serve
soup garnished with chives.

2 Tbsp (30 mL) olive oil

7 oz (200 g) stewing beef
or beef chuck, cut into ¾-inch
(2 cm) cubes

1 onion, chopped

2 cloves garlic, chopped

1 cup (250 mL) sliced mushrooms

6 cups (1.5 L) beef stock (page 46
or 47 for homemade)

1 cup (250 mL) diced butternut
squash (½-inch/1 cm dice)

2 parsnips, cut into
½-inch (1 cm) dice

⅓ cup (80 mL) Scotch
or pot barley, rinsed

1 bay leaf

¼ tsp (1 mL) ground cinnamon
(optional)

Salt and pepper, to taste

¼ cup (60 mL) chopped fresh chives
or parsley, for garnishing

SALADS

SPICED POTATO AND LENTIL SALAD

This recipe has an interesting spice mixture that is sweet and hot and delicately scents the lentils and potatoes. If possible, marinate for 30 minutes or longer. My 21-year-old son, Cameron, always likes to pack this into a pita to eat before an exam. —NETTIE

RINSE LENTILS IN a strainer under cold running water. Drain and transfer to a saucepan. Add the 2½ cups (625 mL) water and bring to a boil over high heat. Cover, reduce heat, and boil gently for 20 minutes or until tender. Drain and rinse under cold water. Set aside.

Meanwhile, place potatoes in a saucepan and cover with water. Bring to a boil over high heat. Cover, reduce heat, and simmer for 10 to 15 minutes or until tender. Drain and rinse under cold water. Set aside.

Heat oil in a skillet over medium-high heat. Add onion and cook, stirring frequently, for 5 minutes or until soft. Add garlic and cook, stirring constantly, for 1 minute. Add salt, pepper, cinnamon, cumin, coriander, cayenne pepper, and cloves. Cook, stirring constantly, for 1 minute or until fragrant.

Combine cooked lentils and potatoes, onion-spice mixture, and lemon juice in a bowl. Toss to mix well.

1 cup (250 mL) red lentils

2½ cups (625 mL) water

3 potatoes (I prefer waxy potatoes), cut into cubes

3 Tbsp (45 mL) olive oil

1 onion, chopped

2 cloves garlic, chopped

½ tsp (2 mL) salt

½ tsp (2 mL) freshly ground pepper

½ tsp (2 mL) ground cinnamon

½ tsp (2 mL) ground cumin

½ tsp (2 mL) ground coriander

¼ to ½ tsp (1 to 2 mL) cayenne pepper

Pinch of ground cloves

Juice of 1 lemon

SQUASH AND LEEKS WITH ASIAN DRESSING

There are many types of Asian squash to choose from: Delica, Hoka, and Sweet Mama, to name but a few. They are turban-shaped and green, and have almost fibreless flesh. The flavour is somewhere between pumpkin and sweet potato.

Most winter squash varieties will keep for up to a month at room temperature. Before using, scoop out and discard the seeds and fibres. —NETTIE

SALAD

3 cups (750 mL) cubed squash (1-inch/2.5 cm cubes)

2 leeks, white and pale green tender parts only, cut into ½-inch (1 cm) rounds

1 cup (250 mL) thinly sliced snow peas

1 cup (250 mL) matchstick-cut carrots or parsnips

One 14 oz (398 mL) can chickpeas, drained

¼ cup (60 mL) toasted sesame seeds (sidebar, page 26), for garnishing

DRESSING

2 Tbsp (30 mL) peanut oil

1 Tbsp (15 mL) toasted sesame oil

1 tsp (5 mL) tamari or soy sauce

Juice of 1 lime

ADD ENOUGH WATER to reach the bottom of a collapsible steamer set in a saucepan and bring to a boil on high heat. Place squash in steamer basket, cover, and steam for 6 minutes. Add leeks, snow peas, and carrots, cover, and steam for 4 to 5 more minutes, or until all vegetables are tender. (Or cover squash cubes with water in a saucepan and bring the water to a boil. Reduce heat and lightly boil for 5 minutes. Add leeks, snow peas, and carrots, cover, and simmer for 4 to 5 minutes, or until all vegetables are tender.) Drain and plunge vegetables into cold water to stop the cooking; drain and pat dry. Arrange cooked vegetables on a platter and scatter chickpeas overtop.

Combine dressing ingredients in a bowl (or in a jar with a tight-fitting lid). Whisk (or shake) to combine. Pour dressing overtop salad ingredients and garnish with sesame seeds.

MÂCHE WITH ROASTED BEETS, WALNUTS, AND BLUE CHEESE

Mâche is available in specialty markets year-round, sold in a bunch with roots attached. It is highly perishable, delicious, and expensive. With its velvety texture, which is enhanced by the presence of walnut oil, it must not be dressed until everyone is seated at the table for fear of soggy greens. Roasted beets bring out the earthy flavour of this delicate green. —NETTIE

MÂCHE WITH ROASTED BEETS AND GRILLED BEEF

Cooking the beef in one piece to your exact preference is easy and fast. I have found that if I flash-freeze the grilled steak for about 45 minutes in the coldest part of the freezer, I can slice it close to paper thin, which is what you want for this salad garnish. You may find that you have enough beef left over for one more meal, since three or four slices will be more than enough for each serving. —PAT

6 medium-sized beets,
trimmed and quartered

2 Tbsp (30 mL) + 1 Tbsp (15 mL)
olive oil

6 oz (175 g) sirloin tip steak

1 clove garlic, crushed

1 tsp (5 mL) smoked paprika

Sea salt and freshly ground pepper,
to taste

3 Tbsp (45 mL) toasted walnut oil
or toasted sesame oil, divided

Two 6-inch (15 cm) corn or flour
tortillas, cut into ½-inch-wide
(1 cm) strips (about
2 cups/500 mL total)

2 Tbsp (30 mL) red wine vinegar

2 cloves garlic, minced

6 cups (1.5 L) mâche or mixed
tender salad greens

⅓ cup (80 mL) diagonally
sliced green onions

3 oz (90 g) blue cheese, crumbled

½ cup (125 mL) coarsely
chopped walnuts

Aluminum foil

(continued)

(continued from previous page)

PREHEAT THE OVEN to 375°F (190°C).

Arrange beet quarters in the centre of a large sheet of aluminum foil and drizzle with 2 Tbsp (30 mL) olive oil. Bring 2 long edges of foil together and pleat to enclose beets. Roll up 2 side edges of foil so packet is sealed. Bake in preheated oven for 1 hour, or until beets are tender when pierced with the tip of a knife.

Spread both sides of steak with garlic and sprinkle with paprika. Heat 1 Tbsp (15 mL) olive oil in a skillet or ridged grill pan over medium-high heat. Add steak and cook for 6 to 8 minutes (use a thermometer to gauge degree of doneness— see sidebar), turning once. Remove from heat and let stand until cooled down a bit. Season with salt and pepper. Wrap tightly in plastic wrap and flash-freeze for 45 minutes, or until firm enough to slice.

Cool beets until cool enough to handle, and then slip off and discard skins. Set roasted quarters aside in a bowl.

Meanwhile, heat 2 Tbsp (30 mL) of the walnut oil in a skillet over medium heat. Add tortilla strips and fry, turning often with tongs, for 4 minutes or until golden brown. Transfer to a paper towel–lined plate and set aside.

Combine remaining walnut oil, vinegar, and garlic in a small bowl. Drizzle half of this dressing overtop the baked beets. Combine mâche and green onions in a large bowl. Drizzle remaining walnut oil dressing overtop and toss with tongs to coat greens. Divide greens evenly among 6 salad plates.

Spoon 4 roasted beet quarters into centre of greens on each plate. Sprinkle salads with blue cheese, walnuts, and fried tortilla strips.

Slice the steak into very thin slices. Divide steak slices into 2 portions and add to 2 salad plates. Wrap leftover beef slices and store in the refrigerator for up to 2 days.

DONENESS TEMPERATURES FOR BEEF	
Rare	120°F (49°C)
Medium Rare	125°F (51°C)
Medium	130°F (54°C)

SPELT SALAD WITH GRILLED VEGETABLES AND TOFU

Spelt kernels and wheat berries are the hulled whole kernels of wheat from which the flour is milled. Because their bran is intact, they can take an hour or more to cook. Spelt is a specific type of wheat that is remarkable for its high protein content, as high as 17 percent. —NETTIE

1 cup (250 mL) whole spelt kernels or wheat berries

4 cups (1 L) water

DRESSING

1 cup (250 mL) chopped seeded tomatoes (canned or fresh)

½ cup (125 mL) olive oil

¼ cup (60 mL) balsamic vinegar

2 tsp (10 mL) Dijon mustard

1 tsp (5 mL) salt

GRILLED VEGETABLES

One 14 oz (440 g) pkg firm tofu, rinsed and cut into 1-inch (2.5 cm) cubes

1 small eggplant, cut into 1-inch (2.5 cm) cubes

1 red bell pepper, seeded and cut into 1-inch (2.5 cm) squares

1 green bell pepper, seeded and cut into 1-inch (2.5 cm) squares

2 onions, quartered

2 cups (500 mL) baby arugula, spinach, or mâche

About ten 10-inch (25 cm) skewers (wooden or metal)

PREHEAT THE GRILL to medium.

Combine spelt kernels and water in a saucepan. Bring to a boil over high heat. Cover, reduce heat, and simmer for 1½ to 2 hours, or until tender (spelt will be chewy). Rinse under cold water and drain thoroughly.

Meanwhile, if using wooden skewers, soak them in water for at least 30 minutes.

Combine tomatoes, oil, vinegar, mustard, and salt in a shallow baking dish. Thread tofu and vegetables onto separate skewers, grouping vegetables by type so that tender vegetables can be removed earlier from the grill while longer-cooking vegetables continue cooking. Place tofu skewers and vegetable skewers in the dressing. Marinate, turning occasionally, for 1 hour at room temperature (or cover and marinate in the refrigerator overnight).

Remove skewers from marinade, and transfer marinade to a large bowl and set aside. Grill tofu and vegetables on preheated grill, turning often. Remove peppers after 2 to 3 minutes, onions after 3 to 4 minutes, tofu after 4 to 5 minutes, and eggplant after 5 to 6 minutes. As vegetables and tofu are removed from grill, slide off skewers directly into bowl containing marinade.

Add cooked spelt and salad greens to the grilled vegetables in the bowl and toss well.

BROCCOLI SLAW WITH LIMA BEANS

Salad is a very good way to use up the tender part of broccoli stems, a valuable and nutriet-rich part of the vegetable.
—NETTIE

IN A SAUCEPAN, cover lima beans with water and simmer over medium-high heat for 4 to 5 minutes. Drain and refresh under cold water, and then pat dry.

Arrange broccoli, carrot, beets, radishes, green onions, cilantro, mint, and cooked beans on a platter (or combine in a bowl). Whisk lemon juice and oil together and pour overtop vegetables. Garnish with sesame seeds. (If using a bowl, toss before serving.)

SHREDDING BROCCOLI

Shredding broccoli stems renders them tender for eating raw. The stems are wrapped in an outer layer of tough skin that when peeled away actually reveals a sweet and tender inner core. Avoid buying broccoli that have a split or opening in the bottom of the stalks, indicating that the broccoli matured too long on the stalk and that the tough and woody outer layer extends almost to the core of the stem.

1. Peel and discard the tough outer layer of skin surrounding the tender broccoli stalks using a paring knife or a vegetable peeler.

2. Using a hand grater or the 4 mm shredding blade of a food processor, shred the peeled stalks into a colander. Let drain over a sink for at least 15 minutes before using in salads or other dishes.

1 cup (250 mL) shelled lima beans,
frozen

1 cup (250 mL) chopped
broccoli florets

2 cups (500 mL) shredded
broccoli stems

1 cup (250 mL) shredded carrot

1 cup (250 mL) shredded beets

½ cup (125 mL) sliced radishes

2 green onions, thinly sliced

¼ cup (60 mL) chopped
fresh cilantro or chiffonade
of Thai basil (page 133)

1 Tbsp (15 mL) chopped fresh mint

2 Tbsp (30 mL) fresh lemon juice

¼ cup (60 mL) olive oil

3 Tbsp (45 mL) sesame seeds,
for garnishing

LIMA BEANS

Lima beans are flat seeds
that have a white to pale
green colour and a waxy texture when cooked. They were
often planted as part of the
First Nations "three sisters"
combination of corn, beans,
and squash. Now lima beans are available fresh, frozen,
and canned.

SWEET POTATO, FENNEL, AND APPLE SALAD

Sweet potatoes come in many varieties, with skins ranging from tan to purple and flesh ranging from pale yellow to red-orange. They combine well with a wide range of ingredients and flavours, from aromatic spices to fleshy fruits, nuts, chiles, and fresh herbs. Combining fruits and vegetables makes the best salads.

—NETTIE

IN A SAUCEPAN, cover sweet potatoes with water and cook over medium-high heat for 15 minutes, or until tender. Drain and rinse under cold water. When cool enough to handle, remove and then discard peels.

Combine apple, fennel, onion, walnuts, cherries, and cooked sweet potato in a bowl.

Whisk together sesame oil, olive oil, vinegar, and Pomegranate Glaze in a bowl (or shake in a jar) to combine. Pour overtop salad ingredients and toss to mix.

FLAVOUR PROFILE

The combination of olive oil, apple cider vinegar, and pomegranate syrup lends a fruity and fragrant essence to the dressing for this salad. Splashes of toasted sesame oil and tart-sweet pomegranate syrup balance the acidic tones of the vinegar. Toasted walnuts complement the hint of sesame oil.

SALAD

3 unpeeled sweet potatoes
(about 2½ lb/1.25 kg),
cut into 1-inch (2.5 cm) pieces

2 apples, halved and thinly sliced

1 cup (250 mL) coarsely chopped
fennel bulb (sidebar, page 165),
into ½-inch-long (1 cm) pieces

½ red onion, thinly sliced

½ cup (125 mL) coarsely chopped
toasted walnuts (sidebar, page 26)

¼ cup (60 mL) chopped dried
cherries or cranberries

DRESSING

¼ cup (60 mL) toasted sesame oil

2 Tbsp (30 mL) olive oil,
or hemp or safflower oil

¼ cup (60 mL) apple cider vinegar

1 Tbsp (15 mL) Pomegranate
Glaze (page 8, or store-bought
pomegranate molasses)

COUSCOUS WITH MINT, CUCUMBER, WALNUTS, AND BRIE

Israeli couscous is pea-sized and is more like pasta. It is made from a type of hard wheat that has been rolled into small balls. You can then toast them to add flavour. You must also toast your walnuts—they will taste great. —NETTIE

TOAST THE COUSCOUS in a dry skillet over medium heat, stirring constantly, for 5 to 7 minutes or until golden brown.

Meanwhile, bring 2 quarts (2 L) salted water to a boil over high heat. Cook the toasted couscous in the water for 10 minutes, or until tender. Drain and rinse under cold running water until cool. Pour couscous into a bowl and add cucumber and mint.

In a bowl (or in a jar with tight-fitting lid), combine olive oil, sesame oil, lemon juice, salt, and pepper; whisk (or shake) to blend. Drizzle over couscous mixture and toss to mix well. Sprinkle salad with walnut pieces and brie slices.

1 cup (250 mL) Israeli couscous or regular couscous

2 cups (500 mL) diced English cucumber

½ cup (125 mL) chopped fresh mint

¼ cup (60 mL) olive oil

1 Tbsp (15 mL) toasted sesame oil

Juice of ½ a medium-sized lemon

½ tsp (2 mL) sea salt

¼ tsp (1 mL) freshly ground pepper

½ cup (125 mL) toasted walnut pieces (sidebar, page 26)

One 4 oz (125 g) wedge brie, cut into thin slices

ISRAELI COUSCOUS

Available in specialty stores and Middle Eastern food stores, Israeli couscous is hand-rolled, moistened semolina wheat and is larger than most regular couscous. Many brands of Israeli couscous are already toasted, which gives it a nuttier flavour. Use it in pasta recipes and in salads.

BARLEY TABBOULEH WITH FETA AND OLIVES

Sweet, chewy barley replaces bulgur in this main course salad. The quality of your olives and feta will determine how tasty the salad will be. Look for fresh ingredients. —NETTIE

4½ cups (1.125 L) vegetable stock (page 40 for homemade) or water

½ tsp (2 mL) salt

1½ cups (375 mL) pot barley, rinsed

⅓ cup (80 mL) olive oil

¼ cup (60 mL) fresh lemon juice

1 cup (250 mL) chopped fresh parsley

¼ cup (60 mL) chopped fresh dill

2 cups (500 mL) diced English cucumber

2 cups (500 mL) cherry tomatoes, halved

¾ cup (185 mL) crumbled feta cheese

½ cup (125 mL) sliced, pitted green or black olives

BRING STOCK AND salt to a boil in a saucepan over high heat. Add barley, cover, reduce the heat, and simmer for 40 minutes, or until tender. Drain off any unabsorbed liquid and transfer barley to a large bowl.

Combine olive oil and lemon juice in a bowl (or in a clean jar with a tight-fitting lid); whisk (or shake) and pour overtop cooked barley. Let sit for 5 minutes, and then stir. Add parsley, dill, cucumber, and tomatoes, and toss to mix well. Let sit for 10 minutes or more at room temperature.

Transfer barley mixture to a platter. Sprinkle feta cheese and olives overtop.

WARM VEGETARIAN COBB SALAD

"This is a perfect flexitarian recipe," declared my 11-year-old son, Emery. He's right: Lots of choice, and once you prepare the salad and garnishes you can decide to add meat. Personally, I think there are enough ingredients to please everyone, but it is all about choice, as demonstrated by his Single A hockey teammates. — NETTIE

WARM COBB SALAD

This is just the dish where meat that's been cooked and frozen into two-portion packets really comes in handy. I have used everything from smoked fish and chicken to roast beef, lamb, pork, and ham (already sliced or cubed) as a garnish for the greens and vegetables in this salad. It takes very little time to thaw and/or warm up the meat using a microwave or toaster oven. (The meat may be served warm or at room temperature here.) If you don't have any precooked meat, poach a chicken breast as directed on page 183. — PAT

SALAD

1 lb (500 g) fresh green beans, trimmed

3 cups (750 mL) fresh spinach

3 cups (750 mL) fresh or frozen chopped Swiss chard (thawed if frozen)

1½ cups (375 mL) cooked chickpeas (or 1 can [14 oz/398 mL] chickpeas, drained)

1 cup (250 mL) grape tomatoes, halved

1 cup (250 mL) diced English cucumber

GARNISHES

½ cup (125 mL) shredded cheddar cheese

¼ cup (60 mL) chopped walnuts or pecans

2 large hard-boiled eggs, cut into wedges

1 avocado, cubed

½ red bell pepper, chopped

¼ cup (60 mL) cubed cooked meat (see recipe introduction)

DRESSING

¼ cup (60 mL) olive oil

1 red onion, thinly sliced

2 cloves garlic, chopped

3 Tbsp (45 mL) fresh lemon juice

2 Tbsp (30 mL) red wine vinegar

1 Tbsp (15 mL) Dijon mustard

1 Tbsp (15 mL) liquid honey

2 tsp (10 mL) tamari or soy sauce

CUT BEANS INTO 1½-inch (4 cm) pieces. Add enough water to reach the bottom of a collapsible steamer set in a large saucepan and bring to a boil over high heat. Place beans in steamer basket, cover, and steam for 8 to 10 minutes, or until tender. (Or cover beans with water in a saucepan and bring the water to a boil. Reduce heat and lightly boil for 10 to 12 minutes, or until tender.) Cool slightly.

Meanwhile, assemble spinach, Swiss chard, chickpeas, tomatoes, and cucumber on a platter, or toss in a salad bowl. Add warm, cooked green beans to platter or bowl when ready.

Assemble cheese, walnuts, eggs, avocado, and red pepper as well as cooked meat on a platter for guests to garnish their own salads.

Make dressing by heating oil in a skillet over medium-high heat. Add onion and cook, stirring frequently, for 5 minutes or until soft and translucent. Add garlic and cook, stirring constantly, for 1 minute or until fragrant. Whisk in lemon juice, vinegar, mustard, honey, and tamari. Cook, stirring constantly, for 1 minute or until bubbly. Drizzle over greens and vegetables on the platter, or toss with greens and vegetables if using a bowl. Pass salad along with garnishes at the table.

VEGETABLE PLATTER WITH COCONUT SAUCE

Served with warmed pita-bread wedges, cooked rice, or couscous, this dish makes a deliciously light Middle Eastern–style lunch. —NETTIE

ARRANGE SPINACH ON a large platter and pile chickpeas, zucchini, tomatoes, and onions overtop. Sprinkle with cheese, olives, and sesame seeds. Drizzle with about ½ cup (125 mL) Coconut Sauce, and pass around remaining sauce.

2 cups (500 mL) baby spinach or shredded lettuce

One 14 oz (398 mL) can chickpeas, drained and rinsed

2 small zucchini (or 1 English cucumber), cut into chunks

3 tomatoes, cored and cut into chunks

1 small red onion, sliced

¼ cup (60 mL) crumbled feta cheese

¼ cup (60 mL) sliced pitted black olives

¼ cup (60 mL) sesame seeds

2 cups (500 mL) Coconut Sauce

1 eggplant, thickly sliced

1 red bell pepper, halved and seeded

3 Tbsp (45 mL) + 2 Tbsp (30 mL)
olive oil, divided

1 onion, chopped

1 or 2 jalapeño peppers,
seeded and chopped

2 cloves garlic, chopped

1 Tbsp (15 mL) garam masala
(sidebar, page 36)

1 tsp (5 mL) red or green curry paste
(page 9 for homemade)

One 14 oz (398 mL) can
coconut milk

1 Tbsp (15 mL) tahini

2 Tbsp (30 mL) fresh lemon juice

1 tsp (5 mL) salt

Rimmed baking sheet, lightly oiled

COCONUT SAUCE

MAKES: 2 cups (500 mL)

Roasting the eggplant gives this sauce a nutty flavour. This sauce makes an excellent finish for steamed vegetables.

PREHEAT THE OVEN to 375°F (190°C).

Arrange eggplant slices and red pepper halves cut side down in one layer on prepared baking sheet. Drizzle 3 Tbsp (45 mL) oil overtop. Roast in preheated oven for 15 to 20 minutes, or until peppers are charred and eggplant is browned and tender. Let cool.

Meanwhile, heat remaining 2 Tbsp (30 mL) oil in a skillet over medium heat. Add onion and jalapeño peppers and cook, stirring frequently, for 5 minutes. Add garlic, garam masala, and curry paste. Cook, stirring constantly, for 2 minutes or until onions are soft. Stir in coconut milk and simmer for 2 minutes. Stir in tahini, lemon juice, and salt. Remove from heat and let cool.

Remove and discard peels from roasted red peppers and then quarter them. Combine quartered peppers and roasted eggplant in a food processor and blend until smooth. With motor running, add onion mixture to the eggplant purée through the opening in the lid. Blend until smooth. Add more lemon juice if the sauce is too thick.

GREEN GODDESS POTATO SALAD

When she was a young girl, my 19-year-old daughter, Mackenzie, was responsible for watering the tarragon plants in our backyard. She always associates the smell of spring with the arrival of the tarragon plants. French tarragon has a distinctive anise aroma due to an essential oil in the cavities along the veins of the leaves. Basil is sweet, and the smaller oregano leaf is much stronger and not as sweet—you can exchange one leaf for the other. —NETTIE

BRING A LARGE saucepan of salted water to a boil. Cook beans for 3 to 5 minutes, or until tender-crisp. Lift out using a strainer or tongs and plunge into ice-cold water to stop the cooking. Drain, pat dry, and cut into ¼-inch (6 mm) pieces.

Add potatoes to the boiling water and cook for 10 to 12 minutes or until tender-crisp. Drain in a colander and plunge the colander into ice-cold water to stop the cooking.

Drain, pat dry, and transfer to a large bowl. Add cooked beans and toss to mix.

Combine green onions, parsley, basil, and tarragon in a food processor or blender. Pulse until onions and herbs are coarsely chopped. Add Cashew Cream and pulse until blended with the herbs. Taste and add salt and pepper, adding more as required. Toss dressing with the beans and potatoes.

12 oz (375 g) green beans (trimmed if using fresh)

4 cups (1 L) cubed potatoes

DRESSING

3 green onions, chopped

¼ cup (60 mL) packed fresh parsley leaves

4 or 5 fresh basil leaves or oregano leaves

2 tsp (10 mL) chopped fresh French tarragon

1 cup (250 mL) Cashew Cream (page 6) or mayonnaise

1 tsp (5 mL) salt

½ tsp (2 mL) freshly ground pepper

SIDES

HERBED BASMATI RICE

This is a simple recipe nicely flavoured by the herbs, and it's the perfect accompaniment to Tempeh Sausage (page 206), allowing the spicing of the sausage to shine through. —NETTIE

COMBINE WATER AND salt in a saucepan and bring to a boil over high heat. Add rice, stir, and bring back to a boil. Cover, reduce heat, and simmer gently for 10 to 15 minutes, or until water is absorbed and rice is tender. Toss with butter, herbs, and pepper.

3 cups (750 mL) water

1 tsp (5 mL) salt

1½ cups (375 mL) white basmati rice, rinsed

2 Tbsp (30 mL) butter or olive oil

½ cup (125 mL) chopped mixed fresh herbs (flat-leaf parsley, dill, cilantro, basil)

¼ tsp (1 mL) freshly ground pepper

1 lb (500 g) sweet potatoes
(2 large-sized), cut into chunks

⅓ cup (80 mL) goji berries
or raisins

2 Tbsp (30 mL) toasted sesame oil

2 Tbsp (30 mL) Pomegranate
Glaze (page 8, or store-bought
pomegranate molasses)
or brown rice syrup

1 Tbsp (15 mL) minced fresh ginger

Sea salt and pepper, to taste

1 cup (250 mL) toasted sunflower
seeds (sidebar, page 26),
for garnishing

MASHED SWEET POTATOES

You can use Yukon Gold potatoes in this recipe instead of sweet potatoes, or try half Yukon Gold and half sweet. The goji berries and fresh ginger add a refreshing twist. —NETTIE

COVER SWEET POTATOES with water in a saucepan and bring the water to a boil over high heat. Reduce heat and lightly boil for 10 to 15 minutes, or until tender.

Meanwhile, place goji berries in a bowl and cover with hot water. Let stand for 7 to 10 minutes, or until plump. Drain and coarsely chop.

When sweet potatoes are cooked, drain, reserving ¼ cup (60 mL) of the cooking water. Transfer potatoes to a bowl and mash, drizzling with oil and mashing it into the potatoes. If necessary, add some reserved cooking water for a soft mashed texture. Add Pomegranate Glaze, ginger, and rehydrated goji berries. Season to taste with salt and pepper. Garnish with sunflower seeds and serve immediately.

GOJI BERRIES

This raisin-like dried fruit, also known as "wolfberries," has been used for centuries by Asian chefs in healing soups and stews. Rehydrated berries are also used as a meat substitute. They have more vitamin C than oranges and more beta carotene than carrots, and are high in immune-system-boosting antioxidants. I like to plump them up, in hot cider or in water, and then use them the way one would use raisins or cranberries in baked goods, smoothies, and cooked oatmeal.

MASHED ROOT VEGETABLES WITH ROASTED GARLIC

We all know that we should eat more root vegetables. Combining them with potatoes is an excellent way to showcase their flavour and also add variety to your traditional mashed potato recipe. The red of the beets dominates this dish, so if you can find golden beets at a farmers' market, use them for a lighter and more golden result. —NETTIE

8 oz (250 g) potato (1 large-sized Yukon Gold or russet)

8 oz (250 g) celery root (1 medium-sized)

8 oz (250 g) parsnips (2 medium-sized)

8 oz (250 g) beets (2 medium-sized)

1 Tbsp (15 mL) salt

1 large-sized head roasted garlic (see sidebar)

½ cup (125 mL) butter (¼ lb/125 g), cut into small pieces

PREHEAT THE OVEN to 450°F (230°C).

Cut potato, celery root, parsnips, and beets into 1-inch (2.5 cm) cubes. Place in a large pot and cover with 2 inches (5 cm) water. Add salt and bring the water to a boil over high heat. Cover, reduce heat, and boil gently for 30 minutes, or until the tip of a knife meets with no resistance.

Strain vegetables and return to warm pot. Add roasted garlic cloves and butter. Mash the vegetables by hand or use a food mill, incorporating the garlic and butter.

ROASTING GARLIC

Roasting vegetables caramelizes their sugars, making them sweet, mellow, and nutty-tasting—and thus very appealing to those who dislike vegetables. In the case of garlic, the cloves become sticky with the sugars. Often the whole head is used as in the recipe opposite. Follow the steps below for perfect roasted garlic. You can roast one or several heads at the same time.

Preheat the oven to 400°F (200°C). Remove the loose, papery skin from the outside of a whole head of garlic by rubbing the head between your palms. Slice off and then discard the top ¼ inch (6 mm) of the tips of all the cloves.

Place the garlic head cut side up in an ovenproof baking dish and drizzle with 2 tsp (10 mL) olive oil. Cover with a lid or foil. Bake in the preheated oven for about 30 minutes, or until garlic is quite soft. Transfer to a cooling rack.

When garlic is cool enough to handle, squeeze the cloves from their skins. The roasted cloves will be soft enough to mash and use in spreads, dips, sauce, and other recipes.

BEET VARIETIES

Beets have long been a favoured vegetable because their leafy green stalks are edible and the roots store very well for fresh eating. They also make an excellent preserve. In addition to the red-bulb beet we call the garden beet, there are other edible subspecies: chard, the sugar beet (a white root, used for table sugar), and mangold (used for fodder).

Some varieties in addition to the popular red beet:

Chioggia is a heritage type with white rings in the flesh, sometimes called Candystripe or Bull's Eye.

Orange and purple beets are becoming more common at markets in the fall. Ask the grower about sweetness and texture before canning large quantities.

SERVES: 6 | 4 veggie + 2 meat servings (if using bacon)

SOBA NOODLES WITH RED CABBAGE

These noodles may be eaten hot or cold. I prefer noodles made from a combination of buckwheat and regular wheat noodles (rather than just buckwheat) because they are less dense and cook quickly. It should say right on the label or package. —NETTIE

SOBA NOODLES WITH CABBAGE AND BACON

Crispy bacon is the perfect garnish for the wilted cabbage and soba noodles. Be sure to cook the bacon until most of the fat has been rendered, and drain well on paper or cloth towels. —PAT

2 slices side bacon, for garnishing

¼ cup (60 mL) peanut butter or almond butter

3 Tbsp (45 mL) toasted sesame oil

3 Tbsp (45 mL) soy sauce or tamari

3 Tbsp (45 mL) mirin

2 Tbsp (30 mL) rice vinegar

¼ tsp (1 mL) dried red chile flakes or cayenne pepper

10 oz (300 g) soba noodles

4 cups (1 L) shredded red cabbage

¼ cup (60 mL) diced green onions

½ cup (125 mL) shredded carrot (about 1 medium-sized)

¼ cup (60 mL) chopped fresh cilantro or parsley

ARRANGE BACON SLICES on a grill pan or skillet in one layer, making sure they don't touch. Cook, turning once or twice, over medium-high heat for 3 to 5 minutes or until bacon is browned and crisp. Transfer to a paper towel–lined plate to drain.

Whisk together peanut butter, sesame oil, soy sauce, mirin, vinegar, and red chile flakes in a bowl. Set aside.

Cook noodles according to package directions. Place shredded cabbage in a large colander over the sink. Drain cooked noodles over cabbage to wilt it. Transfer noodtles and cabbage to a large bowl. Add green onions, carrot, and cilantro. Drizzle prepared sauce overtop and toss until combined.

Using tongs, divide noodle mixture among 6 bowls. Crumble bacon into bite-sized pieces and garnish 2 bowls.

BROCCOLI AND TOASTED PECANS

Broccoli is a perfect side for its speed, ease, and ability to pair with almost anything. Steaming is the best way to cook broccoli: the vegetable turns a bright, vibrant green that looks beautiful. —NETTIE

- 1 cup (250 mL) pecan halves
- 2 Tbsp (30 mL) granulated sugar
- 2 Tbsp (30 mL) water
- 3 cups (750 mL) broccoli florets (1½-inch/4 cm pieces)
- 1 tsp (5 mL) toasted sesame oil
- 1 tsp (5 mL) tamari or soy sauce

TOAST PECANS IN a skillet over medium-high heat, shaking the pan to flip the pieces, for 5 minutes or until fragrant. Transfer to a bowl.

Add sugar and water to the skillet. Cook over medium-high heat, stirring to dissolve sugar, for 1 minute. Add toasted pecans and simmer, stirring frequently, for 5 minutes or until sugar sticks to pecans and pecans are golden brown. Set aside.

Add enough water to reach the bottom of a collapsible steamer set in a saucepan and bring to a boil over high heat. Place broccoli in steamer basket, cover, and steam for 5 to 7 minutes, or until tender.

Transfer broccoli to a serving bowl, toss with sesame oil and tamari, and garnish with the sugared pecans.

STUFFED POTATOES
WITH FETA AND PINE NUTS

The creamy-textured potato is a blank canvas waiting for us
to transform it into an exciting taste adventure. Nestled in the
potato cavity are feta, pine nuts, and olives. Choose potatoes of
the same size and shape. — NETTIE

STUFFED POTATOES
WITH BACON OR HAM

See page 63 for directions on adding crispy bacon as a garnish to
the cheesy stuffing. — PAT

PREHEAT THE OVEN to 400°F (200°C).

In a saucepan, combine potatoes with enough water to
cover; salt the cooking water. Bring water to a boil over high
heat. Reduce heat and simmer for 10 to 15 minutes, or until
potatoes are tender. Drain, rinse with cool water, and set aside.

Place feta cheese into a medium-sized bowl. Add pine nuts,
olives, cherries, oregano, lemon zest, oil, and pepper. Toss to
mix well.

Scoop out the flesh from the centre of each cooked potato
half using a small spoon or melon baller. Combine potato flesh
with feta mixture. Arrange potato halves on prepared baking
sheet and spoon 2 Tbsp (30 mL) feta-potato filling into each
one. Garnish 12 halves with crumbled bacon or chopped ham.

Bake potatoes in preheated oven for 20 minutes, or until
heated through.

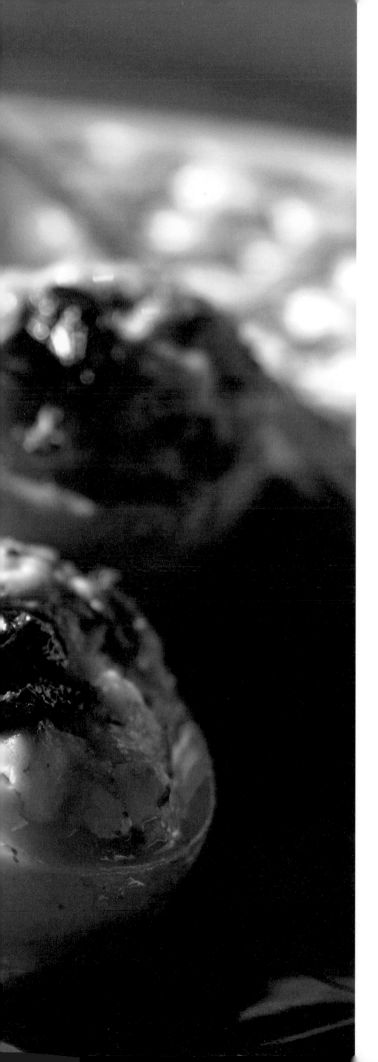

18 small new potatoes, halved

1 cup (250 mL) crumbled
feta cheese

½ cup (125 mL) toasted pine nuts
(sidebar, page 26)

½ cup (125 mL) chopped pitted
black olives

2 Tbsp (30 mL) chopped dried
cherries or currants

1 Tbsp (15 mL) chopped fresh
oregano

1 tsp (5 mL) lemon zest

2 Tbsp (30 mL) olive oil

½ tsp (2 mL) freshly ground pepper

½ cup (125 mL) chopped
fresh parsley

¼ cup (60 mL) crumbled cooked
bacon or chopped cooked ham

2 rimmed baking sheets,
parchment-lined

SAUTÉED BRUSSELS SPROUTS
WITH POMEGRANATE GLAZE

Always buy the smallest Brussels sprouts; they are more tender and sweeter. You can also roast Brussels sprouts, halved and tossed with 2 Tbsp (30 mL) olive oil, in a 450°F (230°C) oven for 20 to 25 minutes or until tender. I often add a tablespoon (15 mL) of good-quality balsamic vinegar just before serving. — NETTIE

2 lb (1 kg) Brussels sprouts, halved and trimmed

3 Tbsp (45 mL) olive oil

1 shallot, finely chopped

2 Tbsp (30 mL) Pomegranate Glaze (page 8, or store-bought pomegranate molasses)

1 cup (250 mL) shelled pistachio nuts, for garnishing

ADD ENOUGH WATER to reach the bottom of a collapsible steamer set in a large saucepan and bring to a boil over high heat. Place Brussels sprout halves in steamer basket, cover, and steam for 8 to 10 minutes, or until tender. (Or cover Brussels sprouts with water in a saucepan and bring the water to a boil over high heat. Reduce heat and lightly boil for 10 to 12 minutes, or until tender. Or roast as directed in the recipe introduction.)

Meanwhile, heat oil in a large skillet over medium-high heat. Add shallot and cook, stirring frequently, for 3 to 5 minutes or until soft and translucent. Add cooked Brussels sprouts. Cook, stirring constantly, for 2 to 3 minutes or until lightly browned. Drizzle with pomegranate glaze and toss to mix well. Transfer to a serving bowl and garnish with pistachio nuts.

POMEGRANATE GLAZE
OR MOLASSES

A thick, dark syrup made from cooked-down pomegranate juice. Its concentrated, tart, fruity flavour is used in salad dressings, marinades, and sauces. See page 8 for a recipe.

5 large eggs

½ cup (125 mL) olive oil
or melted butter

2 cups (500 mL) buttermilk

⅓ cup (80 mL) honey

¾ cup (185 mL) whole wheat
pastry flour

2½ tsp (12 mL) baking powder

1 tsp (5 mL) baking soda

2½ cups (625 mL) cornmeal

9- × 13-inch (23 × 33 cm)
baking pan, parchment-lined
or lightly oiled

BUTTERMILK CORNBREAD

Rich and moist, this cornbread is the perfect accompaniment to Black Bean Chilli (page 184). Leftover cornbread can be used to make breadcrumbs.
—NETTIE

PREHEAT THE OVEN to 350°F (180°C).

Beat eggs until light and fluffy in a large mixing bowl. Add oil, buttermilk, and honey.

Combine flour, baking powder, baking soda, and cornmeal in a separate bowl. Beat the dry ingredients into the wet mixture until combined.

Pour batter into prepared pan and spread evenly. Bake in preheated oven for 30 to 35 minutes or until a tester comes out clean when inserted into the centre of the bread.

POTATO PARSNIP GRATIN

An ideal combination of potatoes, cream, and cheese. The beauty
of this dish is that it can be assembled before company arrives,
then baked as you prepare the rest of your dinner. Use sharp
cheddar because the flavour is more intense. —NETTIE

1 cup (250 mL) 35% cream
(whipping cream)

1 cup (250 mL) milk or buttermilk

2 shallots, finely chopped
(or ⅓ cup/80 mL
finely chopped onion)

1 clove garlic, minced

1 Tbsp (15 mL) fresh thyme leaves

1 tsp (5 mL) chopped
fresh rosemary

1 tsp (5 mL) salt

½ tsp (2 mL) freshly ground pepper

2 lb (1 kg) Yukon Gold
or russet potatoes, sliced

2 cups (500 mL) shredded parsnips

1 cup (250 mL) shredded cheddar
or Parmesan cheese

1 cup (250 mL) shredded Gruyère
or Emmental cheese

9- × 13-inch (23 × 33 cm) shallow
baking dish, buttered

Rimmed baking sheet

(continued)

(continued from previous page)

PREHEAT THE OVEN to 375°F (190°C).

Combine cream, milk, shallots, garlic, thyme, rosemary, salt, and pepper in a bowl. Pour 1 cup (250 mL) of this mixture over bottom of prepared baking dish.

Layer one-third of the potato slices overtop, pressing the potatoes into the cream mixture. Spread half of the parsnips over the potatoes. Pour ½ cup (125 mL) of the cream mixture overtop. Spread the cheddar cheese over the parsnips and cream.

Layer another third of the potato slices overtop the cheddar cheese, and then add remaining parsnips. Spread remaining potatoes overtop. Pour remaining cream mixture over all.

Spread Gruyère cheese evenly over the top. Cover with foil and place gratin dish on a baking sheet.

Bake in preheated oven for 50 minutes. Remove the foil and bake for another 15 to 20 minutes, or until the vegetables are tender when pierced with the tip of a knife and the top is crisp and golden brown. Let stand for 2 to 3 minutes, or until the potatoes have absorbed the extra liquid.

TIP

As an alternative to parsnips, wash and thinly slice 1 leek and slice 1 small onion. In place of the first layer of parsnips, spread all of the leek slices overtop the potatoes, and use the onion slices in place of the second half of the parsnips.

Combine cream, milk, shallots, garlic, thyme, rosemary, salt, and pepper

Layer one-third of the potato

Spread half the parsnips over the potatoes

Pour in ½ cup (125 mL) of the cream mixture

Spread the cheddar cheese overtop

Layer another third of the potato slices

Spread Gruyère cheese evenly over the top

¼ cup (60 mL) olive oil

2 cloves garlic, minced

8 cups (2 L) lightly packed thinly sliced kale leaves (about 2 lb/1 kg)

½ cup (125 mL) water or vegetable stock (page 40 for homemade)

½ cup (125 mL) dried cranberries or raisins

¼ cup (60 mL) fresh lemon juice

½ cup (125 mL) toasted pine nuts (sidebar, page 26)

1 tsp (5 mL) salt

½ tsp (2 mL) freshly ground pepper

5 oz (150 g) hot-smoked salmon

BRAISED KALE WITH PINE NUTS, CRANBERRIES, AND GARLIC

Lacinato kale stands apart from other greens. It has long, crinkled green leaves, whose colour intensifies with cooking, making it a very beautiful dish to serve. Remove the centre ribs and chop or thinly slice the leaves for this dish. Have the extra water or stock on hand, but if your wok or skillet is heavy and the heat is low enough, the kale won't stick and you won't need it. —NETTIE

BRAISED KALE WITH SMOKED SALMON, PINE NUTS, AND CRANBERRIES

There are sweet hits from the cranberries or raisins, and buttery, nutty bites from the toasted pine nuts, rendering the greens richly complex. Trout, whitefish, tuna, and grilled seafood are also very nice with the braised kale. You can add Tempeh Sausage and Ground Pork Patties (page 206) to this dish for a complete meal in a pan. —PAT

HEAT OLIVE OIL in a wok or large skillet over medium-high heat. Add garlic and cook, stirring frequently, for 30 seconds. Reduce heat to medium and add kale in 2-cup (500 mL) batches. Stir for about 1 minute and, as kale begins to shrink, add another 2 cups (500 mL), along with a small amount of water (about 2 Tbsp/30 mL) to keep kale from sticking as it cooks. Repeat until all the kale has been added. Cook, stirring and tossing, for 5 to 7 minutes or until tender.

Add cranberries, lemon juice, and pine nuts. Cook for 2 minutes, stirring and tossing to coat the kale. Season with salt and pepper and divide among 6 plates. Separate the salmon into large flakes using a fork. Divide the flakes in half and use them to garnish 2 of the plates.

GRILL

MARINATED GRILLED EGGPLANT

Grilling fresh vegetables brings out their flavour. In this recipe, eggplant is marinated twice. Before grilling, the eggplant is brushed with oil, garlic, and ginger. After grilling, the slices are steeped in hoisin sauce—a thick, rich brown sauce made from soybeans, garlic, sugar, and chiles (see page 3). Hoisin sauce is sold in cans, jars, and bottles; keep in the fridge once opened.
—NETTIE

MARINATED GRILLED PORK AND EGGPLANT

Marinating the pork chop and cooking it whole help to keep the meat moist during grilling. The double-marinade technique that Nettie has developed for eggplant works beautifully for boneless cuts of meat. Use a heavy, ridged grill pan on the stovetop or a barbecue grill to cook the vegetables and meat. —PAT

5 Tbsp (75 mL) roasted peanut oil

2 cloves garlic, minced

2 Tbsp (30 mL) minced fresh ginger

3 Tbsp (45 mL) hoisin sauce

3 Tbsp (45 mL) tamari or soy sauce

3 green onions, thinly sliced

3 to 5 oz (90 to 150 g) boneless
pork loin chop

2 lb (1 kg) eggplant, peeled and cut
crosswise into ½-inch (1 cm) slices

¼ cup (60 mL) sesame seeds

Rimmed baking sheets, lined with
parchment or waxed paper

EGGPLANT

Eggplants vary in length—from 2 to 12 inches (5 to 30 cm)— and in shape. They can be round, oblong, or pear-like. Most North Americans think of eggplants as being deep purple and shiny, but eggplants can also be pure white, pink, burgundy, violet, blue, red, green, and black, and even striped. Any of the varieties may be used fresh or frozen.

(continued)

(continued from previous page)

PREHEAT THE GRILL to medium-high. (You can also use a grill pan on the stove over medium-high heat.)

Combine oil, garlic, and ginger in a small bowl. Combine hoisin sauce, tamari, and green onions in a separate small bowl. Set both bowls aside.

Place the chop between sheets of plastic wrap on a cutting board. Pound, using a meat pounder (or a rolling pin), until about ¼ inch (6 mm) thick. Lay chop flat on a prepared baking sheet.

Lay eggplant flat on a prepared baking sheet. Brush both sides of eggplant slices with oil mixture. Brush both sides of pork chop with remaining oil mixture. Let stand for 5 minutes.

Cook eggplant and pork chop on preheated grill for 5 minutes; turn eggplant and pork and cook on other side for 3 to 5 minutes. Remove eggplant. Check pork for doneness: internal temperature should be 160°F (71°C), or the internal colour should have changed to white with traces of pink in the centre. Continue grilling if necessary.

Place grilled eggplant on a serving dish. Baste the cooked eggplant slices with hoisin mixture. Cut pork chop into thin strips and toss with remaining hoisin mixture, and transfer to the serving dish. Sprinkle evenly with sesame seeds. Serve immediately.

Cook on preheated grill

Baste the cooked slices with hoisin mixture

GRILLED CORN AND RADICCHIO ON TOMATO AND RED ONION SALAD

Soak corn in cold water for one hour. Wrap in aluminum foil. Place on the grill and turn every five minutes. Follow these simple steps and the results will be delicious. Serve with grilled bread or your favourite pasta. — NETTIE

GRILLED CORN AND SIRLOIN ON TOMATO AND RED ONION SALAD

As for the Mâche with Roasted Beets and Grilled Beef recipe (page 76), grilling beef for a salad is quick and easy, and you will probably have more than enough meat for an extra serving the next day. — PAT

8 ears corn, husks and silk removed

2 heads radicchio (1 lb/500 g total), quartered lengthwise

2 Tbsp (30 mL) + 1 Tbsp (15 mL) + ¼ cup (60 mL) olive oil, divided

One 4 to 6 oz (125 to 175 g) sirloin tip steak

1 clove garlic, crushed

2 tsp (10 mL) chopped fresh rosemary

4 large ripe tomatoes
(2 lb/1 kg), diced

1 red onion, minced

½ tsp (2 mL) salt

½ tsp (2 mL) freshly ground pepper

Sea salt and freshly ground pepper

2 Tbsp (30 mL) red wine vinegar

½ cup (125 mL) chiffonade
of fresh basil (page 133)

12 cups (3 L) salad greens
(romaine, spinach, mesclun)

PREHEAT THE GRILL to medium-high.

Soak corn in cold water for 1 hour. Pat dry and wrap individual ears in aluminum foil. Cook, turning every 5 minutes, on preheated grill for 20 to 30 minutes, or until light brown spots begin appearing on the kernels. Remove foil and let cool.

When corn is cool enough to handle, cut ears in half crosswise. Stand each piece on its cut end on a plate (rather than a cutting board— the corn may release a lot of juice) and slice downward along the cob several times to remove all the kernels. Place kernels in a serving bowl and discard cobs.

Place radicchio in a bowl and toss with 2 Tbsp (30 mL) oil to coat. Brush both sides of the steak with 1 Tbsp (15 mL) oil. Spread both sides with garlic and rosemary.

Cook radicchio and steak (at the same time) on the preheated grill for 6 to 8 minutes. Turn radicchio several times and cook until lightly charred on all sides. Turn steak after 4 minutes, and cook for 2 to 4 minutes on the other side, or until cooked to your preference (use a thermometer to gauge degree of doneness).

Remove radicchio from the grill and let cool. Add to corn in bowl. Add tomatoes and onion. Season with salt and pepper and toss to mix well.

Remove steak from the grill and season with sea salt and pepper. Let cool enough to slice into strips. Set aside.

Combine remaining oil and the vinegar in a clean jar with a lid and shake to mix. Drizzle one-third of dressing overtop vegetables, add basil, and toss to coat.

Place salad greens in a bowl. Drizzle remaining dressing overtop, and toss to coat. Divide greens among 6 plates. Spoon grilled corn mixture over greens. Garnish 2 portions with sirloin strips.

DONENESS TEMPERATURES FOR BEEF	
Rare	120°F (49°C)
Medium Rare	125°F (51°C)
Medium	130°F (54°C)

PENNE WITH CHICKPEAS, SPINACH, AND GRILLED ASPARAGUS

Unlike the ordinary canned chickpeas you usually find at the supermarket, canned *organic* chickpeas contain no salt, allowing the cook more freedom to season to taste. (Chickpeas are sometimes labelled garbanzo beans.) Terrific hot, this pasta is also delicious when served cold in a pita lined with salad greens. Rotini, gemelli, or another similarly shaped pasta may be substituted, if you wish. —NETTIE

PENNE WITH CHICKPEAS, GRILLED ASPARAGUS, AND CHICKEN

Grilling the chicken with the skin on helps to baste the chicken as it cooks and keeps it moist. —PAT

1 lb (500 g) dried penne, about 4 cups (1 L)

3 to 5 oz (90 to 150 g) bone-in chicken breast with skin

1 Tbsp (15 mL) + 3 Tbsp (45 mL) olive oil, divided

1 Tbsp (15 mL) + ½ cup (125 mL) finely chopped fresh basil

½ tsp (2 mL) + ½ tsp (2 mL) sea salt or smoked salt

15 stalks fresh asparagus, woody ends snapped off

Pinch of salt and freshly ground pepper (for asparagus)

3 large cloves garlic, minced

1 onion, finely chopped

2 carrots, finely shredded

½ cup (125 mL) thinly sliced
sun-dried tomatoes

One 19 oz (540 mL) can chickpeas,
drained and rinsed
(or 1½ cups/375 mL cooked)

3 cups (750 mL) lightly packed
baby spinach leaves,
washed and thinly sliced

1 cup (250 mL) vegetable stock
(page 40 for homemade) or water

¼ tsp (1 mL) freshly ground pepper

¾ cup (185 mL) finely grated
Parmesan cheese

9-inch-square (23 cm) baking pan,
lightly oiled

Vegetable grill basket, lightly
oiled, or rimmed baking sheet,
parchment-lined or lightly oiled

PREHEAT THE GRILL to medium-high, or the oven to 450°F (230°C).

Bring a large pot of salted water to a boil. Add pasta and boil uncovered for 10 to 12 minutes, or until al dente. Drain and set aside.

Brush chicken breast all over with 1 Tbsp (15 mL) oil. Rub 1 Tbsp (15 mL) of the basil over the skin and sprinkle with ½ tsp (2 mL) salt. Place on grill or in prepared baking pan, skin side up. If roasting in the oven, cover pan with foil. Grill or roast for 15 to 20 minutes, or until the meat turns opaque and reaches an internal temperature of 165°F (74°C), and the juices run clear.

Cut asparagus into 1-inch (2.5 cm) lengths. Toss with 1 Tbsp (15 mL) oil, salt, and pepper. Spread out in grill basket or on prepared baking sheet. Grill or roast for 8 minutes or until asparagus is tender-crisp and slightly browned. Remove asparagus and set aside.

Check internal temperature of chicken and continue cooking or remove from oven and set aside. When cool enough to handle, remove skin and bones and discard. Cut or pull chicken into strips and set aside.

Heat remaining 2 Tbsp (30 mL) oil in a large skillet over medium heat. Add garlic and cook, stirring frequently, for 30 seconds. Stir in onions and cook, stirring frequently, for 5 minutes or until softened. Add carrots, basil, and ½ tsp (2 mL) salt, and cook, stirring frequently, for 3 minutes. Stir in sun-dried tomatoes, chickpeas, spinach, and stock. Bring to a boil, and then lower heat and simmer for 5 minutes, or until vegetables are tender.

Toss warm pasta with cooked vegetables in a large bowl. Stir in ¼ tsp (1 mL) pepper and Parmesan cheese. Add additional salt and pepper to taste. Add grilled/roasted asparagus and toss well. Serve in warmed pasta bowls sprinkled with additional Parmesan cheese. Add chicken strips to 2 portions.

MARINATED TOFU AND TEMPEH KABOBS WITH VEGGIES

You have been warned! Raw tofu is probably eaten only by monks in self-published recipe books from the '60s. On its own, tofu has no flavour. That is why we marinate it. There are two marinades in this recipe, one for the tofu and one for the kabobs. They can be grilled or broiled. Tempeh, a fermented soy food sold fresh or frozen, must always be cooked. (See page 11 for information on soy products.) Serve these delicious kabobs with quinoa, steamed sushi rice, or short-grain brown rice. —NETTIE

MARINATED PORK KABOBS

Pork tenderloin and pork chops are perfect for grilling, and when marinated with Nettie's delicious marinade, they are spectacular. You have some options here: you can follow the regular vegetarian instructions to make ten veggie kabobs and grill one or two pork skewers separately (using the six cubes of pork); or for two of the skewers you can mix vegetables and pork (using three pork pieces in place of the tofu and tempeh). Because it freezes well, I like to marinate and grill a much larger amount of pork so that I have plenty of cooked pork on hand. —PAT

MARINATED PORK, TOFU & TEMPEH

1 cup (250 mL) water

½ oz (15 g) dried
porcini mushroom pieces

½ cup (125 mL) olive oil

1 cup (250 mL) dry red wine

¼ cup (60 mL) red wine vinegar

½ cup (125 mL) tamari
or soy sauce

3 cloves garlic, chopped

2 whole cloves

1 Tbsp (15 mL) chopped
fresh marjoram

½ tsp (2 mL) salt

½ tsp (2 mL) freshly ground pepper

One 1 lb (500 g) pkg extra-firm tofu,
rinsed and cut into
½-inch (1 cm) cubes

8 oz (250 g) tempeh, thawed and cut
into twenty ½-inch (1 cm) cubes

Six 1-inch (2.5 cm) cubes trimmed
pork (from chops or tenderloin)

KABOB INGREDIENTS

10 small potatoes, halved

10 button mushrooms, stems removed

2 red bell peppers, each cut into 5 equal-sized squares

1 large red onion, cut into 10 wedges

3 medium-sized zucchini, each cut into 6 chunks

20 cherry tomatoes

KABOB BASTE

2 Tbsp (30 mL) red wine vinegar

1 Tbsp (15 mL) Dijon mustard

1 Tbsp (15 mL) finely chopped fresh basil

3 cloves garlic, chopped

¾ cup (185 mL) olive oil

Pinch of salt and pepper

9- × 13-inch (23 × 33 cm) casserole dish

Ten 10- or 12-inch (25 or 30 cm) wooden or metal skewers (if using wooden skewers, be sure to soak them in water for 30 minutes beforehand to prevent scorching)

TO PREPARE THE marinade, bring water to a boil in a medium-sized saucepan over medium-high heat. Add dried mushrooms. Reduce heat and simmer for 15 minutes, or until mushrooms are tender and rehydrated. Remove from heat.

Add oil, wine, vinegar, tamari, garlic, cloves, marjoram, salt, and pepper to the pot. Bring to a boil over medium-high heat. Lower heat and simmer for 5 minutes. Let cool.

Arrange tofu and tempeh in a single layer in casserole dish. Purée the cooled marinade ingredients in a food processor or blender until smooth. Pour marinade overtop tofu and tempeh, reserving 1 cup (250 mL); use this to marinate the pork cubes separately in a bowl. Cover and marinate tofu and tempeh as well as the pork in the refrigerator for at least 6 hours, or overnight. Bring to room temperature before skewering.

In a medium-sized pot, add enough water to reach the bottom of a collapsible steamer and bring to a boil. Cover and steam the potatoes over boiling water until tender, about 12 minutes. Set aside until cool enough to handle safely.

To prepare kabob baste, whisk together vinegar, mustard, basil, garlic, olive oil, and salt and pepper in a bowl. Set aside.

Prepare veggie kabobs by skewering, in the following order, potato, mushroom, red pepper, tofu, onion, zucchini, tofu, tomato, tempeh, zucchini, potato, tomato. Reserve the marinade for brushing on skewers after grilling.

Add 3 pieces of pork to 2 of the kabobs, replacing the tofu and tempeh with the pork. (Place the extra pieces of tofu and tempeh onto a separate skewer, or wrap and store them in the fridge for use in a salad or with rice.) Or make pork-only skewers.

Place all kabobs in a large pan or on a rimmed baking sheet and brush them generously with kabob baste.

Preheat the grill to medium heat. Position rack about 8 inches (20 cm) above the grill.

Cook kabobs for 8 to 10 minutes, or until vegetables, tofu, and tempeh are tender and browned, brushing them every 2 minutes with reserved marinade. Check doneness of the pork by slicing through a piece. If centre is opaque and white with just a tinge of pink, pork is cooked. Transfer to serving platter and brush with any remaining marinade.

GRILLED WHOLE WHEAT PIZZA

There are several advantages to grilled pizza: the cheese melts evenly, and the crust is incredibly crunchy because you grill it on both sides. After grilling the bottom of the crust, the dough needs to sit over the indirect heat source of your grill (to avoid scorching). It all depends on the number of burners involved. If you have a two-burner grill, turn off one burner and put the dressed crust back over the burner you just turned off. This method is called indirect grilling because there is no heat directly under the food. Your grill must have a lid, which turns the grill into a convection oven and cooks your pizza. Feel free to form the dough into a square or rectangle instead of a circle if that fits better with the grill that you have.

Making dough from scratch is comparable to homemade veggie broth. Make extra. This dough is easy to make, requiring just one rising, not two, and can be frozen for up to three months in oiled plastic wrap. I recommend defrosting the dough in the fridge overnight, and then letting it stand at room temperature for at least an hour before using.

All-purpose flour is made from a blend of hard wheat flour, which has a high protein (gluten) content, and soft wheat flour. It is a good combination for pizza dough. I mix all-purpose with whole wheat here, and it's the perfect pizza dough for cooking on the grill. —NETTIE

1 cup (250 mL) warm water

1 pkg active dry yeast
(2¼ tsp/11 mL)

1 tsp (5 mL) granulated sugar

½ tsp (2 mL) salt

1 cup (250 mL) whole wheat flour

1 cup (250 mL) all-purpose flour

4 Tbsp (60 mL) yellow cornmeal,
divided

2 Tbsp (30 mL) olive oil

**SUGGESTED PIZZA
TOPPINGS**

Olives: whole, chopped, or sliced

Nuts: chopped pumpkin seeds,
pine nuts

Herbs: whole fresh leaves
or chopped

Garlic: chopped or dehydrated

Cheese: grated Pecorino, Parmesan
(Note: Mozzarella gets too tough
and rubbery on the grill.)

Citrus zest: grated orange, lemon,
or lime rind

Roasted red peppers

Artichoke hearts

Green onions, thinly sliced

Sliced pepperoni

Sliced or chopped cooked ham
or chicken

Chopped cooked bacon

Whole or chopped seafood

PREHEAT THE GRILL to high with lid closed; after 10 minutes, reduce heat to medium.

Stir water, yeast, sugar, and salt together in a large mixing bowl. Let stand for 5 minutes as yeast dissolves. Stir in whole wheat flour, all-purpose flour, and 2 Tbsp (30 mL) cornmeal. Stir until dough forms a ball and place on a lightly floured cutting board.

Knead dough for 10 minutes, until smooth and elastic. (If using a stand mixer or food processor, mix dough ingredients until they form a ball and mix for 1 minute more.) Transfer dough to a large oiled bowl and turn to coat entire surface of the ball. Cover with a lint-free dish towel and place in a warm, draft-free environment for 1 hour, or until dough has doubled in size.

Meanwhile, prepare ingredients for topping your pizza (see left for suggestions).

Punch dough down using your fist. To roll out dough, sprinkle a clean work surface with remaining cornmeal. Using cornmeal gives the pizza a more authentic texture. Turn dough out onto the middle of the surface and flatten with the palm of your hand. Use a rolling pin to roll into a circle 14 inches (35 cm) in diameter. Dough should be ⅛ to ¼ inch (3 to 6 mm) thick.

Brush both sides of dough generously with oil. Pick up dough by the 2 corners nearest you and lay dough flat on the cooking grate, cornmeal-coated side down. Close the lid and grill for 3 to 4 minutes, or until bottom is nicely browned.

Using tongs, transfer crust from the grill to a baking sheet. Turn grill off and close lid to retain heat. Flip crust on baking sheet, so that the browned underside is now facing up. Add pizza toppings (suggestions are listed to the left), or use as directed in the recipe that calls for this dough.

Place dressed dough back on grill. Grill with the lid closed until the bottom is browned, about 8 to 10 minutes.

TEMPEH GRILLED PIZZA

Follow the preceding recipe for making homemade dough for the grill. Tempeh is a fermented soy food; see page 12 for more information. —NETTIE

HAM, SPINACH, AND TEMPEH GRILLED PIZZA

Try this pizza without any meat and see if you like it; I do! When I do use ham, however, sometimes I add a ½ cup (125 mL) of drained pineapple tidbits for a Hawaiian-style topping. Alternately, you could use Italian salami, pepperoni, or other deli meats in place of ham as long as they are already cooked. —PAT

½ cup (125 mL) olive oil, divided

1 lb (500 g) tempeh, thawed and crumbled

1 cup (250 mL) chopped shallots

1 clove garlic, minced

One 5½ oz (156 mL) can tomato paste

1 cup (250 mL) vegetable stock (page 40 for homemade)

3 Tbsp (45 mL) red wine vinegar

2 Tbsp (30 mL) Pomegranate Glaze (page 8, or store-bought pomegranate molasses)

2 Tbsp (30 mL) tamari or soy sauce

1 tsp (5 mL) Dijon mustard

2 tsp (10 mL) chile powder

2 Tbsp (30 mL) chopped
fresh flat-leaf parsley

2 cups (500 mL) spinach leaves

1 cup (250 mL) cornmeal

2 lb (1 kg) pizza dough (page 120,
or store-bought), rolled out into
two 14-inch (35 cm) pizza rounds

1 cup (250 mL) diced cooked ham
(½-inch/1 cm dice)

2 Tbsp (30 mL) pine nuts

RESERVE 1 TBSP (15 ML) oil and set aside. Heat remaining oil in a wok or skillet over medium-high heat. Add tempeh and cook, stirring often, for 15 minutes or until tempeh is reddish brown. Drain on paper towels or a lint-free dish towel.

Wipe wok clean. Heat reserved oil over medium heat. Add shallots and garlic. Cook, stirring frequently, for 5 minutes or until shallots are soft. Add tomato paste, vegetable stock, vinegar, Pomegranate Glaze, tamari, and mustard. Bring to a boil over high heat, then reduce heat and simmer, stirring frequently, for 5 minutes. Add chile powder, parsley, spinach, and cooked tempeh. Simmer for 5 minutes or until spinach has wilted. Set aside.

Preheat the grill to low. Divide cornmeal in half and sprinkle evenly over 2 large baking sheets. Press 1 pizza round into the cornmeal on each sheet, making sure underside of dough is coated with cornmeal. Slide crusts onto grill rack and pierce dough using a fork. Close grill lid and cook for 4 minutes, or until lightly browned on underside. Using tongs, or a large spatula, flip crusts upside down.

Meanwhile, divide tempeh topping mixture into 2 equal portions. Spread tempeh mixture on the crusts, leaving a 1-inch (2.5 cm) border around the edge. Sprinkle ham over one of the crusts. Garnish both crusts with pine nuts.

Close grill lid and cook for 8 to 10 minutes, or until tempeh mixture is bubbling and bottom of the crust is browned.

TIP

Pizza can be baked in the oven on a low rack at 500°F (260°C) using the same cooking times as for grilling. Pizza can also be baked on a preheated pizza stone or on a mesh pizza pan, both of which allow the crust to bake without condensing moisture between the crust and pan.

LENTIL AND ARTICHOKE GRILLED PIZZA

Use any canned bean. I really like the size and colour of red lentils and adzuki beans. Serve with salsa, sour cream, and/or extra grated cheese. Grilling melts the cheese evenly. —NETTIE

GRILLED LENTIL PIZZA WITH SEAFOOD AND ASPARAGUS

I love this lentil pizza as it is, but sometimes if I have the ingredients and the desire for a bit of a change, I add shrimp or scallops and fresh or canned asparagus to one half of the pizza. Scallops are cooked when they turn opaque and shrimp are cooked when they turn bright pink; for both, the flesh should be firm, not hard or rubbery. I recommend using the very small scallops or shrimp for this pizza. —PAT

> **TIP**
>
> To cook pizza in the oven, preheat the oven to Broil (500°F/260°C). Broil for 8 minutes, or until cheese is melted and underside of crust is browned.

1⅓ cups (330 mL) canned red
or green lentils or adzuki beans,
drained and rinsed, divided

One 14 oz (398 mL) can artichoke
hearts, drained, divided

1 clove garlic

½ to 2 tsp (2 to 10 mL) chile powder

½ tsp (2 mL) salt

1 Tbsp (15 mL) toasted sesame oil

¼ cup (60 mL) yellow cornmeal

1 lb (500 g) pizza dough
(page 120, or store-bought)

1 cup (250 mL) grape tomatoes,
halved

1¼ cups (310 mL) shredded white
cheddar cheese, divided

½ cup (125 mL) thinly sliced
green onions

½ cup (125 mL) pitted black olives,
thinly sliced

2 Tbsp (30 mL) chopped fresh basil

1 cup (250 mL) fresh small scallops
or peeled and deveined shrimp
(about 3 oz/90 g)

½ cup (125 mL) fresh or canned
asparagus pieces (drained if canned)

2 Tbsp (30 mL) olive oil

(continued)

(continued from previous page)

PREHEAT THE GRILL to low.

Combine 1 cup (250 mL) lentils, 2 artichoke hearts, garlic, chile powder, and salt in a food processor. Process for 3 seconds and with motor running, add sesame oil through opening in the lid. Process until mixture reaches desired consistency—chunky or smooth. Transfer to a bowl and stir in remaining lentils.

Sprinkle cornmeal onto a large baking sheet. On a lightly floured surface, roll out dough into a 14-inch (35 cm) round. Press rolled dough round into the cornmeal to coat one side. Transfer round to the grill with cornmeal-coated side down.

Slide crust directly onto grill rack—do not cook on grill using stone or baking sheet—and pierce dough using a fork. Close lid. Cook for 4 minutes, or until underside is lightly browned. Using tongs or a large spatula, flip crust and slide back onto the grill. Close the lid of the grill to keep it hot until ready to dress.

DRESS THE PIZZA: Slice remaining artichoke pieces and assemble all other vegetarian pizza toppings. Combine scallops, asparagus pieces, and 1 Tbsp (15 mL) of the olive oil in a bowl and toss to coat. Heat remaining 1 Tbsp (15 mL) oil in a skillet over medium-high heat. Add the scallops and asparagus and cook, tossing and stirring constantly, for 3 to 5 minutes or until scallops have turned opaque and asparagus is tender-crisp.

Spread lentil-artichoke mixture over crust, leaving a 1-inch (2.5 cm) border around outside rim. Spread grape tomatoes skin side down over entire pizza and sprinkle ¼ cup (60 mL) cheddar cheese overtop. Spread onions over cheese and tomatoes, and then olives over onions.

Sprinkle ½ cup (125 mL) cheddar cheese over olives.

Spread artichoke pieces evenly over one half of the pizza. Spread grilled scallops and artichoke pieces evenly over the other half of the pizza. Sprinkle remaining cheddar cheese evenly overtop.

Return pizza to grill rack and cook with lid closed for 8 minutes, or until cheese is melted and underside of crust is browned.

GRILLED PINEAPPLE, TOFU, AND ZUCCHINI WITH RED ONION

Vegetarians can share a grill with meat eaters. A perforated stainless steel grill basket allows the aroma of the grill to be absorbed, prevents small pieces of vegetables from falling into the fire, and is easy to clean. —NETTIE

GRILLED STEAK

The most tender cut of beef cooked over an open flame is possibly the quintes-sential meat-lover's dish, and I have chosen it to accompany Nettie's fruit and vegetable combination. You can go ahead and serve one steak per person, but for healthy portions, I recommend serving one-half of a steak instead. Start with an organic, well-marbled, 1-inch-thick (2.5 cm) sirloin, centre-cut rib-eye, T-bone, or porterhouse steak. Salt only after the steak is grilled, since salt draws the liquid to the surface where it steams and evaporates. Follow my no-fail grill-ing instructions and you will have a tender and juicy steak that is cooked to the perfect degree of doneness. —PAT

One 1 lb (500 g) pkg
extra-firm tofu, rinsed

½ cup (125 mL) tomato sauce
(page 159 for homemade)

2 Tbsp (30 mL) Dijon mustard

2 Tbsp (30 mL) rice vinegar

2 Tbsp (30 mL) maple syrup

2 Tbsp (30 mL) orange juice

⅛ tsp (0.5 mL) each salt
and freshly ground pepper

2 cups (500 mL) cubed pineapple
(1-inch/2.5 cm cubes) (fresh,
or canned and drained)

1 cup (250 mL) sliced red onion
(1-inch/2.5 cm rounds)

3 Tbsp (45 mL) olive oil, divided

One 5 to 7 oz (150 to 200 g) steak
(see recipe introduction)

1 cup (250 mL) zucchini chunks
(1-inch/2.5 cm chunks)

11- × 7-inch (28 × 18 cm)
baking dish

Grill basket

PREHEAT THE GRILL to medium heat.

Cut tofu crosswise into eight ½-inch (1 cm) strips. Place in a single layer in a shallow baking dish.

Combine tomato sauce, mustard, vinegar, maple syrup, orange juice, salt, and pepper in a small bowl. Set aside ¼ cup (60 mL) sauce for brushing steak. Pour sauce over tofu in baking dish. Let stand for 30 minutes.

Combine pineapple and onions in grill basket and brush all sides with 2 Tbsp (30 mL) olive oil. Add marinated tofu strips to basket. Set aside the marinade.

Brush steak with some of the reserved sauce and then place on preheated grill. (Get the grill basket with vegetables on the grill at the same time as the steak—see next step.) To get a cross-hatched pattern on the steak, place at a 45-degree angle to grill bars. Grill for 2 minutes. Using tongs, rotate the steak 90 degrees without flipping. Grill for

4 to 6 minutes, or until tiny beads of blood begin to form on top of the steak.

Place grill basket containing tofu, pineapple, and onions on grill. Flip once after 4 minutes. Brush remaining marinade over tofu slices. Brush remaining olive oil over zucchini and add to grill basket. Grill for 4 minutes.

After the first 6 to 8 minutes for the steak are up, flip using tongs. Brush grilled top side of steak with reserved sauce. Grill second side of steak for 2 minutes for rare, 4 minutes for medium, or 6 minutes for well done.

Turn over zucchini once. Leave basket on grill for another 4 minutes.

Remove steak to a shallow dish and pour remaining sauce overtop. Let sit for 3 minutes and divide into 2 servings. Divide grilled fruit and vegetables to 6 plates, placing tofu evenly over 4 plates. Top the remaining 2 plates with the steak.

RICOTTA AND ASIAGO-STUFFED PORTOBELLO MUSHROOMS

Stuffed mushrooms can be served in a bun, or open-faced, or between slices of crusty bread. Their meaty, earthy flavour combines so well with classic Italian ingredients. This may remind you of lasagna, with large grilled mushroom caps used in place of the noodles. —NETTIE

LAMB AND CHEESE-STUFFED PORTOBELLO MUSHROOMS

Ground lamb and mushrooms are a perfect flavour combination, and with the fresh basil and asiago cheese, this is truly a Mediterranean experience. —PAT

8 large portobello mushroom caps

3 Tbsp (45 mL) + 2 tsp (10 mL)
olive oil

1 tsp (5 mL) salt

1 tsp (5 mL) freshly ground pepper

6 oz (175 g) ground lamb

1 cup (250 mL) ricotta
or cottage cheese

¾ cup (185 mL) finely grated asiago
cheese, divided

¼ cup (60 mL) diced pitted
green olives

2 Tbsp (30 mL) chiffonade
of fresh basil (sidebar, page 133)

1 cup (250 mL) tomato sauce
(page 159 for homemade)
or marinara sauce

Rimmed baking sheet

(continued)

(continued from previous page)

PREHEAT THE GRILL to medium-high.

Lightly brush both sides of mushrooms with 3 Tbsp (45 mL) oil. Sprinkle with salt and pepper. Place mushrooms, gill side up, on the grill. Cook for 8 minutes, or until softened, turning once. Transfer to a rimmed baking sheet, gill side up.

Meanwhile, heat 2 tsp (10 mL) oil in a skillet over medium-high heat, and then add ground lamb, stirring and breaking it up with the back of a wooden spoon. Cook lamb for 4 to 6 minutes, or until browned through and there is no trace of pink remaining. Drain off the fat and let meat cool.

Combine ricotta cheese, ½ cup (125 mL) asiago cheese, olives, and basil. Reserve ¼ cup (60 mL) of cheese mixture in a separate bowl and combine with lamb once cooled.

Heat tomato sauce in a small pot over the grill, or on the stovetop, over medium-high heat for 3 minutes or until bubbling.

Spoon 1 to 2 Tbsp (15 to 30 mL) tomato sauce into each mushroom cap. Spoon vegetarian ricotta mixture evenly over-top, stopping after topping 6 mushrooms. Divide meat ricotta mixture into 2 equal portions and top remaining 2 mushrooms.

Sprinkle remaining asiago cheese evenly over all mushrooms. Transfer the entire baking sheet onto the grill, and grill the stuffed mushrooms for 5 minutes, or until asiago cheese has melted and filling is hot and bubbling.

HOW TO CUT LEAVES IN CHIFFONADE

Large-leafed herbs like basil, sage, and chicory, and green-leafed vegetables like spinach, kale, and chard may be finely shredded for use as an ingredient or garnish. Chiffonade of leaves keep their texture in sauces and other dishes, like in the ricotta-cheese stuffing opposite, and they are an interesting shape for a garnish.

1. If using leaves such as spinach or sorrel, remove thick vein from leaves first. This is not necessary for most herbs, as in the basil, below. Stack 3 or 4 similar-sized leaves on top of one another.

2. Roll up leaves tightly, starting from a long side.

3. Hold roll in one hand and use a sharp French knife to cut roll of leaves crosswise into very fine slices.

4. The rolls will unfurl into long thin shreds.

BEANS

ANCHO CHOCOLATE CHILLI

Dried chiles offer deep, smoky, and earthy flavours that are the base for many spicy sauces. They are also a rich source of vitamin A. Ancho, a dried version of the fresh poblano chile, is the most commonly used chile in Mexico. It is brick red to dark mahogany in colour and medium hot. If anchos are not available, use other dried red chiles. Unsweetened chocolate is a combination of cocoa solids and cocoa butter. It is too bitter to nibble on but ideal for cooking, as its intense taste is not easily overpowered by competing flavours. —NETTIE

ANCHO CHOCOLATE CHILLI WITH BEEF

There are lots of garnish options for this richly spiced chilli: chopped fresh tomatoes, sour cream or drained natural yogurt, chopped fresh cilantro, chopped sweet or green onions, cornbread, and nuts or seeds, such as roasted, salted cashews or sunflower seeds. The chile peppers and the chocolate are a powerful taste combination that can stand up to beef, lamb, or even game meats, and I recommend tender satay-style meat strips as an excellent way of complementing this delicious dish. —PAT

CHILLI SPICE MIXTURE

3 medium-sized dried ancho chiles (or 1 tsp/5 mL chile powder)

1 Tbsp (15 mL) chopped fresh oregano

1 tsp (5 mL) Toasted Cumin Dry Rub (page 10) or ground cumin

½ tsp (2 mL) ground cinnamon

2 tsp (10 mL) salt

CYNTHIA'S COMMENTS

If you are using flank steak in this recipe, cutting against the grain is very important. The grain is very evident in flank meat so make sure that you place the lines on the meat horizontally (from left to right) on the cutting board. Skewer the steak with a fork and then slice vertically against the lines of the meat. When choosing your cut of beef, look for a piece with little bits of fat throughout, which will add loads of flavour to the dish.

6 oz (175 g) flank or sirloin tip steak (you can also use lamb)

3 Tbsp (45 mL) tamari or soy sauce

2 Tbsp (30 mL) liquid honey

1 tsp (5 mL) toasted sesame oil

2 Tbsp (30 mL) olive oil

3 cloves garlic, chopped

1 cup (250 mL) thinly sliced red onion

1 cup (250 mL) thinly sliced fresh shiitake mushrooms

½ cup (125 mL) corn kernels, frozen or canned (drain first)

1 cup (250 mL) zucchini, cut into ½-inch (1 cm) pieces

1 lb (500 g) Swiss chard, stalks and veins removed, leaves chopped

½ cup (125 mL) vegetable stock (page 40 for homemade) or water

1 oz (30 g) unsweetened chocolate, finely grated

One 28 oz (796 mL) can diced tomatoes and juice

One 14 oz (398 mL) can pinto beans, drained and rinsed

6 wooden or metal skewers

PREHEAT THE OVEN to Broil (500°F/260°C) and move oven rack to top position. If using wooden skewers, set them in a shallow dish and cover with water to soak.

To make chilli spice mixture, slice chiles in half lengthwise and remove stems and seeds. To toast chiles, heat a small, dry skillet over medium heat. Add chiles and cook for 1 minute, pressing down on them with tongs, before turning over and toasting for 30 seconds on the other side. Let cool and slice each chile into 4 pieces. Pulse in a spice grinder until finely ground. Transfer to a small bowl and combine with oregano, cumin rub, cinnamon, and salt.

Cut thin slices of beef against the grain (see sidebar). Using a meat pounder or a rolling pin, pound meat slices to tenderize them. Rub 3 Tbsp (45 mL) chilli spice mixture over beef strips.

In a shallow dish, combine tamari, honey, and sesame oil. Add beef strips and marinate for at least 20 minutes. (To prepare in advance, cover and marinate in refrigerator for up to 2 days.)

Heat olive oil in a large saucepan over medium heat. Add garlic and sauté for 1 minute. Add onion and cook, stirring frequently, for 5 minutes. Add mushrooms, corn, zucchini, chard, and vegetable stock. Cover, reduce heat, and cook, stirring frequently, for 5 minutes. Onions should be translucent and soft and vegetables should be softened. Stir in chilli spice mixture, chocolate, and tomatoes. Reduce heat and simmer, covered, for 15 minutes.

Meanwhile, remove beef strips from marinade and thread strips onto skewers. Broil in preheated oven for 2 to 3 minutes each side or until cooked through.

Add beans to chilli in the pot and simmer for 5 minutes, or until beans are hot. Ladle into 6 serving bowls. Serve grilled beef skewers with 2 of the bowls of chilli.

BLACK BEAN TORTILLAS WITH CHEDDAR AND COLESLAW

Let's get dinner on the table as soon as we can. With a twist of the wrist, you can open organic black beans from a can, which can be mashed and heated quickly. Prepare some rice or quinoa to either serve as a side or use as another filling. To shave even more time from preparation, you can purchase already-prepared coleslaw and use it straight from the container, omitting the olive oil, chives, cilantro, and salt. Garnish these tortillas with hot sauce or your favourite salsa. —NETTIE

BLACK BEAN TORTILLAS WITH TURKEY AND COLESLAW

I'm with Nettie on this one: it's late and I'm tired and everyone is hungry. Ground beef, chicken, or turkey is fast and easy to serve with tacos and wrap-style dishes. You can add chile powder or cumin (or both) to season the meat, but the seasoned beans add flavour enough for me. —PAT

Two 14 oz (398 mL) cans black beans, drained and rinsed

1 tsp (5 mL) Toasted Cumin Dry Rub (page 10) or ground cumin

½ cup (125 mL) + 1 Tbsp (15 mL) olive oil, divided

3 Tbsp (45 mL) fresh lime juice

4 cups (1 L) coleslaw (homemade or store-bought)

¼ cup (60 mL) diced chives

½ cup (125 mL) chopped fresh cilantro or flat-leaf parsley

⅛ tsp (0.5 mL) salt

½ cup (125 mL) chopped onion

6 oz (175 g) ground turkey

Twelve 6-inch (15 cm) corn or flour tortillas

1 cup (250 mL) shredded cheddar cheese

CYNTHIA'S COMMENTS

Poultry has been part of the rural economy throughout history. Raising poultry was domestic work done by the women of the family. The country yard was a source of income as well as food: chicken and eggs were sold, and were served at the rural family table, although chicken was only for rare special occasions.

Today demand for chicken and turkey has skyrocketed. Many families consume it two to three times per week. Demand for poultry has grown so fast that the industry has changed drastically, unfortunately not for the better. Choosing organically grown poultry is not only ethical, but will bring your family's taste buds back to a time and place where flavour was the best part of a meal. Preparing this recipe with meat adds loads of flavour, which comes not only from the meat but also from the fat. Food without fat is like life without love!

COMBINE BEANS AND cumin rub in a large bowl. Mash to a coarse mixture using a potato masher.

In a separate bowl, mix ¼ cup (60 mL) of the olive oil with lime juice. Add coleslaw, chives, cilantro, and salt.

Heat 1 Tbsp (15 mL) olive oil in a skillet over medium-high heat. Add onion and cook, stirring frequently for 5 minutes. Add ground turkey and reduce heat to medium. Cook, stirring constantly and breaking up any clumps, for 5 to 8 minutes, or until meat is browned with no pink inside. Set aside.

Spoon about a generous ¼ cup (60 mL+) bean mixture onto half of each tortilla. For the last 4 tortillas, spread the bean mixture evenly over the entire surface of each tortilla, to within ½ inch (1 cm) of the edges. Divide the meat mixture evenly among the 4 tortillas, mounding it in the centre of each one.

Fold tortillas in half over filling. Heat 1 Tbsp (15 mL) olive oil in a large skillet over medium heat. Cook tortillas in one layer, about 3 at a time (or whatever the pan will hold) until golden on both sides, turning once, about 1 minute per side. Repeat with rest of tortillas, adding remaining oil to pan as required.

Divide coleslaw mixture evenly among tortillas and spoon over each cooked tortilla. Sprinkle about 2 Tbsp (30 mL) cheese overtop each one, or pass it separately at the table.

PINTO BEAN, QUINOA, AND WILD RICE WRAP

You can use either wild rice or quinoa in this recipe. Wild rice takes longer to cook. Quinoa needs to be rinsed in a fine-mesh strainer under cold running water for three to five minutes to remove the bitter saponin coating. (Merely soaking it won't quite get rid of the saponin.) You can use a canned tomato sauce with herbs. —NETTIE

BEANS AND GRAINS WITH SHREDDED CHICKEN WRAP

I particularly like poached and shredded chicken in this wrap. When the chicken is tossed with mayonnaise or drained yogurt, it adds extra creamy texture to the filling. I like to thin commercial mayonnaise with a small amount of the brine from canned pickles or olives. Of course, you can dice the chicken instead of shredding it or cutting it into strips. —PAT

Six 9- or 10-inch (23 or 25 cm)
flour tortillas

1½ cups (375 mL) chicken stock
(page 45 for homemade)

1 skinless, boneless chicken breast
(about 6 oz/175 g)

1 Tbsp (15 mL) olive oil

1 onion, chopped

½ red bell pepper, chopped

2 cloves garlic, chopped

2 tsp (10 mL) chile powder or flakes

½ tsp (2 mL) ground coriander

½ tsp (2 mL) salt

1 cup (250 mL) tomato sauce
(page 159 for homemade)

One 14 oz (398 mL) can pinto
beans, drained and rinsed

¼ cup (60 mL) chopped fresh
parsley or cilantro

1 cup (250 mL) cooked wild
rice or quinoa, warm or at room
temperature (sidebar, page 142)

1 cup (250 mL) cooked quinoa,
warm or at room temperature
(sidebar, page 142)

¼ cup (60 mL) mayonnaise
or plain yogurt, drained

Sea salt and pepper, to taste

1 avocado, diced

⅓ cup (80 mL) finely chopped
red onion

1 cup (250 mL) shredded cheddar
or Monterey Jack cheese

1 cup (250 mL) sour cream
(optional)

2 rimmed baking sheets, lightly oiled

(continued)

(continued from previous page)

PREHEAT THE OVEN to 300°F (150°C).

Set tortillas in a stack on one of the prepared baking sheets. Cover with foil and place in the oven to warm while filling is being prepared.

In a saucepan, heat chicken stock over high heat until boiling. Add chicken breast and reduce heat to keep stock gently simmering. Simmer, turning the breast once, for 8 to 10 minutes or until chicken is cooked through. Remove pan from heat and leave chicken in the stock until it's cool enough to be handled.

Heat oil in a large skillet over medium-high heat. Add onion and red pepper and cook, stirring constantly, for 5 minutes or until onion is translucent. Add garlic, chile powder, coriander, and salt, and cook, stirring constantly, for 2 minutes.

Add tomato sauce, beans, and parsley. Bring to a boil, reduce heat, and simmer, stirring occasionally, for about 6 minutes or until most of the liquid has evaporated. Remove the skillet from the heat and stir in rice and quinoa.

Lift out poached chicken breast and cut into thin strips and transfer to a bowl. Toss with mayonnaise and season to taste with salt and pepper.

Fill and roll one warm tortilla at a time, replacing foil over remaining tortillas in the oven to keep them warm. Lay tortilla flat on a working surface and spoon about ¼ cup (60 mL) tomato-bean mixture overtop, to within about 1 inch (2.5 cm) of the edges. (If you're making chicken wraps, follow the next step for only 4 of the 6 tortillas.) Spread a portion of the avocado and red onion mixture down the centre of each tortilla. Sprinkle about 3 Tbsp (45 mL) cheese evenly overtop. Roll into a wrap and place on other prepared baking sheet. Tear off enough foil to cover the sheet. Cover and keep filled wraps warm in the oven.

You should have about ½ cup (125 mL) tomato sauce left for the remaining 2 tortillas. Divide chicken evenly into 2 portions and spoon down the centre of the tortillas. Sprinkle remaining cheese evenly overtop and roll up.

Serve with sour cream (if using).

TO COOK WILD RICE

Bring 1½ cups (375 mL) water or stock to a boil over high heat. Stir in ½ cup (125 mL) rinsed rice. Cover and reduce heat to low. Simmer for 40 minutes or until tender. Makes 1 cup (250 mL) cooked rice.

TO COOK QUINOA

Bring 1 cup (250 mL) water or stock to a boil. Stir in ½ cup (125 mL) quinoa that has been rinsed in a fine-mesh strainer under cold running water for 3 to 5 minutes. Simmer for 15 minutes or until tender. Makes 1 cup (250 mL) cooked quinoa.

CYNTHIA'S COMMENTS

Using organic chicken breast will enhance the flavour of this dish. Chicken breast is such a lean cut of meat that it is a true test for organic-versus-conventional. The meat can stand on its own without extra fat and present its true chicken flavour!

THE COWBOY BEAN (PINTO)

The pinto bean is one of the most common of the shell beans (and not just in the southwestern United States and Mexico), and the most consumed bean (at 3.5 lb/1.6 kg per person) in America. (The navy bean is the second-most consumed bean at 1.5 lb/0.7 kg per person.) The pinto or mottled bean is a medium-sized red-clay or tan bean with brown and red splotches, which is called *frijol pinto* ("painted bean") in Spanish. Pinto beans are usually grown to a mature pod. The outside pod is discarded, and the bean itself is cooked fresh in soups, or mashed and refried, but more often than not dried for storage. Growers will sometimes harvest pinto beans before the bean seeds have reached maturity, and the pods are tender enough for eating fresh, but this is rare. If you grow them yourself or can find them at a farmers' market, young, tender pinto beans are delicious in salads, soups, and pasta dishes.

Pinto beans are an important food for Mexicans, and when combined with cornbread, corn tortillas, or rice, they provide a good source of protein to the diet. An authentic Mexican chilli dish always includes pinto beans, although the kidney bean and black bean are growing in popularity. Mexican ranch hands or "cowboys" as they were called were the pinto-bean equivalent to Johnny Appleseed, spreading the colourful bean all along the Texas-Mexico border and encouraging the nickname "cowboy bean."

ROASTED ROOT VEGETABLE BURRITOS

Cans of refried beans may contain lard, so read the label carefully if you want this recipe to be strictly vegetarian. I use toothpicks to designate which burritos contain meat. Share the baking sheet! — NETTIE

ROASTED VEGETABLE AND BEEF BURRITOS

Ground beef (or even turkey) complements the roasted vegetables in this quick and nutritious burrito. — PAT

2 carrots, diced

2 parsnips, diced

2 medium-sized beets, diced

2 medium-sized
sweet potatoes, diced

1 onion, chopped

2 Tbsp (30 mL) + 1 Tbsp (15 mL)
olive oil, divided

2 tsp (10 mL) ground cumin

½ tsp (2 mL) salt

¼ tsp (1 mL) freshly
ground pepper

CYNTHIA'S COMMENTS

I like to use ground beef to convince any skeptic to convert to organic meat! More obviously than with other cuts, organic ground beef tastes and smells like beef should. Ground beef tends to be leaner, so you may have to add some oil for a bit more fat when cooking if your pan is not coated with a non-stick material.

6 oz (175 g) lean ground beef

1 Tbsp (15 mL) chopped
fresh oregano

1 tsp (5 mL) chile powder

2½ cups (625 mL) tomato salsa
(store-bought or Salsa Cruda,
page 220), divided

Six 9- or 10-inch (23 or 25 cm)
corn or flour tortillas

One 14 oz (398 mL) can
refried beans

Rimmed baking sheet,
parchment-lined

9- × 13-inch (23 × 33 cm)
casserole dish, lightly oiled

PREHEAT THE OVEN to 425°F
(220°C).

Toss together carrots, parsnips, beets, sweet potatoes, onion, 2 Tbsp (30 mL) oil, cumin, salt, and pepper in a large bowl. Spread on prepared baking sheet, in one layer if possible. Bake in preheated oven, stirring every 15 minutes, for 50 minutes or until vegetables are tender. Let pan cool on a wire rack for 10 minutes. Reduce oven temperature to 350°F (180°C).

Heat 1 Tbsp (15 mL) oil in a skillet over medium-high heat. Add ground beef and reduce heat to medium. Cook, stirring constantly and breaking up any clumps, for 5 to 8 minutes or until meat is browned with no pink inside. Add oregano and chile powder and cook for 1 minute more. Set aside.

Toss together roasted vegetables and ½ cup (125 mL) tomato salsa in a large bowl. On a clean work surface, lay out 1 tortilla. (If you're making beef burritos, make 4 vegetarian burritos as follows, reserving about ½ cup/125 mL of the roasted vegetable mixture for 2 beef burritos.) Spread about 3 Tbsp (45 mL) refried beans over the tortilla to within 1 inch (2.5 cm) of the edges. Spoon about ¼ cup (60 mL) roasted vegetables down the centre of the tortilla. Roll up the tortilla around the roasted vegetables. Place in prepared dish, seam side down. Repeat.

Add cooked ground beef to the remaining roasted vegetables and divide the filling in half. Lay out 2 tortillas on a clean work surface. Spread about 3 Tbsp (45 mL) refried beans over the tortilla to within 1 inch (2.5 cm) of the edges. Spoon half of the meat filling down the centre of each tortilla. Roll up each tortilla around the filling. Place in prepared dish, seam side down. Mark the meat-filled burritos with toothpicks for easy identification after baking.

Spoon remaining tomato salsa evenly over burritos. Bake in preheated oven for 10 to 15 minutes, or until heated through.

NOODLES

SOBA NOODLES WITH DICED TOMATOES AND GREEN ONIONS

I like the meaty texture of the soba noodles with the tomato in this recipe. A standard-sized package of soba noodles is usually 16 oz (500 g), but to make six servings, you will be using a little more than half the package only. This sauce makes enough broth for leftovers, so you can decide to cook the entire package. I add extra noodles to the leftover sauce, cover, and refrigerate for a great lunch dish the next day. —NETTIE

SOBA NOODLES AND TOMATOES WITH CHICKEN

Black bean–garlic sauce lends depth and richness to the chicken, but it can also be used with the vegetarian version. Your local supermarket should carry it, as well as any Asian grocer. I like to put some in a small bowl and pass it separately at the table. —PAT

1 Tbsp (15 mL) + 1 Tbsp (15 mL) olive oil

4 green onions, white parts minced, and green parts coarsely chopped for garnishing

1 cup (250 mL) chopped or shredded cabbage

One 14 oz (398 mL) can diced tomatoes and juice

¼ cup (60 mL) soy sauce or tamari

2 Tbsp (30 mL) rice vinegar

1 Tbsp (15 mL) turbinado sugar

2 cups (500 mL) vegetable stock (page 40 for homemade)

10 oz (300 g) soba noodles

6 oz (175 g) chicken strips

2 Tbsp (30 mL) black bean–garlic sauce

CYNTHIA'S COMMENTS

To add some extra flavour to this dish, I would use boneless chicken thighs. The dark meat and bits of fat will taste great when mixed with the shredded cabbage.

SOBA NOODLES

Soba noodles are long, thin Japanese noodles made from either 100 percent buckwheat flour or a combination of buckwheat and unbleached or whole wheat flours. Some varieties are best in soups and salads while others are excellent fried or served like spaghetti. These noodles are eggless as well as lighter and less sticky than Italian pasta.

IN A WOK or large saucepan, heat 1 Tbsp (15 mL) olive oil over medium heat. Add whites of the green onions and cabbage. Stir-fry for 1 minute. Add tomatoes and juice, soy sauce, vinegar, and sugar. Cook for 2 minutes, stirring constantly. Add stock and bring to a boil over high heat. Reduce heat and lightly boil, stirring occasionally, for 15 minutes or until slightly reduced and sauce is thickened.

Meanwhile, cook noodles by bringing 12 cups (3 L) of salted water to a boil in a large pot over high heat. Add soba noodles and bring back to a boil. Reduce heat and lightly boil for 6 to 8 minutes, or until tender. Drain and rinse well with warm water.

Heat 1 Tbsp (15 mL) oil in a skillet over medium heat. Add chicken strips and cook, stirring frequently, for 3 to 5 minutes or until lightly browned on all sides and cooked through. Toss with black bean–garlic sauce.

Divide noodles evenly among 6 bowls. Spoon tomato sauce over each bowl and garnish with green onions. Divide chicken evenly and add to 2 bowls.

TUSCAN FUSILLI WITH LENTILS AND KALE

The sweet, slow-cooked, and caramelized onions in the sauce help to round out the earthy and dense lentils, giving them a nutty-sweet flavour. I use fusilli here because its spiral pockets trap the sauce. *Fusilli* is an ancient Italian word, meaning "rifle," referring to the screw-shaped grooves inside the barrel. You can use any of the short dried pasta shapes in its place. —NETTIE

TUSCAN FUSILLI WITH GROUND TURKEY, LENTILS, AND KALE

Ground turkey or chicken is great for this dish as it's light and lean, although using veal might be more in keeping with a dish from Tuscany. I usually season the meat with only ground nutmeg, but you could add ground coriander or cumin, or both. Be sure to drain the meat before adding it to the pasta and greens. —PAT

½ cup (125 mL) red or green lentils, rinsed

2 cups (500 mL) water

1 tsp (5 mL) salt, divided

2 Tbsp (30 mL) + 1 Tbsp (15 mL) olive oil

2 large onions, chopped

3 cloves garlic, thinly sliced

2 Tbsp (30 mL) chopped fresh rosemary

4 cups (1 L) chopped kale

3 cups (750 mL) dried fusilli pasta

6 oz (175 g) ground turkey or ground chicken

½ tsp (2 mL) ground nutmeg

CYNTHIA'S COMMENTS

Most ground turkey meat from organic birds will yield very little fat but, as far as flavour goes, will still give you huge bang for your buck.

(continued)

(continued from previous page)

COMBINE LENTILS AND water in a saucepan. Bring to a boil over medium-high heat. Reduce heat and simmer gently for 20 to 25 minutes, or until tender but not mushy. Remove from heat, season with ½ tsp (2 mL) salt, and set aside.

Meanwhile, heat 2 Tbsp (30 mL) olive oil in a large heavy skillet or saucepan over medium-high heat. Add onion and cook, stirring constantly, for 1 minute. Reduce heat to low. Cover and cook, stirring occasionally, for 15 to 20 minutes or until onions are soft and moist. Uncover and increase heat to medium. Stir in remaining salt, garlic, and rosemary. Cook, stirring frequently, for 5 to 7 minutes or until golden brown.

Meanwhile, bring a large pot of salted water to a boil over high heat. Add kale and bring back to a boil. Boil gently for 5 minutes or until tender but not soft or mushy. Using a slotted spoon or tongs, remove kale to a colander. Rinse with cold water to stop the cooking and drain well. Cover the pot of water to keep it boiling.

Add pasta to the boiling water and boil, stirring once, for about 7 minutes or until al dente. Reserve 1 cup (250 mL) pasta cooking water and then drain the pasta. Rinse pasta with cool water and drain well.

While pasta is cooking, heat 1 Tbsp (15 mL) olive oil in a skillet over medium-high heat. Add ground turkey and reduce heat to medium. Cook, stirring constantly, and breaking up any clumps, for 5 to 8 minutes, or until meat is browned with no pink inside. Stir in nutmeg and set aside.

Add lentils and their cooking liquid to the onions in the skillet. Using kitchen scissors, cut boiled kale into smaller pieces as you add it to the skillet. Add cooked pasta and enough reserved cooking water to keep pasta and vegetables moist. Increase heat to high. Cook, stirring constantly, until pasta is mixed in and heated through. Remove vegetarian servings and divide among 4 plates.

Using a slotted spoon to allow the meat to drain, transfer the meat to the fusilli and vegetables remaining in the skillet, divide among 2 plates and serve.

COOKING KALE AND OTHER GREENS

Kale is a brassica family vegetable, a leafy-green relative of broccoli and cabbage. It is a powerhouse of fibre and nutrients (rich in antioxidants such as vitamins A, C, and E) and ranks low on the glycemic scale, making it an excellent low-fat essential food. Kale also contains the cancer risk–reducing sulfur phytonutrients known to be present in the brassica plants.

Kale is usually blanched, meaning that it is tossed into a pot of boiling water. It is then plunged into ice water; blanched foods are usually immersed or drained in ice-cold water for as long as they were blanched to stop the cooking. Every fruit and vegetable has a different blanching time. The following instructions on how to blanch kale can also be applied to greens other than kale:

1. Wash greens by immersing and swishing them in a sinkful of water to which a drop of food-grade soap has been added. Rinse, drain, and pat dry.

2. In the Tuscan fusilli recipe, kale is coarsely chopped to make it easier to measure, but you can blanch whole leaves and chop them afterwards. The tough centre rib of the leaf is cut out and discarded. The leaf is folded in half lengthwise and 4 or 5 crosswise cuts are made using a paring knife. Leave the pieces of leaf fairly large—they're easier to remove from boiling water, and you can chop them finer if you wish once they are blanched.

3. This recipe calls for 4 cups (1 L) coarsely chopped kale. The leaves should be lightly pressed into a dry or liquid measuring cup. Five small- to medium-sized leaves will yield about 4 cups (1 L) coarsely chopped kale.

4. To blanch whole or cut leaves, drop them into a large pot of salted, boiling water and bring back to a boil. Adjust the heat to keep the water boiling for 5 minutes. If the water will be used to cook pasta, transfer the blanched kale to a colander set over a bowl or sink. Don't worry about the tiny pieces left in the water because they will be drained with the pasta after it is cooked. Rinse under cold water to stop the cooking and set aside. If you prefer smaller kale pieces for the recipe, you can chop with a French knife or snip them by using scissors to cut through a handful at a time, letting the pieces fall into the pan or mixing bowl.

5. When pasta and greens are ingredients in the same recipe, the pasta is often cooked in the water used to blanch the greens. This adds some colour to the pasta and the expanding pasta also absorbs some of the nutrient-rich water. Bring the kale cooking water back to a boil (you will notice that it is slightly green from the kale) and cook the pasta until al dente. Reserve some of the cooking water—now light green and opaque from the starches in the pasta.

6. Drain the pasta and any bits of kale in a colander set over a sink. Rinse under cool water and set aside.

FARFALLE WITH ROASTED BEET CHIPS AND PINE NUTS

Be sure to look for the freshest possible beets for this dish. You can tell the freshness of beets by their greens—if the greens are bright and vibrant with no signs of yellowing or wilting, the beets are fresh. I use the greens here too, with pasta and toasted pine nuts, because beet greens are packed with calcium, iron, magnesium, phosphorus, potassium, vitamin C, some B vitamins, and 2,404 IU of vitamin A. Beet greens may be interchanged with spinach and other greens in recipes. —NETTIE

FARFALLE WITH ROASTED BEET CHIPS AND BROILED SCALLOPS

When the roasted beet chips come out of the oven, the scallops are then cooked in no time under the broiler. Use sea scallops (as opposed to bay scallops) because they are larger and more suited to the oven method used in this recipe. If only the smaller bay scallops are available, sauté them in oil or butter in a hot skillet over medium heat, turning once, for two to four minutes or until cooked through. Be careful not to overcook scallops because they can turn rubbery. —PAT

6 medium-sized beets with green tops intact

6 Tbsp (90 mL) + 1 Tbsp (15 mL) olive oil, divided

Sea salt and freshly ground pepper, to taste

½ cup (125 mL) pine nuts

2 onions, halved and sliced

3 cloves garlic, chopped

12 oz (375 g) dried farfalle pasta

⅓ cup (80 mL) finely grated Parmesan cheese

8 oz (250 g) sea scallops

2 Tbsp (30 mL) fresh lemon juice

Rimmed baking sheet, parchment-lined

Another rimmed baking sheet, lightly oiled

PREHEAT THE OVEN to 375°F (190°C).

Remove beet tops, rinse them under cool water, drain, and pat dry. Chop leaves and tender red stems and discard tougher stems. Set aside.

Scrub and trim beet bulbs. Slice crosswise into ¼-inch (6 mm) slices. Arrange slices on parchment-lined baking sheet in a single layer and drizzle with 2 Tbsp (30 mL) olive oil. Bake beet chips on top rack of preheated oven for 12 to 15 minutes, or until tender when pierced with the tip of a knife. Remove and season with salt and pepper. You can leave the beet chips whole or cut into ¼-inch (6 mm) strips. Set aside.

Increase oven temperature to Broil (500°F/260°C) for scallops.

Meanwhile, heat a large heavy-bottomed skillet over medium heat. Add pine nuts and dry-roast, stirring constantly, for 2 minutes or until golden and lightly toasted. Transfer to a small bowl and season with more salt and pepper. Set aside.

Add 2 Tbsp (30 mL) oil to the same skillet. Add onion slices and cook over medium heat, stirring frequently, for 7 to 10 minutes or until soft and lightly coloured. Reduce heat to medium-low and continue to cook, stirring frequently, for 15 to 20 minutes or until tender and browned. Add garlic and cook, stirring frequently, for 2 minutes. Add chopped beet greens and drizzle remaining oil overtop. Cover and cook, stirring once or twice, for 5 minutes or until greens are tender.

Meanwhile, bring a large pot of salted water to a boil over high heat. Add pasta to the boiling water and boil, stirring once, for about 5 minutes or until al dente. Reserve about 1 cup (250 mL) pasta cooking water and then drain the pasta. Rinse pasta with cool water and drain well.

Arrange scallops in one layer on oiled baking sheet and drizzle with 1 Tbsp (15 mL) olive oil. Broil on top rack of oven for 2 minutes each side, turning once. Scallops are done when they turn opaque. Remove and drizzle lemon juice overtop.

Return pasta to the pot. Add onion-greens mixture and reserved beet chips or strips. Toss with enough of the reserved pasta cooking water to moisten. Taste and add more salt and pepper if required. Divide farfalle and vegetables evenly among 6 bowls. Divide scallops in half and spoon over 2 bowls. Garnish bowls with the toasted pine nuts and Parmesan cheese.

PAPPARDELLE WITH SPINACH, ASPARAGUS, AND FETA

It is important of course to give readers the option of replacing ingredients with whatever they like, but for this recipe I would stick with the asparagus and mint. My 21-year-old son likes to prepare this recipe after a day of studying at the library and always remarks on the vibrant green colours of the ingredients. —NETTIE

PAPPARDELLE WITH GRILLED SALMON, SPINACH, AND ASPARAGUS

Asparagus, pasta, salmon—it's a spring thing for me. If you can, grill the fish over the flame of a barbecue. Trout, perch, or other medium-textured fish will be delicious with the pasta and greens. It does not take long to grill fish— 10 minutes per inch (2.5 cm) of thickness, in fact—so you can start it around the same time you start cooking the onion, garlic, and asparagus. —PAT

12 oz (375 g) dried
pappardelle pasta

2 lb (1 kg) spinach,
tough stems discarded,
leaves washed but not dried

2 Tbsp (30 mL) + 1 Tbsp (15 mL)
olive oil

1 cup (250 mL) diced red onion

3 cloves garlic, chopped

1 lb (500 g) fresh asparagus
or green beans, cut into
1-inch (2.5 cm) pieces

Salt and pepper

7 oz (200 g) salmon fillet,
skin left on, pin bones removed

⅔ cup (160 mL) crumbled
feta cheese, for garnishing

2 Tbsp (30 mL) chopped
fresh mint or parsley, for garnishing

3 Tbsp (45 mL) chopped
green onions, for garnishing

2 fresh lemon wedges (optional)

COOK PAPPARDELLE IN a large pot of boiling salted water for 6 minutes, or until al dente. Reserve ½ cup (125 mL) of the cooking water. Drain in a colander and rinse under cool water. Set aside.

Meanwhile, in a large, deep saucepan cook the spinach over medium-high heat, stirring and tossing constantly, for 1 minute or until wilted. Drain in a colander set over a bowl and press gently with the back of a spoon to release liquid. Chop spinach and set aside. Reserve liquid.

Heat 2 Tbsp (30 mL) oil over medium-high heat in the same saucepan. Add onion and sauté for 5 minutes or until soft. Add garlic and asparagus. Cover and reduce heat. Cook, stirring occasionally, for 5 to 7 minutes or until asparagus is tender-crisp. Season to taste with salt and pepper.

Brush skinless side of salmon fillet with 1 Tbsp (15 mL) olive oil. Season with more salt and pepper.

Heat a second skillet over medium-high heat. Add salmon, skin side down, and cook for 8 minutes or until just cooked through. Using a lifter, remove fillet from the skin to a plate, leaving the skin in the pan; discard skin. Cover plate with foil until pasta and greens are ready.

Add chopped spinach and reserved spinach liquid to asparagus skillet. Increase heat to medium-high and heat through, stirring constantly, for about 1 minute. Add cooked pasta and reserved pasta cooking water. Heat through, stirring constantly, for 1 to 2 minutes. Spoon pappardelle and greens onto 6 serving plates.

Divide fillet into 2 portions and leave whole or flake salmon into large chunks. Top 2 plates with flaked salmon or whole pieces. Garnish vegetarian plates with feta and mint. Garnish all plates with green onions. Add lemon wedges (if using) to fish portions.

TOFU LASAGNA

What a great way to use tofu. Because it is often bland, combining tofu with wine, garlic, basil, and a tasty tomato sauce turns it into a spectacular source of delicious protein. It's a winner! —NETTIE

TERIYAKI PORK WITH LASAGNA

Marinate the pork strips while making the vegetable lasagna, and cook both in the same oven. It's an easy way to satisfy a hungry, flexible family. If you prepare and bake extra teriyaki pork, you can use it in salads or with roasted vegetables the next day. —PAT

> **TIP**
>
> When you buy prepackaged tofu, always check the best-before date. You should always place tofu in a colander and rinse it in cold water before using. To store tofu, immerse it in water in a covered container and refrigerate. Change the water every 2 days and it should last in your fridge for a week. Leftover tofu freezes well and can be kept frozen for 6 months. Freezing changes the texture of tofu, making it firm and somewhat chewy.

1½ cups (375 mL) Teriyaki Sauce (page 8)

Two 3 oz (90 g) boneless pork chops, cut into 1-inch (2.5 cm) strips (sidebar, page 160)

TOMATO SAUCE

3 Tbsp (45 mL) olive oil

1 onion, chopped

4 cloves garlic, minced

1 green bell pepper, chopped

One 28 oz (796 mL) can crushed tomatoes

One 5½ oz (156 mL) can tomato paste

¼ cup (60 mL) dry red wine or apple juice

2 tsp (10 mL) soy sauce or tamari

1 Tbsp (15 mL) chopped fresh oregano

¼ tsp (1 mL) freshly ground pepper

2 bay leaves

½ cup (125 mL) chopped fresh basil

2 cups (500 mL) ricotta cheese

8 oz (250 g) firm tofu, rinsed and puréed (see Tip)

1 tsp (5 mL) soy sauce or tamari

¼ tsp (1 mL) freshly ground pepper

9 lasagna noodles, cooked and drained

8 oz (250 g) shredded mozzarella cheese

3 Tbsp (45 mL) finely grated Parmesan cheese

Large shallow baking dish or pie plate, for marinating and baking pork

9- × 13-inch (23 × 33 cm) casserole dish

PREHEAT THE OVEN to 375°F (190°C).

Pour Teriyaki Sauce into baking dish. Add pork strips and toss well to coat. Cover with foil and set aside to marinate for 10 minutes, or as long as overnight.

Prepare tomato sauce by heating oil in a large saucepan over medium heat. Add onion and garlic and cook, stirring frequently, for 5 minutes or until soft. Add green pepper, tomatoes, tomato paste, wine, soy sauce, oregano, pepper, and bay leaves. Lower heat to medium-low. Cover and simmer, stirring often, for 30 minutes or until vegetables are tender and sauce is thick. Remove and discard bay leaves. Stir in basil and set aside.

Prepare filling by mixing together ricotta, puréed tofu, soy sauce, and pepper in a bowl. Set aside.

Assemble lasagna by spreading 3 Tbsp (45 mL) tomato sauce over the bottom of the dish. Cover with 3 noodles in one layer. Spread half of filling evenly over the noodles. Cover filling with one-third of the tomato sauce. Sprinkle half of mozzarella cheese overtop sauce. Cover with another 3 noodles, remaining filling, one-third of tomato sauce, and remaining mozzarella cheese. Cover with remaining noodles and remaining tomato sauce. Sprinkle Parmesan cheese evenly over the top of the lasagna.

Cover and bake in preheated oven for 20 minutes. Add dish of pork strips to the oven after lasagna has been in for 10 minutes. Uncover lasagna and bake for 10 minutes, or until sauce is bubbling and cheese is browned. Check pork. Stir and remove if done or re-cover and continue to cook until done. Let lasagna and pork stand for 5 minutes before serving.

Serve 1 or 2 pork skewers alongside the lasagna. If you have leftover pork, wrap and refrigerate or freeze.

(continued)

POUNDING AND MARINATING MEAT FOR TASTE AND TENDERNESS

One of the traditional meat techniques, especially for less tender cuts of meat, is to pound it using a utensil especially designed for this purpose. Meat pounders may be wood or metal, but stainless steel is the best due to its durability and the fact that it can be sterilized or put through a dishwasher.

1. Have your butcher prepare two boneless pork chops that are no more than ¾ inch (2 cm) thick. Rinse and trim meat of all traces of visible fat.

2. Soak wooden skewers in a bowl or sinkful of cool water for at least 30 minutes, or overnight. Prepare metal skewers by oiling them.

3. Pound the meat, using a meat pounder or wooden rolling pin. A stainless steel meat pounder is heavy enough to flatten the meat to a uniform thickness and it pierces the meat so that the sauce or marinade can penetrate it. Be careful not to pound too much or meat will tear.

4. Cut pork into 1-inch-wide (2.5 cm) strips.

5. Thread meat onto prepared skewers.

6. Combine Teriyaki Sauce ingredients in a shallow baking dish. Lay pork skewers in the marinade and let sit for at least 15 minutes. (May be prepared the day before. Cover tightly and refrigerate overnight. Bring to room temperature before baking.)

CYNTHIA'S COMMENTS

My favourite meat is pork. I use it to make my Sunday tomato sauce, which takes on all the lovely subtle flavour of the pork. Today's pork is very lean, and what fat there is blends well with the pasta, adding just the right amount of flavour.

SESAME OIL

Sesame oil, obtained by pressing sesame seeds, is used as a spike of flavour for Asian dishes and also as a cooking oil, particularly in India.  Regular sesame oil is light in both colour and fragrance, while toasted sesame oil is darker and nuttier in taste. Both make very good oils for sautéing grains and vegetables, but toasted sesame oil spoils faster and must be refrigerated after opening. Sesame oil is high in polyunsaturated fats, ranking fourth behind safflower, soybean, and corn oil.

PAD THAI

I always add more peanuts, store-bought chile vinegar sauce, and dried red chile flakes depending on my mood. Omit the eggs to make it vegan. Delicious hot or cold. —NETTIE

SHRIMP PAD THAI

In Bangkok, Pad Thai or Phat Thai is the quintessential street food, perfected by food-cart cooks. The noodles are dry and easy to eat with chopsticks, and it has a balanced, fresh flavour. Traditionally, a fish sauce is always used, and although there are vegetarian, chicken, pork, and beef versions, shrimp is by far the most popular choice. If you purchase shrimp unpeeled and/or with the head attached, buy 1 lb (500 g) for every two people. —PAT

TAMARIND

Tamarinds are the fruit of a tall tree (80 feet/24 metres) that grows in tropical climates all over the world. Tamarinds resemble wide beans with long, reddish-brown seedpods. When ripe, their sour green flesh turns brown and gains a complex, roasted aroma. It's used as a flavouring in sauces, soups, and beverages, and is best known as an essential ingredient in Worcestershire sauce. It is sold in rectangular blocks of pressed pulp that must be softened first, or as a jelly concentrate that typically comes in a jar.

To use the tamarind pulp, place a piece in a small non-metallic pot or glass bowl, cover with boiling water, and set aside for a minimum of 30 minutes and a maximum of 3 hours. Next, force the pulp through a sieve, discarding any seeds and fibres. Press down on the tamarind pulp to extract as much liquid as you can. It will keep in the fridge for 3 days. Freeze leftover liquid in ice cube trays (available at kitchen stores).

8 oz (250 g) dried rice noodles

6 Tbsp (90 mL) + 2 Tbsp (30 mL) peanut oil or olive oil, divided

8 oz (250 g) firm tofu, rinsed and cut into 1-inch (2.5 cm) cubes

½ cup (125 mL) vegetable stock (page 40 for homemade)

2 Tbsp (30 mL) rice vinegar

2 Tbsp (30 mL) soy sauce or tamari

2 tsp (10 mL) red or green curry paste (page 9 for homemade)

1 Tbsp (15 mL) tamarind liquid (see sidebar) or fresh lime juice

4 cloves garlic, coarsely chopped

1 cup (250 mL) sliced mushrooms

1 cup (250 mL) diced red bell pepper

1 cup (250 mL) snow peas or green peas

2 green onions, finely chopped

2 large eggs, lightly beaten

¾ lb (375 g) shrimp, peeled and deveined

2 Tbsp (30 mL) fish sauce

1 cup (250 mL) fresh bean sprouts

2 Tbsp (30 mL) chopped fresh cilantro

3 Tbsp (45 mL) salted roasted peanuts, coarsely ground

3 limes, cut into quarters

RICE NOODLES

Dried rice noodles are made from finely ground rice flour and water. The pasta is then extruded into opaque noodles of varying thicknesses and sizes. Because they are absorbent and have little flavour of their own, they readily take on the taste and fragrance of the foods with which they are cooked. In Asian cuisine, rice noodles are a basic and popular food. Dried rice noodles are perfect for quick and easy cooking as they take little time to soften and can be cooked with almost any vegetable, meat, or seafood.

Dried rice noodles stored in a dry, cool cupboard will last indefinitely. They are very easy to use. Simply soak them in hot water for 15 minutes, or until they are soft. Drain them in a colander and use in soups or stir-fries.

SOAK NOODLES IN a bowl in hot water according to package instructions. Drain and set aside.

Heat 2 Tbsp (30 mL) of oil in a skillet over medium heat. Add tofu cubes and fry, turning to cook evenly, for 3 minutes or until crispy and golden. Using a slotted spoon, transfer to a lint-free dishtowel or paper towel–lined plate to drain excess oil.

Combine vegetable stock, rice vinegar, soy sauce, curry paste, and tamarind liquid in a bowl. Whisk and set aside.

Heat 2 Tbsp (30 mL) of oil in a large wok over medium-high heat. Add garlic and toss for about 1 minute or until golden. Add mushrooms, pepper, snow peas, and green onions. Stir-fry for 2 minutes and set aside in a separate bowl.

Add 2 Tbsp (30 mL) oil to the wok. When oil is hot, pour eggs into the centre, scramble well, and leave

in the wok. Add the vegetable stock mixture, drained rice noodles, fried tofu, and stir-fried vegetables. Cook, stirring constantly, for 5 minutes or until noodles are tender and mixture absorbs the sauce.

Meanwhile, heat 2 Tbsp (30 mL) oil in a small skillet over medium heat. Add shrimp and sauté for 2 to 3 minutes, or until flesh has turned bright pink and is opaque. Turn heat off and toss with fish sauce. Transfer shrimp to a serving bowl for non-vegetarians to pass at the table to add to their plates.

Add ½ cup (125 mL) bean sprouts, all the cilantro, and 2 Tbsp (30 mL) of the peanuts to the wok. Toss well and cook for 1 minute. Transfer to a serving platter and squeeze two of the fresh lime quarters over the mixture. Garnish platter with remaining bean sprouts, peanuts, and lime quarters and serve at the table..

PENNE WITH BEANS AND FENNEL

Cabbage comes in many colours and sizes. Add a cup (250 mL) at a time to the pan, allowing each addition to wilt before adding the next one. Always remove the core from cabbage and slice it thinly. — NETTIE

PENNE WITH SAUSAGE, BEANS, AND FENNEL

For this Italian dish, I chose hot Italian sausage to complete the Mediterranean flavours but you can also use a sweet sausage. — PAT

8 oz (250 g) dried penne pasta

1 Tbsp (15 mL) + 1 Tbsp (15 mL) olive oil

6 oz (175 g) hot or sweet Italian sausage, cut into 1-inch (2.5 cm) pieces

1 onion, chopped

1 cup (250 mL) diced red bell pepper

1 cup (250 mL) diced fennel bulb

1 cup (250 mL) diced zucchini

1 cup (250 mL) diced seeded tomatoes

1 cup (250 mL) vegetable stock (page 40 for homemade)

One 14 oz (398 mL) can cannellini beans, drained and rinsed

2 cloves roasted garlic (sidebar, page 97)

1 Tbsp (15 mL) chopped fresh oregano

1 Tbsp (15 mL) fresh thyme leaves

1 tsp (5 mL) salt

3 cups (750 mL) chopped green cabbage

1 Tbsp (15 mL) chopped fresh rosemary

CYNTHIA'S COMMENTS

When choosing Italian sausage, take a close look at the list of ingredients. You should be able to understand all the words! Look for simple, quality ingredients. The quality of the pork should speak for itself, with extra ingredients added to enhance the flavour, not mask it.

IN A LARGE pot, bring salted water to a boil. Stir in pasta and boil for 8 to 10 minutes, or until al dente. Drain and rinse with cold water to stop the cooking. Set aside.

Heat 1 Tbsp (15 mL) olive oil in a skillet over medium heat. Add sausage and cook, stirring occasionally, for about 10 minutes or until browned and cooked through.

Meanwhile, heat 1 Tbsp (15 mL) olive oil in a large saucepan over medium-high heat. Add onion and cook, stirring frequently, for 3 minutes or until softened. Add red pepper, fennel, and zucchini and sauté over medium-low heat for 3 to 5 minutes. Add tomatoes, vegetable stock, beans, garlic, oregano, thyme, and salt, and the cabbage 1 cup (250 mL) at a time. Bring to a boil over high heat, reduce heat, and simmer, stirring occasionally, for 5 minutes. Cabbage should be tender-crisp. Toss sauce with warm pasta.

Serve, but leave some pasta behind for the 2 meat portions. Toss cooked sausage with rosemary and add to remaining penne.

FENNEL

The type of fennel we eat as a vegetable is called Florence or Roman fennel (sometimes called Finocchio, which is "fennel" in Italian). Fennel is bulbous shaped and is fragrantly like anise (licorice) in both taste and smell. The leaf stalks of *Foeniculum vulgare* var. *dulce* grow wider at the bulbous end, so much so that they overlap and form a tight core in their centre. Fennel is used raw in salads, or cooked with garlic, onions, and tomatoes in sauces and/or Mediterranean dishes.

Choose bulbs that are firm and show no signs of drying out. Some slight yellowing or bruising is acceptable since the outer layers can be removed. Store fennel tightly wrapped in the refrigerator for up to several days. To slice fennel:

1. Cut the bulb in half lengthwise and remove the hard, wedge-shaped centre core.

2. Lay one half, cut side down, on a cutting surface. Thinly slice across the bulb and then dice the stack of slices, or cut into smaller pieces.

CURRIES, CASSEROLES, AND CHILLIS

TOFU CURRY WITH LIME AND NUT BUTTER

The secret behind this recipe lies in the toasting of its spices. Fenugreek, cumin, and coriander are a magical trio. Fenugreek seeds are used in chutneys and Indian pickles. I suggest that you invest in a second coffee bean grinder and use it exclusively for spices. —NETTIE

SHRIMP CURRY WITH LIME AND NUT BUTTER

The sauce for this curry is outstanding, and like any coconut sauce spiked with red or green Thai curry spices, it is perfect for firm fish (such as cod, monkfish, or bass), chicken, pork, and seafood, like the shrimp I use here. I love gently cooking shrimp right in the curry sauce, but you can opt to cook the shrimp in a separate pan (see sidebar, page 171) and serve as a garnish or on the side. Note: If adding shrimp, I recommend using only one package of tofu. —PAT

Two 14 oz (440 g) pkgs firm tofu,
rinsed (if using shrimp,
see note in recipe introduction)

2 tsp (10 mL) whole fenugreek seeds

1 tsp (5 mL) whole cumin seeds

1 tsp (5 mL) whole coriander seeds

1 Tbsp (15 mL) crushed
cinnamon stick

1 Tbsp (15 mL) ground turmeric

2 Tbsp (30 mL) olive oil

1 onion, finely chopped

4 cloves garlic, minced

1 Tbsp (15 mL) grated fresh ginger

1 tsp (5 mL) red curry paste
(page 9 for homemade) or 1 dried
cayenne pepper, crushed

½ tsp (2 mL) salt

One 14 oz (398 mL) can
coconut milk

¼ cup (60 mL) peanut butter

2 tsp (10 mL) lime zest

3 Tbsp (45 mL) fresh lime juice

1 Tbsp (15 mL) brown sugar

1 red bell pepper, cut into
½-inch (1 cm) dice

1 cup (250 mL) sliced carrots

1 cup (250 mL) broccoli florets

¼ to 1 cup (60 to 250 mL) water

4 oz (125 g) shrimp, peeled
and deveined (about 8 to 12)

(continued)

(continued from previous page)

DRAIN TOFU IN a large colander over a bowl or in the sink. Cut into 1-inch (2.5 cm) cubes and set aside.

Heat a large heavy-bottomed skillet over medium-high heat and then add fenugreek, cumin, coriander, and cinnamon. Dry-roast spices, stirring constantly, for 2 minutes or until golden and lightly toasted. Remove to a small bowl and let cool. Using a mortar and pestle, or an electric grinder, grind toasted spices. Add turmeric, mix well, and set aside. You should have about ¼ cup (60 mL) of curry spice blend.

Heat oil in the same skillet, over medium-high heat. Add onion, garlic, and ginger and cook, stirring frequently for 3 to 5 minutes or until onions are soft and translucent. Stir in 1 Tbsp (15 mL) of the curry spice blend, red curry paste, and salt. Cook, stirring constantly, for 30 seconds. Add coconut milk and bring to a simmer, stirring constantly. Add peanut butter, lime zest, lime juice, and brown sugar. Bring back to a simmer, stirring constantly.

Add red pepper, carrots, and broccoli, and bring to a light simmer. Reduce heat to medium-low and simmer, stirring occasionally, for 15 minutes. Taste and add more curry spice blend if desired. Stir in water, ¼ cup (60 mL) at a time, if sauce appears to be too thick. Transfer 2¼ cups (560 mL) of the vegetables and sauce to a separate saucepan for the shrimp portions.

Add tofu cubes to the skillet and simmer, stirring occasionally, for 10 minutes or until vegetables are tender. Bring other saucepan to a gentle simmer over medium-low heat. Add shrimp and simmer gently, stirring frequently, for 3 to 5 minutes or until shrimp has turned bright pink. Remove from heat and keep warm. (Do not overcook shrimp because it will become tough and rubbery.)

GRINDING WHOLE CURRY SPICES

When the toasted spices have cooled, grind them to your preference, whether fine or coarse. This recipe makes about ¼ cup (60 mL) with the addition of the ground turmeric. In this recipe, use 1 to 2 Tbsp (15 to 30 mL) of the curry spice according to your taste. Store the remaining curry blend in an airtight container in a cool, dark place for up to 6 months.

CURRY SPICE

Fresh whole curry spices are blended and toasted for optimum flavour. In the bowl, clockwise from the top, are coriander seeds, cumin seeds, and fenugreek seeds. In the measuring spoon is a crushed cinnamon stick. Fenugreek is key to the essential curry flavour in curry blends. Ground turmeric (not shown) is also added to the sauce and provides its bright yellow colour.

COOKING SHRIMP IN A STOVETOP GRILL PAN

1. Peel and devein shrimp. Rinse under cool water in a colander. Drain and pat dry. Lightly oil a grill pan or skillet. Heat pan over medium-high heat. Reduce heat to medium-low and place shrimp in the pan. Cook for 2 to 3 minutes or until the bottom edges start to turn bright pink (see the 2 shrimp centre bottom).

2. Using tongs, turn shrimp and cook for 2 to 3 minutes on flip side, or until undersides are bright pink. Remove from grill pan or, if pan is large enough, move cooked shrimp to a section that is not directly over the heat. The tender protein in shrimp turns tough and rubbery when overcooked.

 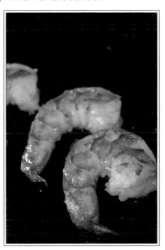

FLAVOUR PROFILE

A wide range of flavours are combined in this complex curry. Coconut milk provides a slightly sweet background that balances out the spikes of fresh ginger, grated lime rind, and fresh lime juice. Peanut butter lends richness and a slightly sweet nutty essence. Spices (see sidebars on opposite page) are toasted whole and ground to a coarse or fine consistency, depending on your preference.

TEMPEH MOLE

Moles are slow-cooked Mexican sauces whose flavour comes from a classic mixture of chiles, chocolate, and sweet spices. Using tempeh, a fermented soy food (see page 12), is a truly East meets West approach, and also means eating lower on the food chain. —NETTIE

CHICKEN MOLE

The Aztecs called their spicy drink made from chocolate *cacahuatl.* This drink and the national dish of Mexico known as *mole* have a lot in common. Of course chocolate is the key to both, but they also have spices in common—chiles, allspice, and cinnamon. Markets all over Mexico sell prepared mole pastes, powders, and spreads, and there are as many variations of these as there are cooks. Chicken is a favoured ingredient for mole, and I could not resist adding it to Nettie's wonderful adaptation. —PAT

4 Tbsp (60 mL) + 2 Tbsp (30 mL) olive oil, divided

1 lb (500 g) tempeh, cut into ½-inch (1 cm) dice

2 large onions, halved and sliced

2 cloves garlic, crushed

½ tsp (2 mL) ground cinnamon

¼ tsp (1 mL) ground allspice

One 14 oz (398 mL) can diced tomatoes and juice

CYNTHIA'S COMMENTS

Choosing organic chicken for this recipe will make all the difference. The chicken will have 10 times the taste and will impress even the pickiest of eaters.

One 14 oz (398 mL) can red kidney
beans, drained and rinsed

2 smoked, dried chipotles,
soaked and chopped (reserve
2 cups/500 mL soaking water)

2½ oz (75 g) dark chocolate
(60% cocoa solids), coarsely
chopped, divided

Two 4 oz (125 g) boneless,
skinless chicken breasts

⅛ tsp (0.5 mL) salt

Dutch oven or casserole
dish with lid

10-inch (25 cm) casserole dish
with lid, lightly oiled

PREHEAT THE OVEN to 300°F
(150°C).

Heat 3 Tbsp (45 mL) oil in a
large skillet over medium-high heat.
Cook tempeh, turning frequently,
for 8 to 10 minutes or until reddish
brown on all sides. Using a slotted
spoon or tongs, lift out and set aside
on a towel-lined plate.

Heat remaining olive oil in Dutch
oven over medium heat. Add onions
and garlic and sauté for 5 minutes,
or until soft and golden. Stir in cinnamon and allspice. Add tomatoes
and juice, beans, chiles and reserved
soaking water, and all of the chocolate except 1 Tbsp (15 mL). Bring to
a boil and then remove from heat.
Remove 1 cup (250 mL) chocolate
mixture and set aside for the meat
portions.

Stir cooked tempeh into chocolate mixture in the Dutch oven.
Cover the pot and bake in preheated
oven for 1½ hours.

Heat oil in a skillet over medium
heat. Add chicken breasts and
brown, turning several times, for
3 or 4 minutes or until meat is
browned on the outside. Place in
prepared casserole dish and cover
with chocolate mixture. Cover with
lid (or foil) and add to the oven
after the tempeh mole has been in
the oven for 30 minutes. Bake for
45 minutes to 1 hour, or until centre
of chicken pieces is no longer pink
and juices run clear.

Taste, and then add salt (if
required) and reserved chocolate.

BROCCOLI RABE AND PECAN CRÊPES

Company is coming and you want to showcase your flexitarian chops? This is a great recipe to serve both veg and with Pat's suggested Italian sausage. You can prepare the filling and sauce a day ahead and assemble the crêpes an hour before baking. —NETTIE

BROCCOLI RABE CRÊPES WITH ITALIAN SAUSAGE

Sweet Italian sausage is the perfect note to balance the slight bitterness of the broccoli rabe in these robust crêpes. For a filling like this one, I like to squeeze the meat out of the casing and then cook it, but if you prefer, you can leave the casing and slice the sausage then cut the slices in half. This will give the filling a chunky texture. The crêpe recipe makes about 20 to 24 crêpes, depending on how long it takes you to get the knack of making the thin, versatile pancakes. Freeze any extra crêpes and use with other savoury or sweet fillings. —PAT

CRÊPES

¾ cup (185 mL) all-purpose flour

1 Tbsp (15 mL) granulated sugar

½ tsp (2 mL) salt

1¼ cups (310 mL) milk

3 large eggs

4 Tbsp (60 mL) melted butter, divided

7-inch (18 cm) crêpe pan or heavy-bottomed skillet

Parchment or waxed paper

BROCCOLI RABE FILLING WITH ITALIAN SAUSAGE

1 lb (500 g) broccoli rabe

3 Tbsp (45 mL) + 1 Tbsp (15 mL) olive oil

4 cloves garlic, chopped

½ tsp (2 mL) dried red chile flakes

1 cup (250 mL) coarsely chopped pecans

2 Tbsp (30 mL) dry breadcrumbs (page 178 for homemade)

5 oz (150 g) Italian sausage, casing removed

BÉCHAMEL SAUCE

¼ cup (60 mL) butter

¼ cup (60 mL) all-purpose flour

2 cups (500 mL) milk or rice milk

½ cup (125 mL) finely grated
Parmesan cheese

½ tsp (2 mL) ground nutmeg

¼ tsp (1 mL) salt

¼ tsp (1 mL) freshly
ground pepper

FOR ASSEMBLING CRÊPES

3 Tbsp (45 mL) dry breadcrumbs
(page 178 for homemade)

1 cup (250 mL) shredded Italian
fontina or mozzarella cheese

¼ cup (60 mL) finely grated
Parmesan cheese

12 crêpes (opposite),
room temperature

Broccoli rabe filling
with Italian sausage (opposite),
room temperature

Béchamel sauce (above),
room temperature

9- × 13-inch (23 × 33 cm) casserole
dish, lightly oiled

8-inch-square (20 cm) baking dish,
lightly oiled

MAKE CRÊPES

Combine flour, sugar, and salt in a bowl. Measure milk into a 2-cup (500 mL) liquid measure and add eggs. Beat together eggs and milk. Add 2 Tbsp (30 mL) melted butter and whisk to combine with milk and eggs.

Pour milk mixture into flour mixture all at once. Whisk with a fork until most of the lumps are gone. Whisk using a wire whisk until batter is smooth. Cover and refrigerate for 1 hour, or overnight. Return to room temperature before cooking crêpes.

Lightly brush crêpe pan with some of remaining melted butter and heat over medium-high heat. Pour batter into hot pan, using a 1 fl oz (30 mL) ladle (or 2 Tbsp/ 30 mL measure). Tip pan to coat bottom with a thin layer of batter. Adjust heat so that pan is hot but won't scorch batter. For a heavy-bottomed pan, once hot, temperature can be lowered to medium-low to low. When crêpe is browned, puffed up, and has pulled away from the sides of the pan, turn it using tongs or your fingers. It should not take more than 1 minute to brown the crêpe—if it does, the pan is not hot enough and batter may stick. Brown other side of crêpe.

Slip crêpe onto a piece of parchment or waxed paper placed over a wire rack to cool. Repeat until batter is finished, brushing pan with melted butter as required and stacking crêpes with parchment or waxed paper in between them.

Crêpes may be made in advance. Wrap crêpes tightly and refrigerate for up to 2 days or wrap tightly, place in an airtight container, and freeze for up to 3 months. When ready to use, remove from refrigerator or freezer and return to room temperature.

MAKE FILLING

Trim and discard woody stem ends of rabe. Blanch rabe by boiling it in a large pot of boiling salted water for 5 minutes. Drain in a colander and rinse with cold water to stop the cooking. Drain and squeeze out liquid. Coarsely chop and set aside.

In a large skillet, heat 3 Tbsp (45 mL) oil over medium-high heat. Add garlic, chile flakes, and pecans. Cook, stirring constantly, for 6 minutes or until lightly golden. Stir in blanched broccoli rabe and cook, tossing to coat with garlic and pecans, for 2 to 3 minutes or until heated through. Set aside ⅔ cup (160 mL).

(continued)

(continued from previous page)

In the same skillet, heat 1 Tbsp (15 mL) oil over medium-high heat. Add sausage and cook, stirring and breaking up meat with back of a wooden spoon, for 5 minutes or until the meat is no longer pink inside. Combine sausage with reserved ⅔ cup (160 mL) rabe filling and stir to mix well. Store in a separate covered container in the refrigerator.

Crêpe filling may be made up to 2 days in advance; return to room temperature when ready to use.

MAKE BÉCHAMEL SAUCE

Heat butter in a heavy-bottomed saucepan over medium-low heat for 1 to 2 minutes, or until foaming subsides. Add flour and cook, whisking constantly, for 3 minutes or until blended into the butter and light golden.

Slowly add milk, whisking constantly, and bring to a simmer. Reduce heat and gently simmer, whisking occasionally, for 5 minutes. Stir in cheese, nutmeg, salt, and pepper and simmer, whisking constantly, for 1 minute or until cheese is completely melted into the sauce.

Sauce may be made up to 2 days in advance. Store in a covered container in the refrigerator and return to room temperature when ready to use.

ASSEMBLE CRÊPES

Preheat the oven to 425°F (220°C). Sprinkle breadcrumbs over bottom of the prepared casserole dish and baking dish. Spoon ¼ cup (60 mL) béchamel sauce over bottom of the larger dish, and 3 Tbsp (45 mL) for the smaller dish (for the meat-filled crêpes). Combine fontina and Parmesan cheeses in a bowl and set aside.

On a clean work surface, lay out and fill one crêpe at a time. Spoon about ⅓ cup (80 mL) of the rabe filling down centre of each crêpe and then fold sides over. Use up all vegetarian filling, reserving 4 crêpes for the meat filling. Working in the same way, fill 4 crêpes with ¼ cup (60 mL) of the rabe and sausage filling. Place filled crêpes, seam side down, in prepared pans in a single layer, separating meat-filled crêpes by placing in smaller dish.

When all crêpes have been assembled, ladle remaining béchamel sauce over crêpes and sprinkle fontina and Parmesan cheeses overtop.

Bake, uncovered, in preheated oven for 20 minutes or until top is bubbling and golden. Let crêpes sit in the pan on a wire cooling rack for 10 to 15 minutes before serving.

BROCCOLI RABE

Broccoli rabe (also known as rapini), considered a leafy green vegetable, is used in Chinese, Italian, and Portuguese cooking. A relative of cauliflower, broccoli, cabbage, and Brussels sprouts, it contains many of the same bitter components as other brassica vegetables.

Make batter

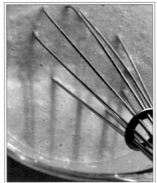

Cook crêpes

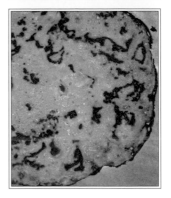

LENTIL MUSHROOM MOUSSAKA

The many fleshy and edible "meaty" types of mushrooms that are now available can make for a very robust, multi-textured casserole. You can use just one variety or a combination of any of the mushrooms listed on page 57. It may seem like a lot of mushrooms, but they will cook down. Add them to the wok in batches; the key is to cook them until they are soft and reduced before adding the next batch. —NETTIE

LENTIL MUSHROOM MOUSSAKA WITH BAKED SALMON

Nettie's moussaka is delicious and filling, making it a perfect meatless main dish. The mushrooms are rich and earthy and complement the nutty taste of the lentils. However, if staunch meat lovers still want their meat, I suggest salmon or trout—rubbed with a dry spice combination, smothered with some of the mushroom sauce, and baked at the same time as the moussaka. I particularly like the Toasted Cumin Dry Rub (page 10) for the fish. —PAT

2 medium-sized eggplants, cut crosswise into ½-inch (1 cm) slices and then peeled

1 cup (250 mL) green lentils, rinsed

3 cups (750 mL) vegetable stock (page 40 for homemade) or water

7 oz (200 g) salmon fillet

2 Tbsp (30 mL) Toasted Cumin Dry Rub (page 10) or ground cumin

1 Tbsp (15 mL) + 2 Tbsp (30 mL) olive oil

4 cloves garlic, minced

2 medium-sized onions, thinly sliced

12 cups (3 L) sliced mushrooms (page 57)

HOMEMADE BREADCRUMBS

For every cup (250 mL) of breadcrumbs required, use three medium-sized slices of white sandwich bread or a 5-inch (12 cm) piece of baguette, bottom crust removed. Tear or coarsely chop bread into 1-inch (2.5 cm) pieces (and toast the bread pieces if you want dry breadcrumbs), then pulse in a food processor until they are fine crumbs. Store in an airtight container in a cool, dry place for up to 2 weeks. Breadcrumbs also freeze well.

½ cup (125 mL) dry red wine
or apple juice

One 5½ oz (156 mL) can
tomato paste

1 Tbsp (15 mL) tamari or soy sauce

½ cup (125 mL) breadcrumbs (dry
or fresh; see sidebar for homemade)

¼ cup (60 mL) chopped fresh basil

¼ cup (60 mL) butter

¼ cup (60 mL) unbleached flour

1¼ cups (310 mL) milk
or plain soymilk

½ cup (125 mL) finely grated
Parmesan cheese

½ tsp (2 mL) salt

¼ tsp (1 mL) freshly ground pepper

Pinch of ground nutmeg

2 rimmed baking sheets, lightly
oiled or parchment-lined

8-inch-square (20 cm) baking pan,
lightly oiled

9- × 13-inch (23 × 33 cm) casserole
dish, lightly oiled

PREHEAT THE OVEN to 350°F (180°C).

Place eggplant slices on prepared baking sheets. Bake in preheated oven for 15 minutes, or until browned. Let pans cool on a wire rack.

Combine lentils and stock in a saucepan. Bring to a boil over high heat. Reduce heat to medium and simmer for 15 minutes, or until tender. Drain in a colander and set aside.

Rub both sides of salmon with cumin rub and let stand for 10 minutes. Brush 1 Tbsp (15 mL) oil over both sides of salmon and place in prepared baking pan.

Heat 2 Tbsp (30 mL) olive oil in a large wok or saucepan over medium heat. Add garlic and onions and sauté for 5 minutes, or until soft. Stir in mushrooms, 2 cups (500 mL) at a time. Cook, stirring constantly, for 3 to 5 minutes or until soft, before adding the next batch of mushrooms. Keep adding mushrooms, cooking and stirring until all of the mushrooms are in the wok. Reduce heat to medium-low and stir in wine, tomato paste, tamari, breadcrumbs, and basil. Simmer, stirring occasionally, for 5 minutes or until sauce

thickens. Spread 1 cup (250 mL) mushroom sauce over salmon fillet and cover baking pan with foil.

Meanwhile, melt butter in a saucepan over medium heat. Whisk in flour and cook, whisking constantly, for 2 minutes or until thickened. Gradually whisk in the milk. Cook, whisking constantly, for 5 minutes or until thickened. Stir in cheese, salt, pepper, and nutmeg. Cook, stirring constantly, for 1 or 2 minutes or until cheese is melted. Set cheese sauce aside.

Cover bottom of prepared casserole dish with all of the baked eggplant slices, layering slices as necessary. Cover with mushroom sauce. Spread cooked lentils evenly over mushroom sauce. Spread cheese sauce smoothly overtop. Cover with foil and bake in preheated oven for 15 minutes. Remove the foil and also add baking pan with salmon to the oven. Bake for 15 minutes, or until vegetarian moussaka is bubbling and golden. Check salmon after 10 minutes and remove if cooked—flesh will turn from translucent to opaque and will flake easily with a fork.

VEGETABLE SHEPHERD'S PIE

I often serve this main course with a leafy green salad. The potato-rutabaga combination is so satisfying that I have yet to see anyone leave the table hungry! —NETTIE

VEGETABLE SHEPHERD'S PIE WITH LAMB KABOBS

The Mediterranean flavour of the stewed vegetables and herbs suggests that lamb would be the complementary meat. Combining herbed ground lamb with an egg yolk ensures the meat will hold together around the skewers. If you have ½-inch-wide (1 cm) flat skewers, you can use one per kabob. If you don't have flat skewers, use two regular skewers to help keep the meat from rotating around the skewer when you turn it. Do not oil metal skewers or soak wooden skewers because this may cause the meat to slip around on the skewer.

It is impossible to use a meat or instant-read thermometer for kabobs, so you have to rely on visuals to gauge doneness. These are done when the outside is browned and the inside is light pink, or, for well done, the pink has disappeared completely. Juices should also run clear. —PAT

LAMB KABOBS

½ onion, coarsely chopped

1 clove garlic

7 oz (200 g) ground lamb

1 tsp (5 mL) Toasted Cumin Dry Rub (page 10) or ground cumin

1 egg yolk

¼ cup (60 mL) dry breadcrumbs (approx) (page 178 for homemade)

VEGETABLE SHEPHERD'S PIE

3 cups (750 mL) cubed potatoes

2 cups (500 mL) cubed rutabaga

2 Tbsp (30 mL) butter

3 Tbsp (45 mL) olive oil, divided

2 cups (500 mL) chopped red onion

5 cloves garlic, minced

1 cup (250 mL) sliced carrots

½ cup (125 mL) white wine or water

1 red bell pepper, sliced

3 stalks celery, sliced

1 cup (250 mL) diced tomato

1 cup (250 mL) fresh or frozen peas

2 cups (500 mL) chopped spinach or kale

RUTABAGA

Rutabaga *(Brassicca napobrassica)* is a large round root vegetable, sometimes referred to as "swede," yellow turnip, or Swedish turnip. The skin is purple with yellow and

some green patches. The inner flesh is orange-yellow. Rutabagas are a good source of vitamin C and fibre, and also contain folate and potassium.

1 Tbsp (15 mL) chopped fresh basil

1 Tbsp (15 mL) fresh thyme leaves

1 tsp (5 mL) paprika

1 tsp (5 mL) hot sauce

1 tsp (5 mL) salt

¼ tsp (1 mL) freshly
ground pepper

Four 10-inch (25 cm) wooden
or metal skewers

11- × 7-inch (28 × 18 cm) casserole
dish, lightly oiled

Baking sheet, lightly oiled

CYNTHIA'S COMMENTS

I must confess to not being a much of a lamb eater. That being said, we supply many friends and family with our traditionally raised lamb, and they adore it. We have done taste tests with many of our restaurant chefs, to compare our local lamb to foreign imports, and our Ontario lamb wins every time. Look for local Ontario lamb—or lamb raised in your area—and I promise that you will be pleasantly surprised.

IN A FOOD processor, pulse onion and garlic until roughly chopped. Add lamb and cumin blend and pulse once to mix. Add the egg yolk and pulse until well blended. Transfer meat mixture to a bowl and add enough breadcrumbs to keep the mixture together. (The mixture should be slightly "sticky.")

Divide meat into 2 equal portions. Lay 2 regular skewers (or one wide flat skewer) on a piece of waxed paper, about ½-inch (1 cm) apart. Flatten and shape one meat portion around the 2 skewers so kabob is about 1 inch (2.5 cm) wide and ¼ inch (6 mm) thick. Repeat process to make the second kabob. Cover kabobs and chill for at least 30 minutes, or overnight.

Preheat the oven to 400°F (200°C). Remove kabobs from refrigerator; bring to room temperature.

Bring a large pot of salted water to a boil over high heat. Add potatoes and rutabaga, cover, and reduce heat to medium-low. Simmer for 20 minutes, or until tender when pierced with the tip of a knife. Reserve ½ cup (125 mL) of the cooking water. Drain well.

Return potatoes and rutabaga to the cooking pot and add butter and half of the reserved cooking water. Whip using electric beaters or mash using a potato masher. Add reserved cooking water, 1 Tbsp (15 mL) at a time, if needed. Set aside.

Heat 2 Tbsp (30 mL) oil in a skillet over medium-high heat. Add onion and garlic and cook, stirring constantly for 5 minutes or until soft. Add carrots and sauté for 2 minutes. Stir in wine and cover. Lower heat to medium and simmer for 4 minutes, or until vegetables are tender-crisp. Transfer vegetables and liquid to a large bowl; set aside.

Heat remaining 1 Tbsp (15 mL) oil in the same skillet over medium heat. Add red pepper and celery and sauté for 3 minutes. Add tomato, peas, and spinach. Cover and reduce heat to medium-low and cook, stirring once or twice, for 5 minutes. Add to bowl with onion-carrot mixture and gently stir to combine. Stir in basil, thyme, paprika, hot sauce, and salt and pepper.

Spoon vegetable mixture into prepared casserole dish. Spoon whipped potato-rutabaga mixture overtop and spread evenly with a spatula. Cover with foil or a lid and bake for 10 minutes. Uncover and bake for 15 minutes or until potatoes are light brown and bubbling. Let sit for 10 minutes. Meanwhile, arrange kabobs on prepared baking sheet. Bake, turning once, in preheated oven for 10 to 15 minutes, or until browned and cooked through.

ROASTED CASHEW CURRY WITH CAULIFLOWER AND PEAS

This rich, aromatic dish combines the smooth flavour of cashews with freshly roasted spices and organic canned tomatoes. Cut vegetables into 1-inch (2.5 cm) pieces for even cooking. (Pictured on the cover.)—NETTIE

ROASTED CASHEW CURRY WITH VEGETABLES AND CHICKEN

You can use leftover baked chicken for this recipe but poaching helps to retain the moisture in the meat. —PAT

POACHED CHICKEN

7 oz (200 g) boneless, skinless chicken breast

½ cup (125 mL) white wine

1 bay leaf

3 sprigs fresh parsley

CURRY CASHEW PASTE

¼ cup (60 mL) salted cashews

2 Tbsp (30 mL) whole coriander seeds

HANDLING HOT CHILE PEPPERS

It's essential to use gloves when handling fresh hot chiles.

The active components that give chiles their heat are the *capsaicinoids*. These irritating elements transfer easily from chiles to your hands, the knife, and the cutting surface—anything with which they come into contact. To avoid painful burning of your eyes or lips, use disposable gloves to prepare hot chiles for recipes.

In their *Big Book of Herbs* (Interweave Press, 2000), Arthur Tucker and Thomas DeBaggio recommend that if you do get capsaicin directly onto your hands, you should actually wash with a small amount of chlorine bleach or ammonia because these household products change the irritants into water-soluble salts. Capsaicin is also alcohol-soluble, so if chiles are burning in your mouth, they claim, "cheap vodka makes a good mouthwash."

Tucker and DeBaggio go on to clear up the misinformation about what parts of the chile pepper are hottest. Some sources claim that the seeds are the hottest part, but this is not quite the case. Tucker and DeBaggio note, "The pure seeds themselves contain none or up to 10 percent of the total capsaicinoids; the heat of the seeds primarily arises from contamination from the placenta." According to these experts, it is the thin inner membrane (called the placenta) on the inside of the chile pepper that holds the highest concentration of the fiery elements, and anything that touches this heat centre will be tainted with the heat of the capsaicinoid essences.

2 tsp (10 mL) whole cumin seeds

½ tsp (2 mL) black peppercorns

½ tsp (2 mL) seeded and minced
fresh green chile, or more to taste

1 cup (250 mL) coarsely
chopped fresh cilantro

½ cup (125 mL) water

VEGETABLES

3 cups (750 mL) cauliflower florets

1 cup (250 mL) diced potato

1 cup (250 mL) sliced green beans

1 cup (250 mL) fresh
or frozen green peas

½ cup (125 mL) diced carrot

2 Tbsp (30 mL) olive oil

1 cup (250 mL) finely
chopped onion

2 cloves garlic, chopped

1 Tbsp (15 mL) finely chopped
fresh ginger

One 28 oz (796 mL) can whole
tomatoes with juice

¼ tsp (1 mL) ground turmeric

¼ tsp (1 mL) salt

1 cup (250 mL) water

2 tsp (10 mL) brown sugar

1 Tbsp (15 mL) fresh lemon juice

POACH CHICKEN BY combining chicken breast, wine, and enough water to cover the chicken in a saucepan. Add bay leaf and parsley. Bring to a boil over high heat. Cover, reduce heat, and gently simmer for 15 to 20 minutes, or until chicken is tender. Drain and let cool enough to handle. (Chicken may be poached the day before, covered, and refrigerated. Bring to room temperature or briefly reheat in the microwave or toaster oven before using.)

To prepare cashew paste, roast the cashews, coriander, cumin, and peppercorns in a small dry skillet over low heat, stirring frequently, for 3 to 5 minutes or until very fragrant. Use a spice grinder or a blender to grind into a smooth powder. If using spice grinder, transfer to a food processor. Add chile, cilantro, and water. Blend to a smooth paste. Set aside. (Covered and refrigerated, this paste keeps well for up to 3 days.)

To prepare the vegetables, bring a large pot of salted water to a boil over high heat. Add cauliflower and potatoes. Partially cover, lower heat to medium-low, and simmer for 8 to 10 minutes or until vegetables are tender. Using tongs or a slotted spoon, transfer potatoes and cauliflower to a colander to drain. Rinse under cold water until cool and then

drain. Transfer to a large bowl and set aside.

To blanch remaining vegetables, bring water in the pot on the stove back to a boil over high heat. Add beans, peas, and carrot. Bring back to a boil over high heat and boil for 1 minute. Immediately drain in a colander. Rinse under cold water until cool and then drain. Add to bowl with potatoes and cauliflower. (If making ahead, cover and refrigerate for up to 3 days.)

In a large skillet, heat oil over medium heat. Add onion and cook, stirring frequently, for 5 minutes or until soft. Stir in garlic and ginger and sauté for 2 minutes. Add tomatoes, turmeric, and salt. Cover, reduce heat to medium-low, and cook, stirring occasionally, for 5 minutes.

Stir in cashew paste and water and cook, stirring constantly, for 1 minute or until hot. Add brown sugar, lemon juice, and prepared vegetables. Bring to a boil over high heat, reduce heat to medium-low or low, and simmer for 5 minutes to blend flavours.

Divide curry into 6 portions and spoon onto plates or into bowls. Cut chicken into strips or cubes. Divide in half and add to 2 plates or bowls. Serve with rice or noodles.

BLACK BEAN CHILLI WITH TOFU

Leftover tofu? Freeze it. Freezing tofu changes its soft texture to a chewy meat-like coarse ingredient (similar to ground chuck). It also increases tofu's sponge-like ability to absorb the flavours of ingredients or spices with which it's cooked, ideal for dishes like these. (See page 185.) —NETTIE

BLACK BEAN CHILLI WITH TOFU AND BEEF

In this recipe, I think of the meat as one more condiment for this delicious chilli. In fact, I'm sure you could completely forgo it because the black and kidney beans combined with the chewy texture of the tofu will satisfy most people's craving for some sort of meat. My advice? Try it Nettie's way first. —PAT

CYNTHIA'S COMMENTS

Not to disagree with Nettie's veggie-loving ways, but . . . the sprinkles of ground beef are a real treat, especially for a meat lover. I consider it the equivalent to adding milk chocolate shavings to a bowl of vanilla ice cream!

2 Tbsp (30 mL) + 1 Tbsp (15 mL) olive oil

1 large red onion, chopped

2 cloves garlic, chopped

1 cup (250 mL) chopped carrots

1 cup (250 mL) chopped red bell pepper

½ cup (125 mL) chopped celery

One 1 lb (500 g) pkg frozen tofu, thawed, squeezed dry, and crumbled (see tofu sidebar)

2 jalapeño peppers, finely chopped, or 1 Tbsp (15 mL) chile powder

Two 28 oz (796 mL) cans diced tomatoes and juice

2 Tbsp (30 mL) chopped fresh oregano

1 Tbsp (15 mL) chopped fresh dill

1 Tbsp (15 mL) Toasted Cumin Dry Rub (page 10) or ground cumin

1 Tbsp (15 mL) paprika

1 tsp (5 mL) salt

½ tsp (2 mL) freshly ground pepper

6 oz (175 g) ground beef

3 Tbsp (45 mL) hot tomato
salsa (store-bought
or Salsa Cruda, page 220)

One 14 oz (398 mL) can black
beans, drained and rinsed

One 14 oz (398 mL) can kidney
beans, drained and rinsed

½ cup (125 mL) chopped
fresh basil

GARNISHES
(Optional)

1 cup (250 mL) chopped
roasted cashews

1 cup (250 mL) hot tomato
salsa (store-bought
or Salsa Cruda, page 220)

1 cup (250 mL) sour cream
or plain yogurt, drained

1 cup (250 mL) shredded
cheddar cheese

HEAT 2 TBSP (30 mL) olive oil in a large wok or saucepan over medium-high heat. Add onion and garlic and sauté for 5 minutes or until soft. Add carrots, red pepper, and celery. Cook, stirring frequently, for 3 minutes. Add tofu, jalapeño peppers, and diced tomatoes with juice. Bring to a boil over high heat and stir in oregano, dill, cumin rub, paprika, salt, and pepper. Reduce heat and simmer, stirring occasionally, for 20 minutes.

Meanwhile, heat 1 Tbsp (15 mL) oil in a skillet over medium-high heat. Add ground beef, stirring and breaking it up with the back of a wooden spoon. Cook for 4 to 6 minutes, or until browned through. Drain off fat. Add salsa and toss to combine with ground beef. Set aside.

Add black beans, kidney beans, and basil to the chilli. Simmer, stirring occasionally for 5 minutes or until heated through. Ladle chilli into bowls. Divide ground beef in half and add to 2 bowls. Pass garnishes separately.

DEFROSTING TOFU
Remove tofu from package, place in a deep bowl, and cover with boiling water. Let stand for 10 minutes, then drain. Rinse with cold water, tear into little pieces, and press firmly between your palms to expel all moisture. Squeeze out the excess liquid as if the tofu were a sponge, then crumble.

CANNELLINI AND CHOCOLATE CHILLI

I love the taste of this spicy, rich white bean chilli. The chocolate chips round out the flavours of this chilli, which is full, satifying, and robust thanks to the protein (tofu) and ground chiles. —NETTIE

CANNELLINI AND CHOCOLATE CHILLI WITH CHICKEN SATAY

If you can slow-char the chicken—that is, grill marinated and skewered chicken strips slowly over gently glowing embers—you should definitely do so. Throughout Thailand, it's the authentic method for cooking the flavourful dish known as satay, and this method really brings out the flavour of the spices in the marinade; but broiling is more convenient and still quite tasty. The chicken satay may be prepared, with its marinade, one day in advance and stored, tightly wrapped, in the refrigerator. The traditional method for satay is to cook and serve the meat skewered. You will need four to six soaked wooden or oiled metal skewers if you prefer it this way, but I have chosen instead to broil the meat without skewers, and I simply add the cooked strips directly to the Chocolate Chilli. You may find it easier to cut thin strips from raw chicken breast if it is slightly frozen. —PAT

CHICKEN SATAY

4 to 6 oz (125 to 175 g) skinless, boneless chicken breast

1 clove garlic, crushed

1 tsp (5 mL) ground ancho or chipotle chile (see sidebar)

¼ tsp (1 mL) ground cumin

¼ tsp (1 mL) ground cinnamon

1 tsp (5 mL) granulated sugar

1 Tbsp (15 mL) tamari or soy sauce

1 Tbsp (15 mL) fresh lemon juice

2 tsp (10 mL) toasted sesame oil

GROUND CHILE PEPPERS

Toast 1 large dried chile in a hot dry pan for a minute on each side. Let cool and then grind in a spice grinder. Store remaining ground pepper in a sealed container in a dry, dark, cool place.

CANNELLINI AND CHOCOLATE CHILLI

¼ cup (60 mL) olive oil

6 cloves garlic, minced

1 large red onion, diced

8 oz (250 g) frozen tofu, thawed, squeezed dry, and crumbled (sidebar, page 185)

1 red bell pepper, thinly sliced

1 yellow bell pepper, thinly sliced

1 green bell pepper, thinly sliced

1 cup (250 mL) diced celery

1 tsp (5 mL) ground cumin

2 bay leaves

2 tsp (10 mL) ground ancho or ground chipotle chile (see sidebar)

One 2-inch (5 cm) stick cinnamon

One 28 oz (796 mL) can crushed tomatoes

2 tsp (10 mL) tamari or soy sauce

One 14 oz (398 mL) can cannellini beans, drained and rinsed

2 Tbsp (30 mL) chocolate chips

¼ cup (60 mL) chopped fresh cilantro, for garnishing

Rimmed baking sheet, lightly oiled

CUT THIN SLICES of chicken equal to the length of the chicken breast. The strips will be approximately ¼ inch (6 mm) wide, 1 inch (2.5 cm) thick (the thickness of the breast), and 4 inches (10 cm) long.

In a large bowl, using a pestle or fork, mash garlic, ground chile, cumin, cinnamon, and sugar together. Add tamari, lemon juice, and sesame oil and stir to form a thick paste. Add the chicken strips to the bowl and toss to coat with paste. Cover and marinate in the refrigerator for at least 2 hours, or up to 24 hours.

Heat oil in a wok or large frying pan over medium heat. Add garlic and onion and stir-fry for 8 to 10 minutes, or until lightly browned. Add tofu, bell peppers, celery, cumin, bay leaves, ground chile, and cinnamon stick. Stir-fry for 10 minutes.

Remove chicken from the refrigerator, stir, and let return to room temperature.

Add crushed tomatoes, tamari, and beans to the wok. Increase heat and bring to a boil and stir in chocolate chips. Reduce heat and simmer, stirring frequently, for 15 minutes or until vegetables are tender and chocolate is melted.

Preheat the oven to Broil (500°F/ 260°C) and move the oven rack to the top position. Place chicken strips in one layer on prepared baking sheet. Spoon or brush any remaining marinade overtop strips.

Broil chicken strips on top shelf of preheated oven for 2 minutes. Turn strips using tongs and broil for 2 minutes more, or until chicken is opaque and juices run clear when pierced with a knife. Set aside.

Ladle chilli into 6 bowls. Add chicken satay strips to 2 bowls. Divide cilantro into 6 equal portions and garnish bowls.

GRAINS

VEGETABLE CHILLI WITH WHOLE SPELT

Red kidney beans are most often used in chilli; however, any legume such as black-eyed peas, lima beans, or even chickpeas may be substituted. —NETTIE

VEGETABLE CHILLI WITH SPELT AND CHICKEN DRUMSTICKS

Chicken drumsticks are always popular with both children and adults, but chicken thighs and breasts will work just as well with this dish. You will need to be the judge as to the size of the drumsticks and the size of your meat eaters' appetites. I usually allow two drumsticks per person and cook and serve them with the bone in. —PAT

1 Tbsp (15 mL) olive oil

2 large onions, coarsely chopped

3 cloves garlic, chopped

1 eggplant, coarsely chopped

1 Tbsp (15 mL) chile powder, or to taste

1 tsp (5 mL) Toasted Cumin Dry Rub (page 10) or ground cumin

1 tsp (5 mL) dried chipotle flakes, ground chipotle (sidebar, page 186), or dried red chile flakes

1 tsp (5 mL) ground coriander

One 28 oz (796 mL) can crushed tomatoes

3 Tbsp (45 mL) pomegranate molasses (or Pomegranate Glaze, page 8) or date molasses

1 Tbsp (15 mL) tamari or soy sauce

Salt and freshly ground pepper, to taste

2 to 4 chicken drumsticks (see recipe introduction), skin removed

1 cup (250 mL) cooked whole spelt kernels (see sidebar)

One 10 oz (300 g) pkg frozen corn kernels, thawed

One 19 oz (540 mL) can red kidney beans, drained and rinsed

TO COOK SPELT KERNELS

The night before making the chilli, cover ½ cup (125 mL) spelt kernels with water. Cover bowl and place in refrigerator overnight. Drain and rinse well. Bring 1 cup (250 mL) water or stock to a boil. Stir in the soaked spelt. Cover and reduce heat to low. Simmer for 40 to 60 minutes, or until tender (spelt will remain chewy). Makes 1 cup (250 mL) cooked spelt.

CYNTHIA'S COMMENTS

Despite Pat's recommendation, I have to say I prefer leaving the skin on the drumsticks. I bring up this adage again: "Food without fat is like life without love." Just choose your fat wisely!

HEAT OIL IN a large saucepan over medium heat. Add onions and garlic and cook, stirring frequently, for 5 to 7 minutes or until softened and golden brown. Stir in eggplant, chile powder, cumin rub, chipotle flakes, and coriander and cook, stirring frequently, for 5 minutes or until eggplant is soft.

Stir in tomatoes, pomegranate molasses, tamari, salt, and pepper, and bring to a boil over high heat. Transfer 2½ cups (625 mL) chilli to a separate smaller saucepan for the meat portions. Partially cover, reduce heat, and simmer chilli, stirring occasionally, for 20 to 30 minutes or until sauce thickens.

Make 2 to 3 slashes in the flesh of each drumstick and add to the smaller saucepan with the chilli. Partially cover and cook over medium heat, stirring occasionally, for 20 to 25 minutes or until chicken pulls away from the bone and juices run clear.

Combine spelt, corn, and kidney beans in a bowl. Add to chilli: two-thirds to vegetarian version, one-third to meat version. Cover and cook chilli for about 5 minutes more to heat through.

RICE WITH LENTILS AND GREENS

Tuscan kale is my favourite—it has such a rich colour, a dark green. Use the small French green lentils as they will retain their shape and provide a nice contrast to the brown rice. Lentils are high in protein and iron and are fat free. —NETTIE

PARMESAN LAMB CHOPS WITH RICE, LENTILS, AND GREENS

I am suggesting lamb rib chops as the accompaniment to the nutty flavours of brown rice, lentils, greens, and mushrooms—a robust combination on their own. You could also use thin pork chops, chicken legs, or boneless pork medallions instead. Lamb rib chops are small, so two chops are considered a single serving. Bake the meat in the oven while the lentils and rice are cooking—there is lots of time. —PAT

CYNTHIA'S COMMENTS

Lamb on the bone is a favourite with many of my friends. When buying any meat with the bone still attached, the value for your dollar is greater: you will be spending less per pound as well as adding flavour to your dishes—meat is always tastier with the bone attached. You can also use the bones afterwards to make a great stock.

TIP

For perfectly done lamb chops, use an instant-read thermometer placed in the centre of the meat but not touching the bone, and consult the doneness chart at right.

5 cups (1.25 L) vegetable stock (page 40 for homemade) or water, divided

1 cup (250 mL) brown rice, rinsed

2 bay leaves

1 cup (250 mL) chopped fresh flat-leaf parsley

4 lamb rib chops

1 large egg, beaten in a shallow dish

Salt and pepper, for seasoning

1½ cups (375 mL) breadcrumbs (dry or fresh; see page 178 for homemade)

¼ cup (60 mL) finely grated Parmesan cheese

2 cups (500 mL) lentils, rinsed

¼ cup (60 mL) olive oil

1 cup (250 mL) thinly
sliced red onion

2 cloves garlic, minced

1 cup (250 mL) thinly sliced cremini
or button mushrooms

½ tsp (2 mL) salt

⅛ tsp (0.5 mL) freshly
ground pepper

2 cups (500 mL) finely
chopped Tuscan kale

¼ cup (60 mL) finely
grated Parmesan cheese

½ cup (125 mL) chopped
fresh basil, for garnishing

Rimmed baking sheet, lightly oiled

PREHEAT THE OVEN to 350°F (180°C).

Bring 2 cups (500 mL) of the stock to a boil over high heat in a medium saucepan. Stir in rice, bay leaves, and parsley. Cover, reduce heat, and simmer for 40 minutes, or until rice is tender. Stir with a fork and set aside.

Lightly flatten chops with the side of a cleaver or meat pounder and then dip in the beaten egg. Season with salt and pepper. Combine breadcrumbs and ¼ cup (60 mL) cheese in a shallow dish or pie plate. Coat both sides of chops with breadcrumb mixture. Again dip in egg and coat with breadcrumb mixture. Arrange on prepared baking sheet.

Bake lamb chops in preheated oven for 25 to 45 minutes, depending on the degree of doneness you prefer—see chart. When lamb is cooked, remove from oven, cover, and set aside until vegetables are ready.

Meanwhile, combine lentils and remaining stock in a saucepan. Bring to a boil over high heat. Reduce heat and simmer for 15 minutes, or until tender. Drain in a colander, rinse with cool water, and set aside.

Heat oil in a large skillet or saucepan over medium heat. Add onion and cook, stirring frequently, for 5 minutes or until soft. Add garlic, mushrooms, and salt and pepper. Cook, stirring frequently, for 5 minutes or until mushrooms are soft and release their liquids.

Add kale and cook, stirring and tossing, for 3 to 5 minutes or until wilted. If mixture seems too dry, add up to ¼ cup (60 mL) water. Stir in cooked lentils and brown rice. Cook, stirring constantly, for 1 to 3 minutes or until heated through. Stir Parmesan cheese into the mixture or use as a garnish on top. Serve immediately with lamb chops on the side for the meat portions. Garnish with basil.

DONENESS TEMPERATURES FOR LAMB	
Medium-Rare	145°F (63°C)
Medium	160°F (71°C)
Well Done	170°F (77°C)

PAELLA WITH TEMPEH AND SEITAN SERVED IN ROASTED SQUASH

A great protein-packed main-dish substitute for a traditional turkey. Serve with your usual mashed potatoes and other vegetables. If serving more than six people, this recipe is easily doubled. Use canned olives and bottled capers so that you will have the liquid required for this recipe. Tempeh, arame, and seitan are sold in most health food stores. —NETTIE

PAELLA WITH TURKEY AND TEMPEH SERVED IN ROASTED SQUASH

I love this paella for two reasons. First, it makes a fabulous holiday dish. If you make the vegetarian version, vegetarians can eat this as their main course while those who still want roast turkey can enjoy the stuffed squash as a vegetable side, keeping their traditions firmly in place. Or you can add ground turkey or boneless, skinless turkey strips to the paella as instructed if your meat-eater friends and family are open to the idea of a completely new turkey dinner! Second, I love this recipe because it offers a fabulous way to use leftover, cooked holiday turkey. To make an all-meat version of the paella to serve six, substitute 3 cups (750 mL) cubed cooked turkey for the seitan. —PAT

ARAME

Arame is a mild-flavoured, thinly sliced sea vegetable sold in dried form. It resembles black angel-hair pasta.

SEITAN

Seitan is derived from isolated strips of gluten, the protein found in wheat. Gluten absorbs the flavours it is cooked with, and it is chewy, unlike tofu, which is soft and creamy.

Three 1½ lb (750 g) acorn squashes

3 Tbsp (45 mL) + 2 Tbsp (30 mL) olive oil, divided

2 tsp (10 mL) tamari or soy sauce

2 Tbsp (30 mL) water

8 oz (250 g) tempeh, cut into ¼-inch (6 mm) dice

2 tsp (10 mL) sesame seeds

½ onion, sliced into ¼-inch (6 mm) slices

2 cloves garlic, chopped

½ red bell pepper, cut into ¼-inch (6 mm) strips

½ yellow bell pepper, cut into ¼-inch (6 mm) strips

2 stalks celery, chopped

1 large tomato, seeded and cut into wedges

One 6 oz (170 mL) jar artichoke hearts, drained and coarsely chopped

1 tsp (5 mL) salt, divided

¼ cup (60 mL) sliced pitted
olives, drained, 2 tsp (10 mL)
brine reserved

⅓ cup (80 mL) arame

1 Tbsp (15 mL) drained capers,
1 Tbsp (15 mL) brine reserved

½ tsp (2 mL) chile powder

½ tsp (2 mL) hot sauce

½ tsp (2 mL) freshly ground pepper

4 oz (125 g) plain seitan,
juice squeezed out and reserved,
coarsely chopped

8 oz (250 g) ground turkey or
skinless, boneless turkey strips

9- × 13-inch (23 × 33 cm)
baking pan

Rimmed baking sheet, lightly oiled

TIP

Vegetable- and meat-filled squash halves may be made a day in advance and reheated in a casserole dish covered tightly with foil. Bake in a 350°F (180°C) oven for 40 minutes, or until heated through.

PREHEAT THE OVEN to 375°F (190°C).

Cut squashes in half. Using a large spoon, scrape out seeds and fibrous flesh. Arrange in baking pan, cut sides up. If some of the squash halves don't sit straight, trim a thin slice from their bottom ends. Pour hot water into the pan to a depth of 1 inch (2.5 cm). Cover pan tightly with foil. Bake in preheated oven for 30 to 40 minutes, or until squash is cooked on the inside but firm on the outside. Turn the oven down to 350°F (180°C).

Meanwhile, make paella by first preparing the tempeh. Combine 1 Tbsp (15 mL) oil, tamari, and water in a large bowl. Add tempeh, stir, and let sit for 5 minutes to marinate. Spread tempeh in a single layer on prepared baking sheet. Drizzle marinade mixture overtop and sprinkle with sesame seeds. Bake uncovered in preheated oven for 10 minutes.

Heat 2 Tbsp (30 mL) oil in a large saucepan over medium heat. Add onion and garlic and sauté for 5 minutes, or until soft. Add bell peppers and celery. Sauté for 8 minutes, or until soft. Add tomato,

artichoke hearts, and ½ tsp (2 mL) salt. Cover, reduce heat, and simmer, stirring occasionally, for 8 minutes.

Add olives, olive brine, arame, capers, caper brine, chile powder, hot sauce, pepper, and baked tempeh. Simmer uncovered, stirring occasionally, for 15 minutes. Paella should be thick. Taste and add remaining ½ tsp (2 mL) salt if desired. Remove 2 cups (500 mL) paella for the meat portions. Add seitan and seitan juice to the pot and heat through.

Meanwhile, heat 2 Tbsp (30 mL) oil in a skillet over medium-high heat. Add turkey and brown, stirring constantly and breaking up the meat with a wooden spoon, for 5 minutes, or until cooked through with no pink showing. Add reserved paella to the skillet and cook for 1 to 2 minutes more, stirring and tossing to mix well.

Spoon seitan paella into the cavities of the baked squash halves, reserving 2 squash halves for the turkey paella. Divide the turkey paella in half and spoon into the cavities of 2 baked squash halves. Pass any extra paella separately at the table.

MUSHROOM BUCKWHEAT BURGERS WITH CASHEW BUTTER

Coating the kasha grain with egg and toasting it before simmering allows it to retain its distinct texture. These burgers are delicious served open-faced on dark rye bread. Toasted sesame oil is added to the burger mixture for its flavour; you can also use it in place of the olive oil to cook the onions, mushrooms, and other vegetables. —NETTIE

BACON-WRAPPED MUSHROOM BUCKWHEAT BURGERS WITH CASHEW BUTTER

Wrapping these vegetarian burgers with crisp bacon gives them an authentic diner look and taste without introducing ground meat to the recipe. Because the ingredients in the mushroom burgers are already cooked, the bacon should be cooked too. Do not preheat the pan when cooking bacon, as adding bacon to a hot grill or pan can cause the bacon to stick and curl more than necessary. Cook over medium to medium-high heat to allow the fat to melt and the meat to brown and crisp. Bacon fat will spit and burn in a pan over high heat. —PAT

1 large egg

1½ cups (375 mL) kasha
(buckwheat groats)

2 cups (500 mL) boiling water

1 tsp (5 mL) salt

⅛ tsp (0.5 mL) freshly
ground pepper

1½ cups (375 mL) diced sweet
potatoes (½-inch/1 cm dice)

3 Tbsp (45 mL) olive oil, divided

1 cup (250 mL) diced onion

1 cup (250 mL) thinly sliced
button mushrooms

1 stalk celery, finely chopped

1 carrot, shredded

¼ cup (60 mL) cashew butter
or almond butter

2 Tbsp (30 mL) chopped
fresh basil or parsley

1 Tbsp (15 mL) toasted sesame oil

1 Tbsp (15 mL) tamari or soy sauce

2 slices side bacon or turkey bacon
(sidebar, page 199)

Rimmed baking sheet, lightly oiled

(continued)

(continued from previous page)

LIGHTLY BEAT EGG in a bowl. Add kasha and stir until well coated. Heat a dry, heavy-bottomed saucepan over medium-high heat. Add egg-coated kasha and toast, stirring constantly, over medium-low heat for 3 to 4 minutes until the grains begin to separate, darken, and give off a toasted aroma.

Add boiling water, salt, and pepper. Cover, reduce heat, and simmer for 10 to 12 minutes, or until most of the water is absorbed. Remove from heat and let stand for 10 minutes or until ready to add to the potatoes.

Steam sweet potatoes in a steamer basket over a pot of boiling water for 5 minutes, or until soft when pierced with the tip of a knife. Discard water from the pot and rinse the sweet potatoes under cool water to stop the cooking. Return potatoes to the pot and mash using a potato masher. Set aside.

Heat 2 Tbsp (30 mL) of the olive oil in a skillet over medium-high heat. Cook onion, stirring frequently, for 3 minutes or until softened. Add mushrooms and cook, stirring frequently, for 3 minutes. Add remaining 1 Tbsp (15 mL) olive oil, celery, and carrot and cook for 5 minutes, or until vegetables are tender.

Add cooked kasha to the mashed sweet potatoes in the pot. Add sautéed vegetables, nut butter, basil, sesame oil, and tamari.

When cool enough to handle, use your hands to form patties and place on prepared baking sheet. To yield 6 large patties of equal size (3-inch/8 cm patties about 1 inch/2.5 cm thick), use a 1-cup (250 mL) dry measure to lightly scoop the mixture. For each patty, slightly underfill the cup (loosely packed), and then press the mixture into a solid patty and place on prepared baking sheet. (Burgers may be made ahead to this point, tightly covered, and refrigerated for up to 2 days. Bring to room temperature before baking.)

Preheat the oven to Broil (500°F/260°C) and move oven rack to top position.

Arrange bacon slices on an unheated grill pan or skillet in one layer, without touching. Cook, turning once or twice, over medium-high heat for 3 to 5 minutes, or until bacon is browned and crisp. Transfer to a paper towel–lined plate to drain.

Wrap 2 burgers each with one slice of cooked bacon. Brown burgers on baking sheet, under the broiler for 3 to 5 minutes, or until crisp and lightly browned.

FLAVOUR PROFILE

Toasting the kasha (buckwheat) brings out more of the nutty flavour of the grain. When combined with the earthiness of the mushrooms, the sweet flavour and dense texture of the sweet potatoes, the smoky-toasted nuttiness of the sesame oil, and the rich, oak-brewed salty taste of the tamari, the result is something complex, rich, and deeply satisfying.

CYNTHIA'S COMMENTS

Bacon is one of my favourite meat items. It adds that extra WOW of flavour to any dish such as the one here; it's great for breakfast; and it's wonderful in simple pasta dishes and in vegetable dishes such as with kale. I use our Beretta Bacon a lot when I cook—bacon is simply amazing.

TOASTING KASHA

Kasha (buckwheat groats) is one of the quickest-cooking whole grains—15 minutes tops versus over an hour for spelt and wheat berries. If left too long in simmering water, though, kasha will become soft and mushy. One way to keep the individual grains intact during cooking is to toast them first.

1. For each 1½ cups (375 mL) uncooked kasha, beat 1 large egg in a bowl using a fork. Add the kasha and whisk to coat each grain with egg.

2. Heat a dry, heavy-bottomed saucepan over medium-high heat. Add egg-coated kasha to the hot pan. Reduce heat to medium-low and toast, stirring constantly, for 3 to 4 minutes until the grains begin to separate, darken slightly, and give off a toasted aroma. Once the egg and grains are in the hot pan, be sure to turn the heat down to medium or low. Stir using a fork to scrape up the excess egg bits that congeal on the bottom of the pan. If you are using a heavy-bottomed pan, the heat should toast the grains in about 3 minutes.

3. The grains should not stick to the bottom of the pan if the heat is low enough. Keep stirring until the individual grains start to pop on the bottom of the pan when the fork clears a path. The grains should be lightly browned but not smoking or dark brown. Toasting kasha using

this technique seals the outside of the grain and prevents it from absorbing too much liquid and becoming mushy. As a result, you will need less liquid to cook toasted kasha: 2 cups (500 mL) boiling water for every 1½ cups (375 mL) egg-toasted kasha.

TURKEY BACON

Look closely at the bacon cooking on the grill in the photo. Those white streaks aren't fat, they're white turkey meat, which is one of the main reasons for choosing turkey bacon over pork bacon—it's low in saturated fat. Look for brands that are nitrate free. Cook turkey bacon as you would pork bacon: on a grill pan or in a skillet over medium-high heat, turning once or twice. You will notice that there will be no excess fat accumulating in the pan or on the grill. Turkey bacon will brown as pork bacon does, but will not shrivel or become quite as crisp as pork bacon.

TORTILLA LASAGNA WITH PORTOBELLO AND GREENS

By combining two popular recipes—lasagna and tortillas—you have basic components that everyone enjoys. It has a velvety texture and is baked in a springform pan, a main course that's a welcome break from noodles. What a delicious way to eat your greens. —NETTIE

TORTILLA LASAGNA WITH BAKED PORK CHOP

Baking the pork with some of the tomato sauce keeps the meat moist and fork-tender. It can go in the oven after the lasagna has been cooking for 20 minutes, so that both are ready at the same time. You can use either boneless or bone-in pork chops, but because this is baked, the meat will be more tender if cooked on the bone. —PAT

CYNTHIA'S COMMENTS

Attention to detail when cooking pork is essential. Overcooked pork is dried out completely and isn't much fun to eat. For moist and tender pork chops, cook to an internal temperature of 160°F (71°C), although I usually remove them from the heat at 150°F (66°C) and cover them in order to let them finish cooking.

2 Tbsp (30 mL) olive oil

4 cloves garlic, chopped

1 large onion, thinly sliced

1 cup (250 mL) sliced portobello mushrooms

1 lb (500 g) Swiss chard or kale, tender stems sliced thin and leaves chopped

Two 28 oz (796 mL) cans crushed tomatoes

2 Tbsp (30 mL) chopped fresh oregano

½ tsp (2 mL) salt

¼ tsp (1 mL) freshly ground pepper

½ cup (125 mL) chiffonade of fresh basil (page 133)

2 cups (500 mL) cottage cheese

1 egg, slightly beaten

Eight 6-inch (15 cm) soft
corn tortillas

1⅓ cups (330 mL) shredded
mozzarella cheese, divided

1 Tbsp (15 mL) + ¼ cup (60 mL)
finely grated Parmesan cheese,
divided

10 oz (300 g) bone-in pork chop,
1 inch (2.5 cm) thick

2 Tbsp (30 mL) Toasted Cumin
Dry Rub (page 10)
or ground cumin (optional)

10-inch (25 cm) springform pan,
lightly oiled

8-inch-square (20 cm) baking dish,
lightly oiled

PREHEAT THE OVEN to 375°F (190°C).

Heat oil in a large pot or wok over medium-high heat. Add garlic and onion and cook, stirring often, for 5 minutes or until softened. Add mushrooms and sauté for 3 minutes. Stir in the chard. Cover, reduce heat, and cook, stirring occasionally, over medium-low heat for 5 minutes. Transfer mushroom-chard mixture to a bowl and set aside.

Pour crushed tomatoes into the large pot or wok. Add oregano, salt, and pepper. Simmer, stirring occasionally, over medium heat for 20 minutes. Stir in basil and cook for 2 minutes. Remove pot from the heat, removing 1½ cups (375 mL) of the tomato sauce for the meat portions.

Combine cottage cheese and egg in a medium-sized bowl and set aside.

Spread 1 cup (250 mL) tomato sauce over the bottom of prepared springform pan. Trim a 2-inch-wide (5 cm) strip off one tortilla. Arrange the two cut pieces of this tortilla and a second whole tortilla to create a single layer overtop the sauce. Spread ⅔ cup (160 mL) cottage cheese-egg mixture over tortillas. Cover cottage cheese with ¾ cup (185 mL) tomato sauce. Spread ⅓ cup (80 mL) of the mushroom-chard mixture over tomato sauce using a slotted spoon to eliminate excess liquid. Sprinkle with ⅓ cup (80 mL) mozzarella cheese and 1 Tbsp (15 mL) Parmesan cheese. Repeat this layering twice, placing remaining tortillas on top. Cover with foil and place in preheated oven.

Meanwhile, prepare pork chop. Rub spice blend (if using) over both sides of pork and place chop in prepared dish. Cover with reserved tomato sauce and then cover pan with foil. After lasagna has been in the oven for 10 minutes, add pork chop to the oven and cook for 30 minutes, or until a meat thermometer inserted into the thickest part of the meat, not touching the bone, reaches 160°F (71°C) (or see Cynthia's comments). Keep warm until lasagna is ready to serve.

After 30 minutes, remove foil from lasagna. Sprinkle remaining mozzarella and Parmesan cheese evenly overtop. Bake uncovered for 10 minutes more, or until top is brown and cheese is melted.

Let stand for 5 minutes. Remove springform pan sides and cut lasagna into 6 wedges. Cut meat off the bone and divide in half to serve 2 people.

FOR KIDS

GRILLED FRUIT KABOBS
WITH GUAVA LIME GLAZE

In this recipe, grilling the fruit allows their natural sugars to provide most of the flavour. You can prepare these delicious kabobs indoors with grilling appliances or outdoors on a gas or charcoal grill. Find guava juice in Latin and Asian groceries, or in the ethnic section of supermarkets—it really brings out the sweetness of the fruit. An easy dessert for any time of year. —NETTIE

PREHEAT THE GRILL to medium-high.

Stir together oil, 2 Tbsp (30 mL) lime juice, and cinnamon in a bowl.

Place fruit on each skewer in this order: apple, plum, banana, pear, peach, pineapple, apple, plum, banana, pear, peach, pineapple. Brush kabobs with oil mixture and place on grill rack. Grill, turning often, for 6 to 8 minutes or until fruit begins to brown. Baste grilled fruit with Guava Lime Glaze before serving.

GUAVA LIME GLAZE

MAKES: ¾ cup (185 mL)

BRING GUAVA JUICE to a boil in a medium-sized saucepan over medium-high heat. Reduce heat to low and simmer for 1 hour or until juice is reduced to ½ cup (125 mL). Let cool and add lime juice. Use a basting brush to coat grilled fruit kabobs before serving.

2 Tbsp (30 mL) olive oil

2 Tbsp (30 mL) fresh lime juice

1 tsp (5 mL) ground cinnamon

2 firm apples, each cut into 8 cubes

2 medium-sized firm-fleshed plums, each cut into 8 pieces

2 ripe bananas, each cut into 8 chunks

2 firm pears (such as Bartletts), each cut into 8 cubes

2 fresh firm-fleshed peaches, each cut into 8 pieces

Sixteen 1-inch (2.5 cm) chunks pineapple (fresh, or canned and drained)

½ cup (125 mL) Guava Lime Glaze

Eight 10-inch (25 cm) wooden or metal skewers (if using wooden skewers, be sure to soak them in water for 30 minutes beforehand to prevent scorching)

GUAVA LIME GLAZE

3 cups (750 mL) guava juice or peach nectar

¼ cup (60 mL) fresh lime juice

USING A STOVETOP GRILL

Use a cast iron or heavy grilling pan to grill kabobs indoors on a stovetop. Heat the grilling pan to sizzling hot over medium-high heat. Once grilling pan is hot, reduce heat to medium-low. Place skewers on the grill and cook for 12 minutes, turning the skewers as the fruit browns.

MAKES: 12 pizzas | 8 veggie + 4 meat pizzas (if using chicken)

1 Tbsp (15 mL) olive oil

6 oz (175 g) ground chicken

6 pita pockets, each split into
2 rounds

1 cup (250 mL) tomato sauce
(page 159 for homemade)

2 cups (500 mL) shredded
mozzarella cheese

¼ cup (60 mL) chopped fresh basil

1 cup (250 mL) shredded carrot

1 cup (250 mL) thinly sliced
red bell pepper

1 cup (250 mL) thinly sliced
fresh shiitake mushrooms

2 cups (500 mL) cherry tomatoes,
halved

1 cup (250 mL) pitted olives
(black or green), thinly sliced

1 red onion, thinly sliced

1 medium-sized zucchini,
thinly sliced into rounds

1 cup (250 mL) finely grated
Parmesan cheese

2 rimmed baking sheets

PITA PIZZA

The perfect flex recipe! Gather a bunch of toppings and let everyone assemble their own pizza by letting them choose their favourite ingredients. There are so many topping options, including sliced Tempeh Sausage rounds (page 206).
—NETTIE

PITA PIZZA WITH GROUND CHICKEN

I prefer using ground chicken and also organic bacon for pizza to using nitrate- and nitrite-laced cured meats. Ground Pork Patties (page 206) make another great topping option for these fun and kid-friendly pizzas. —PAT

HEAT OIL IN a skillet over medium-high heat. Add ground chicken, stirring and breaking it up with the back of a wooden spoon. Cook for 4 to 6 minutes, or until browned through. Drain off fat and set aside.

Preheat the oven to Broil (500°F/260°C) and move oven rack to top position.

Arrange pita rounds in one layer on baking sheets. Spread tomato sauce evenly over 12 pita rounds.

Sprinkle mozzarella evenly overtop each round.

Divide and spread cooked chicken evenly overtop 4 tomato-cheese topped pita rounds. Top all pitas with basil, carrot, red pepper, mushrooms, cherry tomatoes, olives, red onion, and zucchini. Sprinkle Parmesan cheese evenly overtop each pita round. Broil for 5 minutes, or until cheese is bubbling and vegetables are golden.

EVERYDAY FLEXITARIAN ∘ 205

TEMPEH SAUSAGES

This is a very versatile recipe. I prefer to roll the mixture into a log, wrap it in plastic, and slice off pieces as required. Serve with sautéed onions and mushrooms, tofu scramble, or plain apple-sauce. Noble Bean Tempeh from Perth, Ontario (www.noblebean .ca) makes an excellent-quality three-grain tempeh. Serve with Herbed Basmati Rice (page 94) as shown in the photo. — NETTIE

GROUND PORK PATTIES

The same spice blend is used for both the pork patties and the tempeh sausages, so you can measure them at the same time in separate small bowls. Roll the meat into a log as directed for the tempeh sausages, or scoop out 2 Tbsp (30 mL) portions and flatten them between your palms prior to frying. — PAT

TEMPEH SAUSAGES

One 8 oz (250 g) pkg tempeh (I like
to use 3-grain), thawed

2 Tbsp (30 mL) whole wheat flour

1 egg, lightly beaten

1 clove garlic, minced

2 tsp (10 mL) brown sugar

1 tsp (5 mL) ground sage

½ tsp (2 mL) dried rosemary

½ tsp (2 mL) ground nutmeg

½ tsp (2 mL) ground cardamom

¼ tsp (1 mL) ground allspice

¼ tsp (1 mL) chile powder

½ tsp (2 mL) salt

¼ tsp (1 mL) freshly ground pepper

¼ cup (60 mL) olive oil

(continued)

(continued from previous page)

SLICE TEMPEH INTO 1-inch-wide (2.5 cm) slices. Place in bamboo basket or stainless steel steamer. Cover and steam for 15 minutes.

Meanwhile, prepare the pork patties. Combine ground pork, breadcrumbs, egg, garlic, sage, rosemary, nutmeg, cardamom, allspice, chile powder, salt, and pepper. Add additional bread-crumbs if the mixture is too wet. Cover and refrigerate for at least 1 hour or up to 8 hours.

Transfer tempeh to a medium-sized bowl and mash using a fork or potato masher. Stir in flour. Add egg, garlic, brown sugar, sage, rosemary, nutmeg, cardamom, allspice, chile powder, salt, and pepper and mix well.

Lay a long piece of plastic wrap or parchment paper out on a work surface. Scrape the sausage ingredients into the centre of the plastic. Bring up the long ends and roll the ingredients into a cylinder shape that is about 1¼ inches (3 cm) in diameter. Wrap tightly, twisting the ends to seal, and use immediately or refrigerate for up to 3 days.

If refrigerated, bring tempeh sausage back to room tempera-ture. Cut into 1-inch (2.5 cm) slices. Form refrigerated pork mixture into 2-inch (5 cm) patties.

Heat ¼ cup (60 mL) oil in a skillet over medium-high heat. Add sausage slices and cook, in batches, in one layer in the pan. Fry for 1 to 2 minutes, turn, and fry on the remaining side for 1 to 2 minutes or until reddish-brown.

At the same time, fry ground pork patties in a separate pan. Heat 2 Tbsp (30 mL) oil in another skillet over medium heat. Add patties and fry in batches for 4 to 6 minutes, or until golden brown on the underside. Flip and fry on the other side for 3 to 5 minutes or until reddish-brown.

Drain on a paper towel–lined plate.

GROUND PORK PATTIES

8 oz (250 g) ground pork

2 Tbsp (30 mL) dry breadcrumbs (approx) (see page 178 for homemade)

1 egg, lightly beaten

1 clove garlic, minced

½ tsp (2 mL) ground sage

¼ tsp (1 mL) dried rosemary

¼ tsp (1 mL) ground nutmeg

¼ tsp (1 mL) ground cardamom

¼ tsp (1 mL) ground allspice

¼ tsp (1 mL) chile powder

¼ tsp (1 mL) salt

Pinch of freshly ground pepper

2 Tbsp (30 mL) olive oil

1½ cups (375 mL) vegetable stock
(page 40 for homemade)

¾ cup (185 mL) quinoa, rinsed

One 14 oz (398 mL) can
cooked chickpeas, drained

2 Tbsp (30 mL) tahini
or cashew butter

2 Tbsp (30 mL) fresh lemon juice

½ tsp (2 mL) ground cumin

¼ tsp (1 mL) cayenne pepper

⅛ tsp (0.5 mL) freshly
ground pepper

¼ cup (60 mL) chopped
fresh cilantro

1 clove garlic, chopped

2 green onions, chopped,
for garnishing

QUINOA HUMMUS

Cook this quinoa using a good-quality vegetable broth, stock, powder, or bouillon. Prepare in advance and allow to stand at room temperature for at least one hour for maximum flavour. Delicious with a crudité platter of carrots, tomatoes, cucumbers, and peppers. —NETTIE

BRING VEGETABLE STOCK to a boil in a saucepan over medium-high heat. Add quinoa. Reduce heat and simmer, stirring occasionally, for 15 minutes or until grain is tender and water is absorbed. Let cool slightly.

Purée quinoa and chickpeas in a food processor. Add tahini, lemon juice, cumin, cayenne, pepper, cilantro, and garlic. Process for 2 minutes, or until smooth. Transfer to a serving dish and garnish with green onions.

APPLE MISO ALMOND BUTTER SANDWICH

This is a new twist on peanut butter and jam. You can use any type of nut butter: cashew, hazelnut, or even soy (soybeans processed to taste like nuts), but I like to use almond. Miso is a salty paste made by cooking and fermenting soybeans and grains. Low in saturated fat and high in protein, it comes in various strengths and colours. The miso in this recipe, shiro miso, is pale yellow and all-purpose. If pasteurized, refrigerate miso after opening. If unpasteurized, keep it refrigerated even if unopened. —NETTIE

½ cup (125 mL) apple butter

2 tsp (10 mL) shiro miso (golden or yellow)

⅓ cup (80 mL) smooth or crunchy almond butter

8 slices whole-grain bread

COMBINE APPLE BUTTER and miso together in a bowl.

For each sandwich, spread about 2 Tbsp (30 mL) apple butter–miso spread on one side of a slice of bread.

Spread about 4 tsp (20 mL) nut butter on one side of a second slice of bread. Put 2 pieces of bread together and slice in half or into quarters.

CHICKPEA FETA SANDWICHES

This spread will last in the fridge for three days and can be served in a sandwich and as a dip for veggies, used in a pita and to fill celery sticks, or rolled up in a tortilla. Using canned chickpeas saves a lot of cooking time. Check the label: if salt is in the list of ingredients, rinse the chickpeas well. — NETTIE

Two 14 oz (398 mL) cans chickpeas, drained and rinsed

1 clove garlic, sliced

⅓ cup (80 mL) fresh lemon juice

⅓ cup (80 mL) tahini

¼ cup (60 mL) olive oil

1 Tbsp (15 mL) minced seeded jalapeño pepper

⅛ tsp (0.5 mL) salt

¼ tsp (1 mL) freshly ground pepper

4 pita pockets or 8 slices of whole-grain bread

1 cup (250 mL) thinly sliced English cucumber

½ cup (125 mL) fresh mint leaves

10 oz (300 g) feta cheese, cut into ¼-inch-thick (6 mm) slices

1 cup (250 mL) fresh bean sprouts

PURÉE CHICKPEAS IN a food processor or blender. Add garlic, lemon juice, tahini, olive oil, jalapeño, salt, and pepper. Purée to the desired consistency, coarse or smooth.

Spread 3 Tbsp (45 mL) chickpea spread over inside of a pita pocket or a bread slice. Repeat with rest of bread. Divide cucumber, mint, cheese, and sprouts into 4 portions and arrange on top of spread for each sandwich.

LEAFY-GREENS SALAD FOR KIDS

Romaine, leaf, Boston, bibb—all of these lettuces are very familiar to kids these days. You know what your kids like to eat. Mix and match leafy greens, add some arugula, spinach, endive—the possibilities are endless! — NETTIE

WASH AND THEN pat dry greens. Tear into bite-sized pieces. Toss together washed greens, green pepper, cheese, onion, and cherry tomatoes in a bowl.

Whisk together oil, vinegar, oregano, garlic, salt, and pepper in a bowl (or shake in a jar with a lid). Pour dressing over salad and toss gently to coat greens. Serve salad in bowls and let kids garnish with their favourite toppings.

4 cups (1 L) leafy greens

1 medium-sized green bell pepper, diced

1 cup (250 mL) shredded cheddar cheese

1 small red onion, thinly sliced

½ cup (125 mL) cherry tomatoes

½ cup (125 mL) olive oil

¼ cup (60 mL) red wine vinegar

1 Tbsp (15 mL) chopped fresh oregano

1 clove garlic, minced

¼ tsp (1 mL) salt

¼ tsp (1 mL) freshly ground pepper

TOPPING SUGGESTIONS
(Optional)

¼ cup (60 mL) shelled pistachio nuts

¼ cup (60 mL) tamari almonds (page 221)

¼ cup (60 mL) toasted sunflower seeds (sidebar, page 26)

¼ cup (60 mL) dried blueberries

¼ cup (60 mL) dried cherries

¼ cup (60 mL) dried cranberries

¼ cup (60 mL) raisins

1 cup (250 mL) long-grain
white rice or arborio rice

1 tsp (5 mL) salt

6 cups (1.5 L) water or stock

1 Tbsp (15 mL) olive oil

6 oz (175 g) ground pork

2 tsp (10 mL) toasted sesame oil

2 cloves garlic, minced

1 Tbsp (15 mL) finely diced
fresh ginger

½ cup (125 mL) diced shallots

1 cup (250 mL) thinly sliced fresh
shiitake mushrooms, caps only

¼ cup (60 mL) tamari or soy sauce

1 Tbsp (15 mL) mirin

2 Tbsp (30 mL) Sweet Thai Chile
Sauce (page 8) or store-bought

¼ cup (60 mL) chopped
fresh cilantro

½ cup (125 mL) roasted cashews,
coarsely chopped, for garnishing
(optional)

GINGER SHALLOT CONGEE

Congee is soup-like breakfast porridge, eaten as a morning meal in Asia. Long-grain rice has long, slender kernels, which are four times longer than they are wide. Their kernels cook separately and are light and easy to digest. Anything can be added to congee. My version might be better served at brunch. —NETTIE

GINGER SHALLOT CONGEE WITH CHILE PORK

Congee is a Chinese rice porridge that is made using eight measures of water for every one measure of rice. Ground pork is very often the meat of choice for congee, although the Chinese also like to add shrimp and other seafood. There are versions of thick soup or porridge all over Asia, including *juk* in Korea, *jok* in Thailand, and *lugao* in the Philippines. It's eaten as a hot porridge first thing in the morning and with meat and vegetables as a soup later in the day. — PAT

RINSE RICE IN a fine-mesh strainer under cold running water. Combine rice, salt, and water in a large pot. Bring to a boil over high heat. Cover, reduce heat to medium, and cook for 20 minutes or until water is absorbed and rice is tender. Remove from heat, fluff with a fork and let stand, covered for 20 minutes or until rice thickens.

Heat olive oil in a skillet over medium-high heat. Add ground pork, stirring and breaking it up with the back of a wooden spoon. Cook for 4 to 6 minutes or until browned through. Drain off fat and set aside.

Meanwhile, heat sesame oil in a large skillet or saucepan over medium heat. Add garlic, ginger, and shallots and cook, stirring constantly, for 5 minutes. Add mushrooms, tamari, mirin, chile sauce, and cilantro. Cook, stirring constantly for 3 minutes. Remove ¼ cup (60 mL) chile sauce and combine with cooked ground pork.

Divide congee into 6 portions and spoon into bowls. Spoon chile sauce on top of bowls, topping 2 bowls with chile-pork sauce instead. Garnish bowls with cashews (if using).

AROMATIC FRUIT CONGEE

For congee, you need to cook the rice in voluminous amounts of water. This method is similar to the method used to cook pasta. Arborio rice is an Italian short-grain—a highly absorbent, starchy white rice. As the kernels release their starch, they create a smooth, creamy sauce. The kernels remain firm yet tender and are a good grain to combine with cooked fruit and spices. This fusion dish offers a nice alternative to oatmeal at breakfast. Use Gala, Fuji, or Empire organic apples (peeling is optional) and Bosc pears for best results. —NETTIE

RINSE RICE IN a fine-mesh strainer under cold running water. Combine rice, salt, and water in a large pot. Bring to a boil over high heat. Cover and reduce heat to low. Simmer, stirring occasionally, for 50 minutes or until thickened.

Meanwhile, combine apples, pears, apricots, dried cherries, and apple juice in a saucepan. Bring to a boil over medium-high heat. Add lemon zest, cinnamon, ginger, nutmeg, and brown sugar. Lower heat to medium and cook, stirring often, for 30 minutes or until sauce is thickened and fruit is soft.

Serve each portion of congee with ¼ to ½ cup (60 to 125 mL) fruit compote. Add more compote if desired.

CONGEE

1 cup (250 mL) arborio
or long-grain white rice

1 tsp (5 mL) salt

8 cups (2 L) water

FRUIT COMPOTE

2 cups (500 mL) apple chunks
(½-inch/1 cm chunks)

1 cup (250 mL) pear chunks
(½-inch/1 cm chunks)

1 cup (250 mL) apricot chunks
(½-inch/1 cm chunks)
(or ¼ cup/60 mL chopped
dried apricots)

½ cup (125 mL) dried cherries

1 cup (250 mL) apple juice
or fruit juice blend

1 tsp (5 mL) lemon zest

½ tsp (2 mL) ground cinnamon

½ tsp (2 mL) ground ginger

¼ tsp (1 mL) ground nutmeg

2 Tbsp (30 mL) brown sugar

BAKED SWEET POTATO AND APRICOT CROQUETTES

Choose firm, smooth tubers that are free of soft spots. I prefer steaming them—it is faster than boiling. You can also fry these croquettes lightly in oil after baking them for a crispier texture. Placed in a pita bun with salad and pickles, they make a delicious lunch or snack. —NETTIE

HAM, SWEET POTATO, AND APRICOT CROQUETTES

A nugget of cooked ham inside these delicious croquettes is a nice surprise. I like to serve these croquettes at Easter. —PAT

1 lb (500 g) sweet potatoes (2 large), cut into chunks

1 cup (250 mL) orange juice

½ cup (125 mL) dried apricots, thinly sliced

1 clove garlic, minced

1 tsp (5 mL) ground cumin

1 cup (250 mL) finely chopped fresh cilantro or parsley

1 Tbsp (15 mL) fresh lemon juice

1 tsp (5 mL) olive oil

1 cup (250 mL) chickpea flour or breadcrumbs (dry or fresh; see page 178 for homemade)

½ tsp (2 mL) salt

¼ tsp (1 mL) freshly ground pepper

½-inch-thick (1 cm) slice
of cooked ham, cut into 6 or
10 pieces depending on size of
croquette (6 for large, 10 for small)

¼ cup (60 mL) black
and tan sesame seeds

2 Tbsp (30 mL) olive oil,
for frying (optional)

2 baking sheets, parchment-lined

PREHEAT THE OVEN to 400°F
(200°C).

Add enough water to reach the
bottom of a collapsible steamer
set in a 4-quart (4 L) saucepan and
bring to a boil over high heat. Place
sweet potatoes in steamer basket,
cover, and steam for 15 to 20 minutes or until tender. Or cover sweet
potatoes with water in a saucepan,
bring the water to a boil, reduce
heat, and then lightly boil for 10 to
15 minutes or until tender.

Combine orange juice and
apricots in a small pot and bring to
a boil over medium-high heat. Turn
off heat and let sit for 10 minutes.
Strain, discarding juice. Transfer
rehydrated apricots to a small bowl.

Combine steamed sweet potatoes, rehydrated apricots, garlic,
cumin, cilantro, lemon juice, olive
oil, chickpea flour, salt, and pepper.
Purée in a food processor or blender
until smooth, scraping down sides
intermittently.

Spoon out 1 Tbsp (15 mL) portions of purée and mould around
10 cubes of ham, or spoon out

2 Tbsp (30 mL) portions to mould
around 6 cubes of ham, shap-
ing them into small or large balls
(croquettes).

Spoon out 1 or 2 Tbsp (15 or
30 mL) portions of purée and mould
and shape into small or large balls
(croquettes). Place vegetarian croquettes and meat croquettes separately on prepared baking sheets and
sprinkle sesame seeds overtop.

Bake in preheated oven: smaller
croquettes for 15 minutes and
larger croquettes for 20 minutes, or
until base of balls is golden brown.
Croquettes may be served at this
stage or fried. (Baking before frying
crisps the outside and prevents the
absorption of oil.)

To fry (optional), heat 2 Tbsp
(30 mL) olive oil in a large skillet
over medium heat. Add about 10 of
the croquettes to the pan in one
layer. Fry, turning with tongs, for
1 minute each side, or until golden
brown. Transfer to a paper towel–
lined plate. Repeat until remaining
balls are lightly browned.

BAKED TORTILLA CHIPS WITH SALSA

Let's lower the fat of nachos without sacrificing the flavour. It's very easy to make your own tortilla chips, using ordinary pantry staples to create a very satisfying kid-friendly snack. — NETTIE

BAKED TORTILLA CHIPS WITH SHREDDED BEEF AND SALSA

This is definitely a make-ahead recipe, but with a slow cooker, you can have the meat ready at the end of the workday. The rest of this dish is fast and easy. Freeze the leftover shredded beef in two- or four-serving amounts so that you always have cooked meat ready. If you wish to make this recipe but don't have time for slow cooking, simply cook ground beef, chicken, or lamb following the directions on pages 185, 205, and 132 respectively. — PAT

SHREDDED BEEF

1 rump or sirloin tip roast beef

One 28 oz (796 mL) can diced tomatoes and juice

1½ cups (375 mL) tomato salsa (store-bought or Salsa Cruda, page 220)

1 Tbsp (15 mL) cornstarch

2 tsp (10 mL) granulated sugar

TORTILLAS

Ten 6-inch (15 cm) soft corn or flour tortillas

1½ cups (375 mL) mild or medium tomato salsa (store-bought or Salsa Cruda, page 220)

1½ cups (375 mL) cooked pinto beans (drained and rinsed if canned)

½ cup (125 mL) cooked corn kernels (drained and rinsed if canned)

2 cups (500 mL) shredded cheddar or Monterey Jack cheese

3 green onions, sliced

GARNISHES

Sour cream

Avocado slices

Additional salsa

Olives

Sliced artichoke hearts

Slow cooker

2 rimmed baking sheets

COMBINE ROAST BEEF, tomatoes and juice, and salsa in the crock of a slow cooker. Cover and cook on low for 6 to 8 hours, or until beef is fork-tender. Remove beef from the crock and let cool on a plate. Transfer tomato-salsa mixture to a large saucepan and bring to a boil over high heat.

Meanwhile, combine cornstarch and sugar in a small bowl. Stir into hot tomato-salsa mixture. Cook on high heat, stirring constantly, for 2 to 3 minutes or until mixture thickens.

When beef has cooled enough to handle, pull it apart into bite-sized pieces. Return beef to saucepan and mix with salsa-cornstarch mixture.

Measure out 2 cups (500 mL) of beef-tomato mixture, to be served with the baked tortilla chips and other garnishes. Let remaining beef and sauce cool. Measure 2-cup (500 mL) portions into a freezer bag or other container, seal, label, and freeze for up to 3 months. (Each

frozen portion will yield 2 servings.)

Preheat the oven to 400°F (200°C).

Cut each tortilla in half, then cut each half into 3 triangles. You will have 60 tortilla triangles. Arrange triangles evenly on 2 rimmed baking sheets in a single layer. Bake on top and bottom racks in preheated oven for 6 to 7 minutes. Flip triangles using a spatula, switching baking sheets from top to bottom rack and bottom to top rack, and bake for 5 or 6 more minutes or until lightly browned and crisp.

Combine salsa, beans, and corn in a saucepan. Simmer for 5 minutes over medium heat. Spread salsa mixture evenly over both pans of tortilla chips. Cover with shredded cheese and bake in oven for 3 to 5 minutes, or until cheese is bubbling.

Remove from oven and sprinkle green onions overtop. Serve with garnishes and shredded beef in separate bowls.

SALSA CRUDA

This thick and chunky salsa can be as hot or as mild as you like. Try roasting the bell peppers and jalapeño peppers for a smoother taste (see page 2). —NETTIE

4 tomatoes, seeded and chopped

½ cup (125 mL) chopped red bell pepper

½ cup (125 mL) chopped green bell pepper

⅓ cup (80 mL) chopped red onion

1 to 3 jalapeño peppers, seeded and chopped

¼ cup (60 mL) chopped fresh cilantro or basil

2 cloves garlic, chopped

2 Tbsp (30 mL) peanut oil or olive oil

1 Tbsp (15 mL) fresh lime juice

Salt and pepper, to taste

COMBINE TOMATOES, BELL peppers, onion, jalapeño pepper(s), cilantro, garlic, peanut oil, and lime juice in a mixing bowl. Taste and add salt and pepper as desired.

CILANTRO

Coriandrum sativum is an aromatic herb of the parsley family. The fresh green parts of the plant are usually called cilantro, and the seeds of the same plant are usually called coriander. Cilantro resembles flat-leaf parsley in appearance but has a much more pungent flavour. People either love the taste and aroma of cilantro, noting its fresh, lemon-ginger flavour, or they hate it, saying that it tastes "soapy." Do not wash the leaves or remove the roots (if still intact) before storing; it will keep for a week in the refrigerator. Also be sure to wrap cilantro in a damp paper towel.

1 cup (250 mL) raw almonds

1 cup (250 mL) raw cashews

1 cup (250 mL) tamari or soy sauce

½ tsp (2 mL) ground cumin

¼ tsp (1 mL) ground coriander

Rimmed baking sheet,
parchment-lined

8 oz (250 mL) spritz bottle

TAMARI ROASTED NUTS

Tamari is a Japanese word that best describes a dark, rich soy sauce. Read your labels carefully: good-quality tamari contains no preservatives, food colouring, or sugar. Tamari roasted nuts are delicious. Fill an all-purpose spray bottle with tamari, and when the nuts begin to brown, spray a coating of tamari. Be careful to cover the nuts and not the pan. — NETTIE

PREHEAT THE OVEN to 300°F (150°C).

Arrange nuts in one layer on prepared baking sheet. Toast nuts in preheated oven, stirring once or twice, for 6 to 8 minutes or until lightly browned.

Remove from oven. Using the spray bottle, mist roasted nuts with tamari. Combine dried spices together in a small bowl and distribute over roasted nuts. Stir nuts and mist again. Return to oven and toast for 3 to 5 minutes, or until browned and crisp. Cool and store in a sealed container for up to 3 weeks.

TRAIL MIX FOR KIDS

This snack is crunchy and satisfying, and seems to be a favourite with six-year-old kids. I even like it and I am not a kid. It is naturally sweetened and a good source of calcium. The coconut flakes form a barrier between the chopped figs and prevent them from sticking together. —NETTIE

1 cup (250 mL) raw almonds

1 cup (250 mL) raw sunflower seeds

½ cup (125 mL) raisins

¼ cup (60 mL) dried cranberries

½ cup (125 mL) chopped dried figs

¼ cup (60 mL) unsweetened coconut flakes

Baking sheet, parchment-lined

PREHEAT THE OVEN to 350°F (180°C).

Spread out almonds on prepared baking sheet and toast, stirring often, on the middle rack of preheated oven for 10 minutes, or until golden brown. Let cool slightly.

Meanwhile, place sunflower seeds in a dry skillet or pan and toast, stirring constantly, over medium heat for 5 minutes or until light brown. Let cool slightly.

Combine toasted almonds and sunflower seeds, raisins, cranberries, figs, and coconut. Stir well. Store in a sealed container for up to 3 months.

1½ cups (375 mL) cottage cheese

1 medium-sized peach, peeled,
halved, and pitted (for purée;
more for topping)

1 tsp (5 mL) pure vanilla extract

¼ cup (60 mL) lightly packed
brown sugar, divided

2 Tbsp (30 mL) finely chopped
dried cherries

1 tsp (5 mL) lemon zest

1 Tbsp (15 mL) fresh lemon juice

1 lb (500 g) pizza dough (page 120),
or one 14-inch-round (35 cm)
prepared dough

1 tsp (5 mL) ground cinnamon

2 Tbsp (30 mL) yellow cornmeal

4 kiwis, thinly sliced

3 ripe peaches, pitted
and thinly sliced

2 cups (500 mL) blueberries

Rimmed baking pan, lightly oiled
or parchment-lined

KIWI, PEACH, AND BLUEBERRY PIZZA

You want to grill this pizza crust on both sides, so leave all the burners on. Spread the cheese mixture onto the dough after it's been grilled, and then add the fruit. Perfect for breakfast or a snack. Move over, toast. —NETTIE

PREHEAT THE GRILL to medium-high.

Purée cottage cheese, peach halves, vanilla, half the brown sugar (2 Tbsp/30 mL), cherries, lemon zest, and lemon juice in a food processor. Set aside.

Place dough on a large floured cutting board. Mix remaining brown sugar with cinnamon and cornmeal in a bowl.

(If using a prepared pizza round, set this mixture aside and omit the following step.) Knead cinnamon mixture into dough, and then roll out into a 14-inch (35 cm) circle (see page 120).

Place on preheated grill and cook for 4 minutes or until bottom is browned. Turn crust over and grill for more 4 minutes, or until bottom is browned. Transfer to a pizza stone or platter. Spread cottage cheese mixture evenly overtop pizza crust. Arrange sliced fruit in overlapping swirls and garnish with berries. (Sprinkle cinnamon mixture over fruit if using a prepared pizza round). Cut into wedges and serve warm.

TEMPEH SCRAMBLE

If you don't want to use fried tempeh, see page 195 for directions on baking it. Either way, this is delicious breakfast food with a kick. Use medium or hot salsa. You can eat the scramble with toast, on its own, or baked in a tortilla as directed here. —NETTIE

HAM SCRAMBLE

Having cooked ham in the freezer is a real time-saver for flexitarian cooking. Whenever I cook meat, I try to freeze leftovers in small amounts to add to casseroles and wraps. —PAT

¼ cup (60 mL) + 1 Tbsp (15 mL) olive oil, divided

One 8 oz (250 g) pkg tempeh, thawed and crumbled

1 cup (250 mL) chopped onion

2 cloves garlic, minced

1 cup (250 mL) thinly sliced red bell peppers

½ cup (125 mL) green peas (fresh or frozen)

2 cups (500 mL) spinach, thinly sliced

1 Tbsp (15 mL) fresh lemon juice

1 large fresh green chile, finely chopped, or 1 tsp (5 mL) chile powder

1½ tsp (7 mL) ground cumin

1½ tsp (7 mL) salt

6 large (9- or 10-inch/23 or 25 cm) tortillas (corn, flour, or mixed grain)

¾ cup (185 mL) chopped fresh cilantro or flat-leaf parsley

⅓ cup (80 mL) chopped cooked ham

3 cups (750 mL) tomato salsa (store-bought or Salsa Cruda, page 220)

Rimmed baking sheet

HEAT ¼ CUP (60 ML) oil in a wok or skillet over medium-high heat. Add tempeh and cook, stirring frequently, for 8 to 10 minutes or until reddish brown. Transfer to a lint-free cloth using a slotted spoon. Wipe wok clean of any residual bits.

Add remaining 1 Tbsp (15 mL) oil to wok and heat over medium heat. Add onion and cook, stirring frequently, for 5 minutes or until it begins to soften. Add garlic and cook, stirring constantly, for 1 minute. Stir in peppers, peas, spinach, lemon juice, chile, cumin, and salt. Cook, stirring constantly, for 4 minutes.

Preheat the oven to 300°F (150°C).

Lay a tortilla on a work surface and spread vegetable mixture down the centre. Spread a portion of cooked tempeh overtop vegetables and sprinkle with 2 Tbsp (30 mL) cilantro. Fold top down and bottom up over the filling. Fold one side over filling and roll up. Place tortilla on baking sheet, seam side down. Make up rest of veggie tortillas following the same procedure but use ham in place of tempeh for 2 of the tortillas, marking these 2 tortillas with toothpicks.

Cover baking sheet with foil and heat tortillas in preheated oven for 10 to 15 minutes. Serve hot with salsa.

OAT AND BARLEY GRAIN PORRIDGE FOR BEGINNERS

Don't use instant or quick-cooking oats. You can cook any kind of rolled or flaked grain this way and it will cook almost as quickly as instant oats. Rolled grains (or flakes) have been steamed and rolled flat, making them cook quickly. To add variety, you can use regular milk or a soy, nut, or grain beverage for half of the water at the beginning of cooking. —NETTIE

3 cups (750 mL) water,
or 1½ cups (375 mL) water and
1½ cups (375 mL) milk

1 cup (250 mL) rolled oats

1 cup (250 mL) barley flakes

3 Tbsp (45 mL) dried fruit (currants,
apricots, mango, raisins, blueberries)

¼ tsp (1 mL) ground cinnamon

1 Tbsp (15 mL) unsalted butter

1 cup (250 mL) fresh fruit
(strawberries, banana, cored and
shredded small apple)

⅓ cup (80 mL) maple syrup, divided

¼ cup (60 mL) toasted seeds
or nuts (sunflower seeds, pecans,
pumpkin seeds) (sidebar,
page 26) (optional)

1 cup (250 mL) milk
or non-dairy milk

BRING WATER TO a boil in a saucepan over high heat.

Reduce heat to medium-low, add oats and barley flakes, dried fruit, and cinnamon. Cover and simmer, stirring frequently, for 5 minutes. Add butter, fresh fruit, and 2 Tbsp (30 mL) maple syrup. Cover and cook over low heat for 3 to 5 minutes, or until flakes are tender and liquid has been absorbed. Add toasted seeds or nuts (if using).

Divide porridge evenly among 4 bowls and serve with remaining maple syrup and milk.

1 cup (250 mL) maple syrup

¼ cup (60 mL) canola oil

1 Tbsp (15 mL) pure vanilla extract

1 cup (250 mL) barley flakes

2 cups (500 mL) rolled oats

½ cup (125 mL) raw, unsalted pumpkin seeds or sunflower seeds

½ cup (125 mL) unsweetened coconut flakes

1 cup (250 mL) almonds or pecans, coarsely chopped

1 tsp (5 mL) ground cinnamon

½ cup (125 mL) dried currants

½ cup (125 mL) chopped dried apricots

Rimmed baking pan, lightly oiled or parchment-lined

GOLDEN GRANOLA

The secret to my beautiful golden granola is slow-roasting it, stirring the mixture every 15 minutes, and rotating the baking sheet. Doing so will guarantee even toasting. Always add the dried fruit after baking. —NETTIE

PREHEAT THE OVEN to 250°F (120°C) and move rack to middle position in oven.

Heat maple syrup and oil in a saucepan over low heat, stirring constantly with a whisk for 5 minutes. Add vanilla and remove from the heat.

Combine barley flakes, oats, pumpkin seeds, coconut, nuts, and cinnamon in a large bowl. Drizzle syrup mixture overtop and stir until dry ingredients are evenly coated. Spread mixture onto prepared baking sheet.

Bake on centre rack of preheated oven for 70 minutes, stirring every 15 minutes and rotating the baking sheet. Remove pan and let cool on a wire rack. Add currants and apricots and toss to mix well. Store in an airtight container for up to 2 weeks or in the refrigerator for up to 2 months.

APPLE-BLUEBERRY MUFFINS

Frozen berries work really well in this recipe. I like mixing and matching the different colours of fruit. Moist and flavourful, these muffins are a hit. You can use just honey or maple syrup as the sweetener, but I like combining them. You can drink the leftover apple juice after soaking the currants—it is sweet! —NETTIE

PREHEAT THE OVEN to 375°F (190°C).

Combine currants and apple juice in a bowl. Soak for 10 minutes, drain, and set aside.

Meanwhile, purée tofu, bananas, maple syrup, honey, egg, oil, and vanilla in a food processor or blender.

Combine apples, 1 tsp (5 mL) cinnamon, lemon juice, and drained currants in a separate bowl.

Combine flour, yeast, baking powder, baking soda, remaining 1 tsp (5 mL) cinnamon, and salt in a large bowl. Make a well in the centre of the dry ingredients. Fold in tofu-banana mixture and mix until moist. Add apple-currant mixture and mix well. Spoon 1 Tbsp (15 mL) batter into each prepared muffin cup. Spoon 1 Tbsp (15 mL) blueberries over batter in each cup. Stir remaining blueberries into remaining batter and top up muffin cups.

Bake in preheated oven for 25 to 30 minutes, or until a toothpick inserted in the centre of a muffin comes out clean.

½ cup (125 mL) dried currants

1 cup (250 mL) apple juice

½ cup (125 mL) drained silken tofu

2 large ripe bananas, mashed

⅓ cup (80 mL) maple syrup

⅓ cup (80 mL) honey

1 egg

⅓ cup (80 mL) olive oil

1 tsp (5 mL) pure vanilla extract

1 cup (250 mL) diced apples

2 tsp (10 mL) ground cinnamon, divided

1 tsp (5 mL) fresh lemon juice

1½ cups (375 mL) whole wheat pastry flour

¼ cup (60 mL) nutritional yeast

2 tsp (10 mL) baking powder

½ tsp (2 mL) baking soda

¼ tsp (1 mL) salt

1 cup (250 mL) fresh or frozen blueberries

Three 6-well muffin tins, filled with paper muffin liners or lightly oiled

¼ cup (60 mL) sesame seeds

½ cup (125 mL) almonds, chopped

½ cup (125 mL) dried apricots, chopped

½ cup (125 mL) dried cranberries

¼ cup (60 mL) coconut flakes (sweetened or unsweetened)

1 cup (250 mL) barley flakes

1¼ cups (310 mL) small-flake rolled oats

½ cup (125 mL) smooth almond butter

½ cup (125 mL) agave nectar

½ cup (125 mL) liquid honey or brown rice syrup

1 tsp (5 mL) pure vanilla extract

Rimmed baking sheet, parchment-lined

8-inch-square (20 cm) cake pan, lightly oiled

CRISPY BARLEY OAT ALMOND SQUARES

Another Halloween is on the horizon. In the days before nuts and seeds were not allowed at kids' events, I made this recipe often. As a parent rep for my son's Grade 2 class, I was determined to include some healthy delicious treats at the class party. I had to stop the other parent volunteers from devouring my squares! These adult- and kid-friendly desserts can be made quickly and will last for five days, covered. Use organic ingredients where possible, especially when it comes to the dried apricots, almonds, and sesame seeds. If you don't have agave nectar, double the amount of honey; note that Tasmanian honey would make this dessert taste sensational. The nut butter increases the chewiness of the squares—use any type such as peanut, cashew, and hazelnut instead of the almond. Other kinds of organic dried fruit (mango, pineapple, or papaya) can be used as well. Not a marshmallow in sight! —NETTIE

PREHEAT THE OVEN to 300°F (150°C).

Spread sesame seeds and almonds out on prepared baking sheet in one layer. Toast in preheated oven, stirring once, for 5 minutes or until lightly browned.

Combine toasted seeds and almonds, apricots, cranberries, and coconut in a large bowl. Mix well. Add barley flakes and oats. Toss to combine.

Whisk together almond butter, agave nectar, honey, and vanilla in a large saucepan over medium-low heat. Heat for 5 minutes, or until mixture is just about to come to a boil. Remove from stove. Pour over apricot-barley-oat mixture and mix well using a large spoon.

Press mixture into prepared cake pan. Let stand for 45 minutes or until firm. Cut into squares. Store in an airtight container for up to 5 days.

ANCHO CHILE CRANBERRY BROWNIES

Ancho chiles—dark red, wrinkled, and medium hot—have a sweet, raisin-y flavour that combines well with tart cranberries and bittersweet chocolate. You can adjust the amount of heat in this recipe, so if you're baking this recipe for adults, use a little more chile powder. The flavour of chocolate depends on the type of cocoa beans, and on how they are grown and roasted. Buy fair-trade cocoa, sugar, and vanilla products (see page 266). The percentage of cocoa solids, usually listed on labels, is very important too. Use only chocolate with 60 percent or higher for this recipe. It's the best! —NETTIE

PREHEAT THE OVEN to 350°F (180°C).

Set aside ¼ cup (60 mL) chopped chocolate. Melt remaining chocolate and butter slowly in a double boiler or heatproof bowl set over a pan of simmering water. (Don't let the bottom of the bowl touch the water.) Stir often for 5 to 6 minutes, or until melted and combined. Remove the bowl from overtop the water and let the mixture cool slightly.

Whisk eggs, sugar, vanilla, and salt together in a large bowl until thick. Add melted chocolate-butter mixture and stir to combine. Add flour and stir until blended. Add cranberries, reserved chocolate, and chile powder. Stir until well mixed. Batter will be stiff.

Scrape batter into prepared pan. Bake for 40 minutes, or until brownies pull away from the sides of the pan. Centre will be moist but not runny. Cool in pan. Lift out and cut into bars. Store bars in an airtight container for up to 3 days.

10 oz (300 g) bittersweet chocolate,
chopped, divided

½ cup (125 mL) unsalted butter,
cut into chunks

2 large eggs

2 cups (500 mL) granulated sugar

2 tsp (10 mL) pure vanilla extract

½ tsp (2 mL) salt

1 cup (250 mL) all-purpose flour

1 cup (250 mL) dried cranberries

½ tsp (2 mL) ancho chile powder

9-inch-square (23 cm) pan,
parchment-lined

BEVERAGES

CHAI LATTE

Organic green tea, Japanese sencha, or red or green rooibos works well in this recipe. Use two tea bags and increase the water to 4 cups (1 L) if loose tea is not available. —NETTIE

3 cups (750 mL) water

1 Tbsp (15 mL) loose organic tea leaves (see recipe introduction)

¼ tsp (1 mL) ground cinnamon

Pinch of ground allspice

Pinch of ground ginger

¼ cup (60 mL) milk or non-dairy milk

BRING WATER TO a boil in a kettle. Meanwhile, combine tea leaves, cinnamon, allspice, and ginger in a non-reactive teapot. Pour boiling water over tea and spices. Cover and steep for 3 minutes. Strain the spiced tea into 2 teacups.

Meanwhile, bring milk to just under a boil in a small saucepan over medium-high heat. Froth the milk, using a milk frother or wire whisk, and spoon over tea in cups.

LEMON MINT ICED GREEN TEA

Use organic green tea or Japanese sencha, but red or green rooibos also works well here. Use four tea bags and 2 cups (500 mL) boiling water to make the double-strength tea. —NETTIE

2 cups (500 mL) chilled double-strength brewed green tea

¼ cup (60 mL) fresh lemon juice

3 Tbsp (45 mL) liquid honey, or to taste

1 Tbsp (15 mL) chopped fresh peppermint

4 ice cubes

COMBINE TEA, LEMON juice, honey, and peppermint in a blender. Process for 30 seconds or until well blended. Taste and add more honey, lemon juice, or peppermint. Pour into a jug and add the ice cubes. Refrigerate until ready to serve. Or divide ice between 2 glasses and pour tea overtop.

HERB COFFEE

I call this beverage blend "coffee" even though there is no substitute for the real thing. However, this nutty-tasting blend is brewed just like coffee and can be a nice gentle and caffeine-free drink in the morning. —PAT

COMBINE DANDELION, BURDOCK, chicory, licorice, cinnamon, and turmeric in a bowl. Spoon into an airtight glass container and store in a cool, dark place. Blend will keep for up to a year.

To make a serving of herb coffee: Grind a small amount of the blend using an electric coffee grinder or a mortar and pestle. Use 1 Tbsp (15 mL) of the ground mix for every serving of herb coffee. Use in a drip machine or in a press as you would regular ground coffee.

1 cup (250 mL) chopped dried dandelion root

½ cup (125 mL) chopped dried burdock root

½ cup (125 mL) chopped dried chicory root

¼ cup (60 mL) chopped dried licorice root

1 Tbsp (15 mL) cinnamon pieces

1 tsp (5 mL) ground turmeric

1 cup (250 mL) pineapple juice

½ cup (125 mL) freshly squeezed
orange juice

One 14 oz (398 mL) can peach
slices, drained

One 14 oz (398 mL) can pineapple
chunks, drained

½ cup (125 mL)
peach-flavoured yogurt

⅛ tsp (0.5 mL) ground cinnamon

Pinch of ground nutmeg

PEACH SPICE COCKTAIL

Use this drink as a non-alcoholic beverage, or add vodka to it for an adult refresher. — NETTIE

PROCESS ALL INGREDIENTS in a blender on high until smooth.

FRUIT SMOOTHIES

Smoothies are a great way to ensure that the required servings of fruit are consumed daily. This is especially true for kids who need the nutrients that fruit provides. Yogurt is a great addition to these tasty drinks, adding calcium and protein. — PAT

FOR ALL THESE smoothies, process all ingredients on high in blender until smooth.

SUNRISE OVER RIO

Pomegranate juice and acai berries are extremely high in anti-oxidants, and their fresh, tart taste makes this a perfect drink to wake up to in the morning. Add 1 Tbsp (15 mL) soy protein powder for an early-morning power drink.

½ cup (125 mL) pomegranate juice

¼ cup (60 mL) freshly squeezed orange juice

¼ cup (60 mL) frozen acai berry pulp

1 mango, peeled and sliced

BERRIES AND CREAM SMOOTHIE

Any berry, or a combination of berries, will work for this fresh and summery drink.

½ cup (125 mL) cranberry juice

¼ cup (60 mL) freshly squeezed orange juice

1 cup (250 mL) frozen berries (raspberries, strawberries, blueberries, blackberries)

3 Tbsp (45 mL) Cashew Cream (page 6)

1 banana, quartered

MELON MARVEL SMOOTHIE

Using muskmelon in this smoothie gives the drink a green glow.

½ cup (125 mL) apple juice

2 cups (500 mL) muskmelon chunks

2 kiwis, halved

1 mango, sliced

CHERRY ALMOND SMOOTHIE

Almond milk is available in whole food stores and some supermarkets, but if you can't find it, substitute the same amount of rice milk or soymilk with ½ tsp (2 mL) pure almond extract added.

¾ cup (185 mL) almond milk

1 cup (250 mL) fresh pitted cherries or drained canned cherries

¼ cup (60 mL) chopped pitted dried dates

2 Tbsp (30 mL) coarsely chopped almonds

3 Tbsp (45 mL) plain yogurt

1 banana, quartered

Pinch of ground cinnamon

STRAWBERRY SMOOTHIE

Use fresh or frozen strawberries in this chiller.

¾ cup (185 mL) raspberry-cranberry juice

1 cup (250 mL) sliced fresh or frozen strawberries

¼ cup (60 mL) fresh or frozen raspberries

¼ cup (60 mL) plain yogurt

RASPBERRY APRICOT SMOOTHIE

When apricots are fresh, use them in this recipe; at other times, substitute ½ cup (125 mL) chopped dried apricots or drained canned apricots.

¾ cup (185 mL) raspberry-cranberry juice

½ cup (125 mL) chopped fresh apricots

¼ cup (60 mL) fresh or frozen raspberries

1 banana, quartered

MANGO-CANTALOUPE SMOOTHIE

Filled with beta-carotene, this cooler is perfect as a morning wake-me-up.

½ cup (125 mL) freshly squeezed orange juice

¼ cup (60 mL) carrot juice

½ cantaloupe, cut into cubes

½ mango, cut into cubes

1 kiwi fruit, peeled and halved

¼ cup (60 mL) plain yogurt

AUTUMN REFRESHER

You can add maple syrup or apple syrup to sweeten this smoothie to your taste.

—NETTIE

PROCESS ALL INGREDIENTS in a blender on high until smooth.

½ cup (125 mL) soft apple cider

¼ cup (60 mL) drained silken tofu

¼ cup (60 mL) applesauce

2 peaches, pitted and sliced

1 apple, cored and cut into chunks

1 pear, cored and cut into chunks

⅛ tsp (0.5 mL) ground allspice

CURRIED TOMATO COCKTAIL

This balanced cocktail is a tasty beverage to use as a starter for the vegetarian main course dishes in this book. It also makes a very nice tomato mixer for Bloody Mary cocktail drinks. —NETTIE

½ cup (125 mL) tomato juice

¼ cup (60 mL) apple juice

2 Tbsp (30 mL) fresh lemon juice

2 tomatoes, seeded and chopped

2 stalks celery, coarsely chopped

1 small zucchini, cut into chunks

½ cucumber, cut into chunks

¼ tsp (1 mL) red or green curry paste (page 9 for homemade), or to taste

Pinch of celery salt

PROCESS ALL INGREDIENTS in a blender on high until smooth.

SPICY TOMATO COCKTAIL

Making your own vegetable cocktail means that you can control the quality of the ingredients. Use this as a before-dinner cocktail, or add vodka to it for a delicious mixer. — NETTIE

PROCESS ALL INGREDIENTS in a blender on high until smooth.

⅓ cup (80 mL) carrot juice

¼ cup (60 mL) tomato juice

¼ cup (60 mL) apple juice

2 tomatoes, cored and quartered

1 ripe pear, cored and quartered

2 stalks celery, coarsely chopped

1 jalapeño pepper, halved
and seeded

½ lemon, peeled, halved,
and seeded

One 1-inch (2.5 cm) slice
candied ginger

1 Tbsp (15 mL) chopped
fresh parsley

DESSERTS

PEACH-RASPBERRY KUGEL

What is a *kugel*? The Yiddish word means "pudding" in English; think bread pudding but with potatoes, noodles, or cheese. They can be either sweet or savoury. My New Age version pairs tofu with cottage cheese, and is delicious hot or cold. —NETTIE

PREHEAT THE OVEN to 350°F (180°C).

Blend tofu, cottage cheese, maple syrup, almond butter, lemon juice, cinnamon, vanilla, orange zest, and coriander in a blender or food processor until smooth. Transfer to a large bowl and stir in peaches, raspberries, and almonds. Turn into prepared pan and sprinkle with coconut.

Cover and bake for 35 minutes or until set. Let stand 10 minutes before serving.

VANILLA

Real vanilla comes from the pod fruit of an orchid from Central and northern South America. In the 19th century, a botanist made it possible to pollinate the vanilla flower and produce the bean in regions that did not have the typical pollinating insects. They took the vine to Madagascar and Indonesia where it was hand-pollinated, requiring a huge labour force.

The flavour of the bean is found in two parts: the tiny sticky seeds and the pod wall. After the seeds are removed, the pod can be soaked to extract more flavour; the soaking liquid is often used for sauces. An essential ingredient in my pantry.

8 oz (250 g) drained silken tofu

1 lb (500 g) 2% cottage cheese

⅓ cup (80 mL) maple syrup

2 Tbsp (30 mL) almond butter

2 Tbsp (30 mL) fresh lemon juice

1 tsp (5 mL) ground cinnamon

1 tsp (5 mL) pure vanilla extract

½ tsp (2 mL) orange zest

½ tsp (2 mL) ground coriander

3 peaches, peeled and thinly sliced

2 cups (500 mL) raspberries or
blueberries

½ cup (125 mL) thinly sliced toasted
almonds (sidebar, page 26)

¼ cup (60 mL) coconut flakes
(sweetened or unsweetened)

11- × 7-inch (28 × 18 cm) baking
dish, lightly oiled

GREEN TEA CUPCAKES WITH GREEN TEA GLAZE

Green tea leaves come from the *Camellia sinensis* plant. In spring, the earliest leaves of the tea plant are picked to make *gyokuro*, Japan's best-quality green tea. These dried leaves are ground to a fine dust to make *matcha*, a type of powdered green tea used in Japanese tea ceremonies. Green tea contains the amino acid L-theanine, which leaves one feeling alert but not overstimulated. Nourish Tea (www.nourishtea.ca), a Canadian-owned company, makes the best organic, fair-trade teas I have ever tried. Matcha tea is perfect for these bite-sized cupcakes. The shade of green is so vibrant and natural. Better than any food colouring. —NETTIE

¼ cup (60 mL) plain yogurt

⅔ cup (160 mL) milk

½ tsp (2 mL) pure vanilla extract

⅓ cup (80 mL) olive oil

1¼ cups (310 mL) all-purpose flour

¾ cup (185 mL) granulated sugar

1 tsp (5 mL) baking powder

¼ tsp (1 mL) baking soda

2 Tbsp (30 mL) matcha tea powder (see recipe introduction)

¼ tsp (1 mL) salt

Two 6-well muffin tins (or one 12-well), filled with paper muffin liners or lightly oiled

PREHEAT THE OVEN to 350°F (180°C).

Whisk together yogurt, milk, vanilla, and oil in a large bowl. Sift in flour, sugar, baking powder, baking soda, matcha tea powder, and salt.

Spoon batter into prepared muffin tin wells to about two-thirds full.

Bake in preheated oven for 20 minutes, or until a cake tester or toothpick comes out clean when inserted into the centre of a cupcake. Let cool on a cooling rack before glazing with Green Tea Glaze.

2 Tbsp (30 mL) non-hydrogenated
shortening

1 cup (250 mL) icing sugar

½ tsp (2 mL) matcha tea powder

1 Tbsp (15 mL) milk,
more if needed

¼ tsp (1 mL) almond extract

¼ tsp (1 mL) pure vanilla extract

GREEN TEA GLAZE

MAKES: ¼ cup (60 mL)

BEAT SHORTENING IN a bowl for about 2 minutes, or until light and fluffy. Add sugar and matcha tea powder and mix with a wooden spoon until it becomes crumbly. Slowly beat in 1 Tbsp (15 mL) milk, the almond extract, and vanilla. If icing is too thick to spread, pour in additional milk, 1 tsp (5 mL) at a time, and mix until you achieve a spreadable texture.

CONFECTIONER'S SUGAR

Regular sugar, ground to a fine powder, with cornstarch added to prevent crystallization. It is used mostly in icing because it dissolves very easily, or can be sifted over desserts.

BANANA LOAF

If possible, buy bananas, chocolate, and sugar that are organic and fair trade. On bananas, this means looking for two different stickers. Banana bread is easy to prepare and welcomes the addition of ¼ cup (60 mL) dried cranberries, fresh or dried pineapple, or chocolate chips. —NETTIE

PREHEAT THE OVEN to 350°F (180°C).

Beat butter with brown sugar in a bowl until light and fluffy. Beat in egg and vanilla. In a separate bowl, combine bananas with buttermilk and baking soda. Set aside.

Combine two flours with baking powder in a separate bowl. Add flour mixture to butter mixture alternating with the banana mixture, beginning and ending with the flour mixture.

Scrape into prepared loaf pan and bake in preheated oven for 50 to 60 minutes, or until a cake tester inserted into the centre of the loaf comes out clean.

½ cup (125 mL) butter,
at room temperature

⅔ cup (160 mL) lightly packed
brown sugar

1 egg

1 tsp (5 mL) pure vanilla extract

1¼ cups (310 mL) mashed ripe
bananas

½ cup (125 mL) buttermilk
or plain yogurt

1 tsp (5 mL) baking soda

1 cup (250 mL) unbleached flour

½ cup (125 mL) whole wheat flour

1 tsp (5 mL) baking powder

Loaf pan, lightly oiled

GINGERBREAD BARS

Not quite a cookie, but a pair of these—moist and brown sugar flavoured—makes fabulous book ends for an ice cream sandwich. Cut into larger pieces if you prefer. —NETTIE

2 cups (500 mL) all-purpose flour

2 tsp (10 mL) ground ginger

1 tsp (5 mL) ground cinnamon

¼ tsp (1 mL) ground cloves

½ tsp (2 mL) baking soda

½ tsp (2 mL) salt

½ cup (125 mL) plus 2 Tbsp (30 mL)
non-hydrogenated shortening
or unsalted butter,
at room temperature

1 cup (250 mL) lightly packed
dark brown sugar

5 Tbsp (75 mL) granulated sugar,
divided

2 large eggs

¼ cup (60 mL) unsulfured molasses

Rimmed baking sheet,
parchment-lined

PREHEAT THE OVEN to 350°F (180°C).

Sift flour into a medium-sized bowl. Transfer 2 Tbsp (30 mL) sifted flour to a small bowl and set aside. Stir ginger, cinnamon, cloves, baking soda, and salt into larger amount of flour.

In a separate bowl, cream shortening, brown sugar, and 4 Tbsp (60 mL) of the granulated sugar until fluffy. Beat in eggs, one at a time. Stir in molasses. Add spiced flour to shortening mixture and beat to blend.

Scrape batter onto prepared sheet. Sift reserved 2 Tbsp (30 mL) flour evenly overtop. Sprinkle evenly with remaining 1 Tbsp (15 mL) granulated sugar. Bake gingerbread in preheated oven for 20 to 25 minutes, or until golden brown. Cool on pan on a cooling rack before slicing.

Cut crosswise into 4 equal strips, and then cut each strip into 6 pieces, for 24 pieces total.

1 cup (250 mL) white sushi rice

2 cups (500 mL) coconut milk

1 Tbsp (15 mL) mirin

1 tsp (5 mL) wasabi powder

1½ tsp (7 mL) water

3 sheets nori

2 Tbsp (30 mL) thinly sliced
pickled ginger

1 ripe mango, peeled
and thinly sliced

3 ripe kiwis, peeled and thinly sliced

1 cup (250 mL) Sushi Dipping
Sauce (page 33)

2 rimmed baking sheets

Sushi mat

MANGO KIWI DESSERT SUSHI

Cooking sushi rice in coconut milk is brilliant. The rice is so moist and smells so good. The combination of sweet (from the mango and kiwi), hot (from the wasabi powder), and acid (from the pickled ginger) makes this sushi a great after-dinner dessert. —NETTIE

PLACE RICE IN a strainer and rinse well under cool running water. Drain.

Bring coconut milk to a boil in a medium-sized saucepan over medium-high heat. Add rinsed rice and mirin. Cover, reduce heat, and simmer, stirring occasionally, for 20 to 22 minutes or until liquid is absorbed. Spread on one of the baking sheets to cool.

Mix wasabi powder with water in a bowl. Stir to form a paste.

Place 1 nori sheet, shiny side down, on the sushi mat. Spoon ¾ cup (185 mL) warm rice onto nori sheet. Leaving a 1-inch (2.5 cm) strip of nori uncovered along the top, press rice firmly with fingers or a fork to cover nori sheet. Spread a horizontal line of wasabi paste across middle of rice. Add a line of pickled ginger alongside the wasabi. Place 3 strips each of mango and kiwi across rice evenly.

To roll sushi, lift sushi mat at the edge closest to you and begin to roll up, holding the filling in place with your index fingers. Roll nori neatly and firmly, like a jelly roll, almost to the end. Using a fingertip, moisten top strip of nori with some water to seal the roll. Place roll, seam side down, on a baking sheet. Repeat with remaining nori, rice, and fruit. Cut each roll into 8 pieces. Serve with Sushi Dipping Sauce.

WASABI

Wasabi is a light green Japanese root vegetable that is very hot, with a taste reminiscent of horseradish. It is usually dried and powdered (see the powder at the top). For cooking or serving as a condiment, the powder is mixed with water and made into a paste. You can do this yourself, or buy tubes with premixed wasabi paste.

OATMEAL SUNFLOWER MUFFINS

The chewy texture comes from the oats! These delicious muffins are loaded with fibre—whole wheat flour, oats, and sunflower seeds. —NETTIE

PREHEAT THE OVEN to 350°F (180°C).

Mix flour, sunflower seeds, oats, baking powder, cinnamon, cardamom, raisins, cherries, and salt in a large bowl.

In a separate bowl, whisk together juice, maple syrup, and oil.

Stir wet mixture into dry ingredients until combined. Wait 5 minutes so that the oats absorb liquids. The batter will thicken. Spoon into 12 prepared muffin cups. Bake in preheated oven for 35 minutes or until a toothpick inserted into the centre of a muffin comes out clean. Let cool in pan for 10 minutes.

4 cups (1 L) whole wheat pastry flour

½ cup (125 mL) sunflower seeds

1 cup (250 mL) rolled oats

4 tsp (20 mL) baking powder

2 tsp (10 mL) ground cinnamon

1 tsp (5 mL) ground cardamom

½ cup (125 mL) raisins

½ cup (125 mL) dried cherries or other dried fruit

1 tsp (5 mL) salt

2 cups (500 mL) apple juice

⅔ cup (160 mL) maple syrup

⅔ cup (160 mL) canola or olive oil

Two 6-well muffin tins (or one 12-well), filled with paper muffin liners or lightly oiled

¼ cup (60 mL) smooth pecan butter
or almond butter

½ cup (125 mL) chocolate
or vanilla soymilk

½ cup (125 mL) cocoa powder

1 cup (250 mL) lightly packed
brown sugar

¾ cup (185 mL) whole wheat
pastry flour

½ cup (125 mL) quinoa flour

½ tsp (2 mL) baking powder

½ tsp (2 mL) baking soda

½ tsp (2 mL) salt

½ cup (125 mL) thinly sliced
dried dates or figs

2 large eggs, separated

1 tsp (5 mL) pure vanilla extract

1 cup (250 mL) plain yogurt

½ cup (125 mL) chopped pecans,
for garnishing

Two 6-well muffin tins
(or one 12-well), filled with paper
muffin liners or lightly oiled

QUINOA PECAN FUDGE CUPCAKES

You need to toast the quinoa flour to remove any bitter aftertaste from the saponin in the quinoa. You can do this in a small saucepan over medium heat, stirring constantly for two to three minutes or until slightly browned. —NETTIE

PREHEAT THE OVEN to 375°F (190°C).

Combine nut butter and soymilk in a small saucepan. Bring to a boil over medium-high heat, whisking until blended. Remove from heat. Add cocoa powder and whisk until smooth. Transfer to a large bowl.

Mix together brown sugar, whole wheat flour, quinoa flour, baking powder, baking soda, salt, and dates in a bowl. Stir into cocoa mixture.

Beat egg yolks, vanilla, and yogurt in a bowl. Add to batter in large bowl.

Beat egg whites until stiff in a bowl, using electric beaters. Fold into batter. Spoon batter into prepared muffin tins, filling each cup to three-quarters full. Bake in preheated oven for 25 minutes or until a cake tester inserted into the centre of a cupcake comes out clean. Garnish with chopped pecans.

BULGUR PUDDING WITH CANDIED GINGER AND DATES

Bulgur in a dessert? Yes! Bulgur is made from wheat berries that have been steamed, dried, and crushed, and comes in fine, mcdium, and coarsely ground textures; the best texture for this recipe is fine. Never rinse bulgur because it will turn to mush. Use any type of non-dairy milk in this recipe; vanilla soymilk was used to test this recipe, but coconut milk is one of my favourites.
—NETTIE

COMBINE WATER, LEMON juice, and salt in a saucepan. Bring to a boil over high heat. Add maple syrup, dates, and ginger. Cook, stirring constantly, for 2 to 5 minutes or until dates and ginger are softened. Stir in bulgur, cover, and remove from heat. Let stand for 5 minutes, or until water is absorbed.

Stir in soymilk, cranberries, and allspice. Bring mixture to a boil, stirring constantly. Reduce heat and simmer, stirring frequently, for 3 minutes or until mixture thickens to the consistency of oatmeal. Stir in pecans. Serve warm or at room temperature, garnished with Cashew Cream Topping (if using).

1⅓ cups (330 mL) water

2 Tbsp (30 mL) fresh lemon juice

Pinch of salt

2 Tbsp (30 mL) maple syrup or
brown rice syrup

1 cup (250 mL) chopped dried dates

¼ cup (60 mL) chopped
candied ginger

¾ cup (185 mL) fine bulgur

1 cup (250 mL) vanilla soymilk

½ cup (125 mL) dried cranberries

¼ tsp (1 mL) ground allspice

½ cup (125 mL) chopped toasted
pecans (sidebar, page 26)

1⅓ cups (330 mL) Cashew Cream
Topping (page 6) (optional)

CHERRY-APRICOT COBBLER

Most cobblers have a biscuit crust, which is usually cut into rounds (cobbles). So, are cobblers really just fruit pot pies? The fruit and dough are arranged in layers and can be baked up to three hours ahead of time, then reheated at 350°F (180°C) for 15 minutes. —NETTIE

PREHEAT THE OVEN to 350°F (180°C).

Combine canned cherries, apricots, blueberries, sugar, almond extract, and allspice in prepared baking dish. Stir well, and then set aside.

Whisk together whole wheat pastry flour, sugar, all-purpose flour, baking powder, and salt in a large bowl. In a separate bowl, beat the eggs with the milk using a fork. Stir in the Pomegranate Glaze, lemon zest, and vanilla. Slowly pour the egg-milk mixture into the flour mixture, stirring with a wooden spoon. Stir well to combine the wet and dry ingredients.

Spoon this topping over the base in the baking dish, smoothing the top with the back of a wooden spoon. Bake in preheated oven for 50 minutes or until topping is golden brown and juices from filling are bubbling thickly at the edges. Serve warm, with Cashew Cream Topping (if using).

BASE

Three 14 oz (398 mL) cans pitted tart cherries, drained

1 cup (250 mL) chopped dried apricots

½ cup (125 mL) dried blueberries or chopped dried cherries

¾ cup (185 mL) granulated sugar

½ tsp (2 mL) almond extract

¼ tsp (1 mL) ground allspice

TOPPING

½ cup (125 mL) whole wheat pastry flour

½ cup (125 mL) granulated sugar

⅓ cup (80 mL) all-purpose flour

¼ tsp (1 mL) baking powder

¼ tsp (1 mL) salt

2 large eggs

½ cup (125 mL) milk

2 Tbsp (30 mL) Pomegranate Glaze (page 8, or store-bought pomegranate molasses)

2 tsp (10 mL) lemon zest

1 tsp (5 mL) pure vanilla extract

Cashew Cream Topping (page 6) (optional)

11- × 7-inch (28 × 18 cm) baking dish, buttered

6 cups (1.5 L) freshly popped, salted popcorn (½ cup/125 mL unpopped kernels)

2 slices side bacon

⅓ cup (80 mL) butter

⅔ cup (160 mL) lightly packed brown sugar

3 Tbsp (45 mL) corn syrup

¼ tsp (1 mL) baking soda

½ tsp (2 mL) chile powder

¼ tsp (1 mL) ground cinnamon

Pinch of ground cloves

SPICY CARAMEL POPCORN

Why does popcorn pop? Popcorn is a flint or dent variety of corn. The popcorn hull conducts heat faster than the hull of ordinary corn. Because the starch and water content is high, the hull explodes in the presence of high heat. Avoid microwavable popcorn because it contains too many unhealthy ingredients (hydrogenated fats and chemical flavourings). For this recipe, I've been known to use extra virgin olive oil instead of butter. —NETTIE

SPICY CARAMEL POPCORN WITH BACON

Here's a twist on a spicy-sweet snack. Adding crispy bacon to caramel popcorn as it cools delivers an intensified saltiness to the sweet and spice. Try a small amount first to see if your taste buds like this combination. I personally love it, but I know that some people find it just too weird. —PAT

PREHEAT THE OVEN to 300°F (150°C). Keep freshly popped popcorn warm in the oven in a heatproof bowl.

Arrange bacon slices on a grill pan or skillet in one layer so they don't touch. Cook, turning once or twice, over medium-high heat for 3 to 5 minutes, or until bacon is browned and crisp. Transfer using tongs to a paper towel–lined plate to drain. When cool, break into small bits.

Melt butter in a heavy-bottomed saucepan over medium-high heat. Stir in brown sugar and corn syrup and bring to a boil, stirring constantly. Boil for 4 minutes, stirring constantly. Remove from heat and stir in baking soda, chile powder, cinnamon, and cloves. Pour over popcorn in a thin, steady stream, tossing to coat the popcorn. Transfer to a shallow baking dish to cool, tossing 2 cups (500 mL) separately with crumbled bacon. Store in airtight containers for up to 1 week.

CHERRY GINGER AND PISTACHIO BISCOTTI

If you have never used agave nectar, this is the perfect recipe to try it out. These twice-baked cookies explode with flavour because of the combination of dried fruit and nuts. —NETTIE

1 cup (250 mL) shelled pistachio nuts, divided

2 cups (500 mL) whole wheat pastry flour

½ cup (125 mL) lightly packed brown sugar

¼ cup (60 mL) finely chopped candied ginger

1 tsp (5 mL) baking powder

½ tsp (2 mL) baking soda

½ tsp (2 mL) ground cinnamon

¼ tsp (1 mL) salt

½ cup (125 mL) water

⅓ cup (80 mL) agave nectar

1 tsp (5 mL) almond extract

½ tsp (2 mL) pure vanilla extract

½ cup (125 mL) dried cherries

2 baking sheets, parchment-lined

PREHEAT THE OVEN to 375°F (190°C).

Grind ½ cup (125 mL) pistachio nuts in a food processor until fine and transfer to a bowl. Stir in pastry flour, brown sugar, candied ginger, baking powder, baking soda, cinnamon, and salt and mix well.

Combine water, agave nectar, almond extract, and vanilla in a separate bowl. Add wet ingredients to dry ingredients, along with remaining pistachios and cranberries. Mix well to combine.

Divide dough in half and transfer each half to a prepared baking sheet. Shape dough into two 13- × 9-inch (33 × 23 cm) logs. Bake on two racks in preheated oven for 15 minutes. Rotate baking sheets and bake for 10 minutes, or until the top of logs is golden brown. Cool for 10 minutes. Reduce oven temperature to 300°F (150°C).

Cut each log into ½-inch (1 cm) slices using a serrated knife. Lay slices flat on same baking sheets. Return to oven and bake for 15 minutes.

¼ cup (60 mL) butter

4 bananas, sliced diagonally
½ inch (1 cm) thick

¾ cup (185 mL) lightly packed
brown sugar

1 cup (250 mL) Cashew Cream
(page 6)

4 oz (125 g) bittersweet chocolate,
finely chopped

½ cup (125 mL) chopped toasted
nuts (walnuts, pecans, almonds)
(sidebar, page 26), for garnishing

CANDIED BANANAS WITH CHOCOLATE CASHEW CREAM

Store bananas at a cool temperature. (If you put them in the fridge they will turn black on the outside but still remain edible on the inside.) Bananas are one of the best sources of potassium. Please buy organic and fair-trade bananas, which are eco-friendly and aren't grown with chemicals that affect the health of the farm workers and soil. —NETTIE

MELT BUTTER IN a skillet over medium-high heat. Add bananas and brown sugar. Cook gently over medium heat, turning the bananas and shaking the skillet occasionally, for 3 to 4 minutes or until sugar is caramelized. Using a slotted spoon, lift bananas out, leaving most of the caramel behind, and divide evenly among 6 bowls.

Add Cashew Cream to the remaining caramel in the skillet and bring to a boil, stirring constantly, for 2 to 3 minutes or until caramel is dissolved. Add chocolate and stir constantly for 1 to 2 minutes, or until chocolate is melted. Drizzle chocolate cashew cream over bananas in bowls and sprinkle with nuts.

WHOLE WHEAT S'MORE COOKIES

Juice from the gummy root of the marshmallow plant was mixed with sugar and eggs then beaten to make the first marshmallows in France, in the early 19th century. Today, gelatin is used in place of the marshmallow sap and then combined with sugar syrup. Health food stores do sell gelatin-free marshmallows so read your labels.

Buckwheat honey combined with chocolate chips ensures that the cookies are sweet enough for most people. — NETTIE

PREHEAT THE OVEN to 350°F (180°C).

Combine flour, baking soda, and salt in a large bowl. Cream butter in a separate bowl, using a wooden spoon. Add brown sugar and beat until light and fluffy. Add eggs one at a time and beat well after each addition. Beat in buttermilk, honey, and vanilla, mixing until well combined. Add flour mixture, stirring until dough is evenly moistened. Stir in chocolate chips, marshmallows, and nuts.

Drop cookie dough by rounded tablespoonfuls (15 mL) onto prepared sheets, spaced about 3 inches (8 cm) apart. Bake in preheated oven, one sheet at a time, for 15 minutes or until golden brown and dry to the touch, but still slightly soft. Let cool on the baking sheet for about 10 minutes before transferring to cooling racks. Store in an airtight container for 3 to 4 days.

3 cups (750 mL) whole wheat flour

½ tsp (2 mL) baking soda

¼ tsp (1 mL) salt

½ cup (125 mL) unsalted butter, at room temperature

1½ cups (375 mL) lightly packed brown sugar

2 large eggs

½ cup (125 mL) buttermilk (see sidebar)

2 Tbsp (30 mL) liquid buckwheat honey

1½ tsp (7 mL) pure vanilla extract

1½ cups (375 mL) chocolate chips

1 cup (250 mL) stale marshmallows

¼ cup (60 mL) coarsely chopped walnuts

3 rimmed baking sheets, parchment-lined

TO MAKE SOUR MILK (A GOOD SUBSTITUTE FOR BUTTERMILK)

Combine ½ cup (125 mL) milk and 1½ tsp (7 mL) lemon juice or vinegar. Milk will curdle immediately.

CRUST

1¼ cups (310 mL) chocolate wafer crumbs

3 Tbsp (45 mL) granulated sugar

¼ cup (60 mL) butter or non-hydrogenated margarine, melted

FILLING

2¼ cups (560 mL) granulated sugar, divided

⅓ cup (80 mL) water

10 oz (300 g) bittersweet chocolate, chopped

Two 1 lb (500 g) pkgs silken tofu, drained

⅓ cup (80 mL) unsweetened cocoa powder

Two 8 oz (250 g) pkgs cream cheese, at room temperature

1 tsp (5 mL) pure vanilla extract

¼ tsp (1 mL) salt

9-inch (23 cm) springform pan, buttered

CHOCOLATE CHEESECAKE

What cookbook would be complete without a cheesecake recipe! This one uses bittersweet chocolate, silken tofu, cream cheese, and cocoa powder. It is very important to cool and chill the cake before serving. Rich and delicious, it will be a favourite. —NETTIE

FOR THE CRUST, preheat the oven to 350°F (180°C).

To make the crust, combine chocolate wafer crumbs, sugar, and butter in a bowl. Press into the prepared springform pan, covering the bottom and 1 inch (2.5 cm) up the side. Bake in the preheated oven for 10 to 12 minutes, or until crust is set. Cool on cooling rack until completely cool, about 45 minutes.

For the cheesecake, preheat the oven to 350°F (180°C). To make the filling, heat 1 cup (250 mL) sugar in a deep, heavy-bottomed saucepan over medium heat, stirring with a fork. When sugar starts to melt, stop stirring, and cook, swirling the pan occasionally, for 3 to 4 minutes or until the sugar melts and is dark amber.

Remove pan from heat and carefully stir in water (mixture will bubble and steam and caramel will harden). Cook over medium-low heat for 1 to 2 minutes or until caramel has dissolved. Remove from heat and whisk in chopped chocolate, stirring until melted. Let fudge sauce cool slightly in the pan over a cooling rack.

Purée tofu and cocoa together in a food processor until smooth. Combine cream cheese and remaining 1¼ cups (310 mL) sugar in a bowl and beat with an electric mixer at medium speed for 3 to 4 minutes, or until fluffy. Beat puréed tofu into cream cheese mixture at low speed. Add vanilla, salt, and fudge sauce, beating until well mixed.

Pour filling into baked crust and bake on middle rack of preheated oven for about 1 hour, or until top of cake is shiny but centre is still slightly wobbly when pan is shaken. Turn off oven and let cheesecake sit in the cooling oven for 1 hour.

Gently loosen the cake from the sides of the pan by running a knife around the edge of the cake and the pan. Let cool completely in the pan, on a cooling rack. Cover and chill cake in the pan in the refrigerator for at least 6 hours, or up to 3 days. Remove sides of the springform pan and transfer the cake on the pan bottom to a serving plate.

APPENDIX

CANADIAN ORGANIC FOOD STANDARDS

HOW DO I KNOW A PRODUCT IS ORGANIC, AND WHAT ARE CANADIAN ORGANIC STANDARDS?

Look for the "Canada Organic/Biologique Canada" seal. Canadian Organic Standards are regulated and enforced by the Canadian Food Inspection Agency. To be certified organic, farmers and food processors are required to not only follow applicable food-safety laws but also support the following:

- Use of land that has been chemical free for three years
- Detailed record keeping and regular audits, which means . . .
- Full food traceability—everything that goes into an organic product is documented and traceable
- Routine on-site inspections to ensure that Canadian Organic Standards are being met
- Good environmental stewardship through land management that supports natural systems

Canadian Organic Standards require that farmers build fertile soil by doing the following:

- Rotating crops to increase and balance nutrients, as well as discourage pests
- Composting and using "green" manures to add nitrogen and organic matter to the soil, keep weeds down, and prevent drought and soil erosion
- Using beneficial insects or mechanical and manual methods to control pests and weeds

THE FOLLOWING ARE PROHIBITED:

- Chemical pesticides and fertilizers and sewage sludge
- Synthetic hormones
- Genetic engineering
- Cloned animals
- Excessive food-processing, artificial ingredients, preservatives, or irradiation
- Antibiotics (except in carefully documented situations to save an animal's life. In these cases, the meat is never sold as organic, and the milk is discarded for a minimum of 30 days.)

IS ORGANIC FARMING BETTER FOR THE ENVIRONMENT AND OUR HEALTH?

There is scientific evidence from Canada and around the world that organic farming results in healthier soil, less erosion, and cleaner waterways, and reduces human and wildlife exposure to persistent toxic chemicals. Organic farming uses 30 to 50 percent less energy than conventional farming. The population of birds and insects is higher on and around organic farms. The Rodale Institute, an agricultural research institute in the U.S., has found organic crop yields to be equivalent to conventional crops in normal years—and higher in drought years.

WHAT DOES "NATURAL" MEAN ON A FOOD LABEL?

"Natural" can mean anything that the manufacturer decides. Products labelled natural are not regulated and are not verified to meet any standards.

WHY IS ORGANIC FOOD MORE EXPENSIVE?

Typically, organic food has higher production costs—more manual labour goes into raising organic crops and animals. Certified organic growers must keep detailed farm plans, work logs, and records for every field. Animals raised organically must have access to the outdoors and be provided more space than conventional farm animals. Processors of organic food must provide proof of organic certification for all ingredients, prevent co-mingling with conventional products, and log storage and pest-control methods. On top of the added record keeping, all certified operators pay for inspections and certification.

The true cost of conventional food is actually higher than the price paid at the till. Consumers also pay through their taxes, footing the bills for subsidies to conventional crops and for cleaning up agrichemical run-off and pollution of our water and soil.

Check out the website of the Canada Organic Trade Association (www.ota.com/otacanada.html) and its site explaining the Canada Organic seal (www .organicbiologique.ca) for more information.

ACKNOWLEDGEMENTS

There are a lot of enlightened chefs and foodies and others working in the food industry, and we would like to thank all of the people who helped and supported the research, writing, development, and testing of the recipes in this book. We are most appreciative of the following people and companies: Cuisinart Canada (www.cuisinart.ca), Jade Stafford at the Calphalon Culinary Centre (www.calphalon.com), John Landsborugh at the Ontario Natural Food Co-Op (www.onfc.ca), Janet Tovey at Eden Foods (www.edenfoods.com), Hyman Weisbord at Smoke (www.smokefinefoods.com), The Big Carrot Health Food Store (www.thebigcarrot.ca), Fairtrade Canada (www.fairtrade.ca), and Cookin' Greens (www.cookingreens.com).

Cynthia Beretta, of Beretta Organics (www.berettaorganics.com), embodies the kind of thoughtful production and consumption of meat that this book is all about. We are grateful to Cynthia for the fine meat that was used in testing the meat recipes, and for her thoughtful and entertaining comments throughout the book.

What fun we had working on this project with Whitecap Books. Robert McCullough, Grace Yaginuma, Mauve Pagé, Taryn Boyd, Holland Gidney, and Michelle Furbacher make an unbeatable team for topnotch Canadian food titles. We thank you all for your love of both food and books—it shines through everything you do.

FROM NETTIE:

For nourishment, both spiritual and physical: Kim DeLallo, Gina St. Germaine, Jocie Bussin, Marilyn Crowley, Caroline Frail, Alison Fryer, Judi Swartz, Barbara Barron, Suzie Siegal, Joanne Lusted, Naomi Duguid, Mary Catherine Anderson, Mary Bullock, Jill Rigby, Bob Brown, Harry Cook, Stephanie Wells, Helen Cronish, Jim Urquhart, Cameron, Mackenzie, and Emery.

FROM PAT:

I, too, have a team of people who support me and make it possible for me to do the kind of work that I do. Thanks to Gary and Shannon McLaughlin, Kate Carlsen, and Laurie Dearie-Bruce.

INDEX

miso *(continued)*
    Buddha Dragon Noodle Bowl with Bacon-
        Broiled Scallops, 60
moussaka
    Lentil Mushroom Moussaka, 178
    Lentil Mushroom Moussaka with Baked
        Salmon, 178
mozzarella cheese
    Eggplant and Lamb Manicotti, 26
    Eggplant Manicotti, 26
    Pita Pizza, 205
    Pita Pizza with Ground Chicken, 205
    Teriyaki Pork with Lasagna, 158
    Tofu Lasagna, 158
    Tortilla Lasagna with Baked Pork Chop, 200
    Tortilla Lasagna with Portobello and
        Greens, 200
muffins
    Oatmeal Sunflower Muffins, 254
mushrooms
    about, 57
    Ancho Chocolate Chilli, 136
    Ancho Chocolate Chilli with Beef, 136
    Bacon-Wrapped Mushroom Buckwheat
        Burgers with Cashew Butter, 196
    Beef and Barley Soup, 70
    Buddha Dragon Bowl with Lemongrass and
        Rice Noodles, 60
    Buddha Dragon Noodle Bowl with Bacon-
        Broiled Scallops, 60
    Chicken Mole, 172
    combining fresh and dried mushrooms for a
        complex flavour, 42
    Ginger Shallot Congee, 213
    Ginger Shallot Congee with Chile Pork, 213
    Lamb and Cheese–Stuffed Portobello
        Mushrooms, 130
    Lentil Mushroom Moussaka, 178
    Lentil Mushroom Moussaka with Baked
        Salmon, 178
    Mushroom Broth, 42
    Mushroom Buckwheat Burgers with Cashew
        Butter, 196
    Mushroom Provençal Stew, 66
    Mushroom Provençal Stew with Lamb
        Shanks, 66
    Pad Thai, 162
    Rice and Mushroom Soup with Braised
        Cod, 54
    Ricotta and Asiago-Stuffed Portobello
        Mushrooms, 130
    Roasted Vegetable Stock, 44
    shiitake, about, 61
    Split Pea and Mushroom Soup with Crispy
        Pancetta, 58
    Split Pea Soup with Shiitake Mushrooms, 58
    Shrimp Pad Thai, 162
    Tempeh Mole, 172
    Tortilla Lasagna with Baked Pork Chop, 200
    Tortilla Lasagna with Portobello and
        Greens, 200
    Wild and Brown Rice Soup with Three
        Kinds of Mushroom, 54
mushrooms, dried
    combining fresh and dried mushrooms for a
        complex flavour, 42

Dried Shiitake Mushroom, Adzuki Bean,
    and Carrot Soup, 64
Marinated Pork Kabobs, 118
Marinated Tofu and Tempeh Kabobs
    with Veggies, 118
Mushroom Broth, 42
Mushroom Provençal Stew, 66
Mushroom Provençal Stew with Lamb
    Shanks, 66
Shiitake, Adzuki Bean, and Carrot Soup
    with Sautéed Shrimp, 64

N
noodles. *See* pasta, rice noodles, soba
nori
    about, 11
    Mango Kiwi Dessert Sushi, 253
nut butter. *See also* peanuts and peanut butter,
    tahini
    about, 6
    Apple Miso Almond Butter Sandwich, 210
    Bacon-Wrapped Mushroom Buckwheat
        Burgers with Cashew Butter, 196
    Mushroom Buckwheat Burgers with Cashew
        Butter, 196
    Shrimp Curry with Lime and Nut Butter,
        168
    Tofu Curry with Lime and Nut
        Butter, 168
nutritional yeast
    about, 4
nuts and seeds. *See also* nut butter
    about, 6
    Braised Kale with Pine Nuts, Cranberries,
        and Garlic, 107
    Braised Kale with Smoked Salmon, Pine
        Nuts, and Cranberries, 107
    Broccoli and Toasted Pecans, 99
    Broccoli Rabe and Pecan Crêpes, 174
    Broccoli Rabe Crêpes with Italian
        Sausage, 174
    Candied Bananas with Chocolate Cashew
        Cream, 261
    Cashew Cream, 6
    Cashew Cream Topping, 6
    Cherry Ginger and Pistachio Biscotti, 260
    Couscous with Mint, Cucumber, Walnuts,
        and Brie, 84
    Farfalle with Roasted Beet Chips and
        Broiled Scallops, 154
    Farfalle with Roasted Beet Chips and Pine
        Nuts, 154
    Green Goddess Potato Salad, 90
    how to toast, 26
    Mâche with Roasted Beets, Walnuts,
        and Blue Cheese, 76
    Mâche with Roasted Beets and Grilled
        Beef, 76
    Mashed Sweet Potatoes, 95
    Oatmeal Sunflower Muffins, 254
    Peanut Lime Sauce, 7
    Quinoa Pecan Fudge Cupcakes, 255
    Rice Paper Rolls with Sweet Red Chile
        Sauce, 18
    Roasted Cashew Curry with Cauliflower
        and Peas, 182

Roasted Cashew Curry with Vegetables
    and Chicken, 182
Sautéed Brussels Sprouts with Pomegranate
    Glaze, 102
Shrimp Rice Paper Rolls with Sweet
    Red Chile Sauce, 18
Spicy Stir-Fried Greens with Peanuts, 30
Spicy Stir-Fry with Greens, Chicken,
    and Peanuts, 30
Stuffed Potatoes with Bacon or Ham, 100
Stuffed Potatoes with Feta and Pine
    Nuts, 100
Sweet Potato, Fennel, and Apple Salad, 82
Tamari Roasted Nuts, 221
Trail Mix for Kids, 222

O
oats
    Crispy Barley Oat Almond Squares, 229
    Golden Granola, 227
    Oat and Barley Grain Porridge for
        Beginners, 226
    Oatmeal Sunflower Muffins, 254
olive oil
    about, 4
olives
    Barley Tabbouleh with Feta and Olives, 85
    Pita Pizza, 205
    Pita Pizza with Ground Chicken, 205
    Stuffed Potatoes with Bacon or Ham, 100
    Stuffed Potatoes with Feta and Pine
        Nuts, 100
onions, green onions, and shallots
    Ginger Shallot Congee, 213
    Ginger Shallot Congee with Chile
        Pork, 213
    Grilled Corn and Radicchio on Tomato
        and Red Onion Salad, 114
    Grilled Corn and Sirloin on Tomato
        and Red Onion Salad, 114
    Grilled Pineapple, Tofu, and Zucchini
        with Red Onion, 128
    Ham, Spinach, and Tempeh Grilled
        Pizza, 122
    Pappardelle with Grilled Salmon, Spinach,
        and Asparagus, 156
    Pappardelle with Spinach, Asparagus,
        and Feta, 156
    Soba Noodles and Tomatoes with
        Chicken, 148
    Soba Noodles with Diced Tomatoes
        and Green Onions, 148
    Tempeh Grilled Pizza, 122
    Tomatillo Soup with Squash and
        Cilantro, 53
orange juice
    Baked Sweet Potato and Apricot
        Croquettes, 216
    Ham, Sweet Potato, and Apricot
        Croquettes, 216
organic, xi

P
Pad Thai, 162
Paella with Tempeh and Seitan Served
    in Roasted Squash, 194